Child Abuse in the Classroom

CROSSWAY BOOKS • WESTCHESTER, ILLINOIS
A DIVISION OF GOOD NEWS PUBLISHERS

Other books by Phyllis Schlafly:

A Choice Not an Echo, 1964
The Gravediggers, 1964
Strike From Space, 1965
Safe Not Sorry, 1967
The Betrayers, 1968
Mindszenty the Man, 1972
Kissinger on the Couch, 1975
Ambush at Vladivostok, 1976
The Power of the Positive Woman, 1977
The Power of the Christian Woman, 1981
Equal Pay for UNequal Work (editor), 1984

Mrs. Schlafly is the subject of a current biography, *The Sweetheart of the Silent Majority*, by Carol Felsenthal (Doubleday).

First Printing, February 1985
Second Printing, May 1985
Third Printing, June 1985

Excerpts from

Official Transcript of Proceedings

BEFORE THE

U.S. DEPARTMENT OF EDUCATION

In the Matter of:

PROPOSED REGULATIONS TO IMPLEMENT
THE PROTECTION OF PUPIL RIGHTS AMENDMENT
SECTION 439 OF THE GEPA
ALSO KNOWN AS THE HATCH AMENDMENT

Child Abuse in the Classroom

DATES: MARCH 13, 16, 19, 20, 21, 23, 27, 1984

PLACES: SEATTLE, PITTSBURGH, KANSAS CITY,
          PHOENIX, CONCORD, ORLANDO, WASHINGTON DC

Edited by PHYLLIS SCHLAFLY

About Phyllis Schlafly

Phyllis Schlafly's interest in education stems from her six children, all of whom she taught to read at home before they entered school. They credit their outstanding academic success to homeschooling and phonics.

Mrs. Schlafly received her B.A. with Honors from Washington University in St. Louis in 1944, her M.A. from Harvard University in 1945, and her J.D. from Washington University Law School in 1978.

Mrs. Schlafly is the President of Eagle Forum, a national pro-family organization. She is a member of the Illinois Bar, the District of Columbia Bar, and of the Administrative Conference of the United States (a federal advisory panel of administrative law experts).

Mrs. Schlafly has written a monthly newsletter since 1967. She is the author of more than 1,000 syndicated columns, has delivered more than 1,000 network television and radio commentaries, has lectured at hundreds of colleges and universities, and has testified before 50 Congressional and State Legislative Committees. Since 1977, she has been listed by "Good Housekeeping" as one of the 10 most-admired women in the world.

COPYRIGHT ©1984 BY PHYLLIS SCHLAFLY
ALL RIGHTS RESERVED

PUBLISHED BY PERE MARQUETTE PRESS
ALTON, ILLINOIS 62002 **AND**
CROSSWAY BOOKS/A DIVISION OF GOOD NEWS PUBLISHERS
WESTCHESTER, ILLINOIS 60153

LIBRARY OF CONGRESS CATALOGUE CARD NUMBER 84-61629
PERE MARQUETTE   ISBN 0-93464-010-6
CROSSWAY BOOKS   ISBN 0-89107-365-5

PRINTED IN THE UNITED STATES OF AMERICA

Note: We have corrected many stenographers' errors in names of persons, programs, and quotations, but some others are unavoidable because all the testimony was taken orally.

This book consists of selected excerpts from the Official Transcript of Proceedings before the United States Department of Education in the matter of the Proposed Regulations to Implement the **Protection of Pupil Rights Amendment** (Section 439 of the General Education Provisions Act, 20 U.S. Code §1232h), also known as the Hatch Amendment. Section 439(a) was enacted in 1974, and Section 439(b) was enacted in 1978.

Seven days of hearings were held by the Department of Education pursuant to the notice of proposed rulemaking to implement Section 439 which was published in the *Federal Register* on February 22, 1984. The all-day hearings were held as follows:

Seattle, Washington	March 13, 1984
Pittsburgh, Pennsylvania	March 16, 1984
Kansas City, Missouri	March 19, 1984
Phoenix, Arizona	March 20, 1984
Concord, New Hampshire	March 21, 1984
Orlando, Florida	March 23, 1984
Washington, D.C.	March 27, 1984

The final Regulations were published in the *Federal Register* on September 6, 1984, and went into effect November 12, 1984.

"An educational heresy has flourished, a heresy that rejects the idea of education as the acquisition of knowledge and skills . . . the heresy of which I speak regards the fundamental task in education as therapy."

The Honorable Samuel I. Hayakawa
former President, San Francisco State College
former United States Senator from California

TABLE OF CONTENTS

Text of the Pupil Rights Amendment 8

Text of the Regulations 9

Foreword 11

Excerpts from the Official Transcript
    of Proceedings before
    the Department of Education

In the Matter of:

Proposed Regulations to Implement
    the Protection of Pupil Rights Amendment
    Section 439 of the General Education Provisions Act
    also known as the Hatch Amendment, enacted 1978:

   I. Seattle, Washington — March 13, 1984 25
  II. Pittsburgh, Pennsylvania — March 16, 1984 105
 III. Kansas City, Missouri — March 19, 1984 173
 IV. Phoenix, Arizona — March 20, 1984 219
  V. Concord, New Hampshire — March 21, 1984 . . . 291
 VI. Orlando, Florida — March 23, 1984 333
VII. Washington, D.C. — March 27, 1984 385

Appendix A: How Parents Can Evaluate Curricula . . . 435

Appendix B: Sample Letter for Parents 440

Subject Index 442

Index of Witnesses 446

Protection of Pupil Rights
20 U.S. Code §1232h

Inspection by parents or guardians
of instructional material.

(a) All instructional material, including teacher's manuals, films, tapes, or other supplementary instructional material which will be used in connection with any research or experimentation program or project shall be available for inspection by the parents or guardians of the children engaged in such program or project. For the purpose of this section "research or experimentation program or project" means any program or project in any applicable program designed to explore or develop new or unproven teaching methods or techniques.

Psychiatric or psychological
examinations, testing, or treatment.

(b) No student shall be required, as part of any applicable program, to submit to psychiatric examination, testing, or treatment, or psychological examination, testing, or treatment, in which the primary purpose is to reveal information concerning:

(1) political affiliations;

(2) mental and psychological problems potentially embarrassing to the student or his family;

(3) sex behavior and attitudes;

(4) illegal, anti-social, self-incriminating and demeaning behavior;

(5) critical appraisals of other individuals with whom respondents have close family relationships;

(6) legally recognized privileged and analogous relationships, such as those of lawyers, physicians, and ministers; or

(7) income (other than that required by law to determine eligibility for participation in a program or for receiving financial assistance under such program),

without the prior consent of the student (if the student is an adult or emancipated minor), or in the case of unemancipated minor, without the prior written consent of the parent.

34 CFR Part 98—Student Rights in Research, Experimental Programs, and Testing

§98.1 Applicability of part.

This part applies to any program administered by the Secretary of Education that—

(a)(1) Was transferred to the Department by the Department of Education Organization Act (DEOA); and

(2) Was administered by the Education Division of the Department of Health, Education, and Welfare on the day before the effective date of the DEOA; or

(b) Was enacted after the effective date of the DEOA, unless the law enacting the new Federal program has the effect of making section 439 of the General Education Provisions Act inapplicable.

* * * * * * *

§98.3 Access to instructional material used in a research or experimentation program.

(a) All instructional material—including teachers' manuals, films, tapes, or other supplementary instructional material—which will be used in connection with any research or experimentation program or project shall be available for inspection by the parents or guardians of the children engaged in such program or project.

(b) For the purpose of this part "research or experimentation program or project" means any program or project in any program under §98.1 (a) or (b) that is designed to explore or develop new or unproven teaching methods or techniques.

(c) For the purpose of the section "children" means persons not above age 21 who are enrolled in a program under §98.1 (a) or (b) not above the elementary or secondary education level, as determined under State law.

§98.4 Protection of students' privacy in examination, testing, or treatment.

(a) No student shall be required, as part of any program specified in §98.1 (a) or (b), to submit without prior consent to psychiatric examination, testing, or treatment, or psychological examination, testing, or treatment, in which the primary purpose is to reveal information concerning one or more of the following—

(1) Political affiliations;

(2) Mental and psychological problems potentially embarrassing to the student or his or her family;

(3) Sex behavior and attitudes;

(4) Illegal, anti-social, self-incriminating and demeaning behavior;

(5) Critical appraisals of other individuals with whom the student has close family relationships;

(6) Legally recognized privileged and analogous relationships, such as those of lawyers, physicians, and ministers; or

(7) Income, other than that required by law to determine eligibility for participation in a program or for receiving financial assistance under a program.

(b) As used in paragraph (a) of this section, "prior consent" means—(1) Prior consent of the student, if the student is an adult or emancipated minor; or

(2) Prior written consent of the parent or guardian, if the student is an unemancipated minor.

(c) As used in paragraph (a) of this section—

(1) "Psychiatric or psychological examination or test" means a method of obtaining information, including a group activity, that is not directly related to academic instruction and that is designed to elicit information about attitudes, habits, traits, opinions, beliefs or feelings; and

(2) "Psychiatric or psychological treatment" means an activity involving the planned, systematic use of methods or techniques that are not directly related to academic instruction and that is designed to affect behavioral, emotional, or attitudinal characteristics of an individual or group.

§98.5 Information and Investigation office.

(a) The Secretary has designated an office to provide information about the requirements of section 439 of the Act, and to investigate, process, and review complaints that may be filed concerning alleged violations of the provisions of the section.

(b) The following is the name and address of the office designated under paragraph (a) of this section: Family Educational Rights and Privacy Act Office, U.S. Department of Education, 400 Maryland Avenue, SW., Washington, D.C. 20202.

§98.6 Reports.

The Secretary may require the recipient to submit reports containing information necessary to resolve complaints under section 439 of the Act and the regulations in this part.

§98.7 Filing a complaint.

(a) Only a student or a parent or guardian of a student directly affected by a violation under Section 439 of the Act may file a complaint under this part. The complaint must be submitted in writing to the Office.

(b) The complaint filed under paragraph (a) of this section must—(1) Contain specific allegations of fact giving reasonable cause to believe that a violation of either §98.3 or §98.4 exists; and

(2) Include evidence of attempted resolution of the complaint at the local level (and at the State level if a State complaint resolution process exists), including the names of local and State officials contacted and significant dates in the attempted resolution process.

(c) The Office investigates each complaint which the Office receives that meets the requirements of this section to determine whether the recipient or contractor failed to comply with the provisions of section 439 of the Act.

§98.8 Notice of the complaint.

(a) If the Office receives a complaint that meets the requirements of §98.7, it provides written notification to the complainant and the recipient or contractor against which the violation has been alleged that the complaint has been received.

(b) The notice to the recipient or contractor under paragraph (a) of this section must—

(1) Include the substance of the alleged violation; and

(2) Inform the recipient or contractor that the Office will investigate the complaint and that the recipient or contractor may submit a written response to the complaint.

§98.9 Investigation and findings.

(a) The Office may permit the parties to submit further written or oral arguments or information.

(b) Following its investigations, the Office provides to the complainant and recipient or contractor written notice of its findings and the basis for its findings.

(c) If the Office finds that the recipient or contractor has not complied with section 439 of the Act, the Office includes in its notice under paragraph (b) of this section—

(1) A statement of the specific steps that the Secretary recommends the recipient or contractor take to comply; and

(2) Provides a reasonable period of time, given all of the circumstances of the case, during which the recipient or contractor may comply voluntarily.

§98.10 Enforcement of the findings.

(a) If the recipient or contractor does not comply during the period of time set under §98.9(c), the Secretary may either—

(1) For a recipient, take an action authorized under 34 CFR Part 78, including—

(i) Issuing a notice of intent to terminate funds under 34 CFR 78.21;

(ii) Issuing a notice to withhold funds under 34 CFR 78.21, 200.94(b), or 298.45(b), depending upon the applicable program under which the notice is issued; or

(iii) Issuing a notice to cease and desist under 34 CFR 78.31, 200.94(c) or 298.45(c), depending upon the program under which the notice is issued; or

(2) For a contractor, direct the contracting officer to take an appropriate action authorized under the Federal Acquisition Regulations, including either—

(i) Issuing a notice to suspend operations under 48 CFR 12.5; or

(ii) Issuing a notice to terminate for default, either in whole or in part under 48 CFR 49.102.

(b) If, after an investigation under §98.9, the Secretary finds that a recipient or contractor has complied voluntarily with section 439 of the Act, the Secretary provides the complainant and the recipient or contractor written notice of the decision and the basis for the decision.

FOREWORD

A remarkable real-life drama took place in seven American cities during March 1984. Hundreds of parents traveled to one of seven locations to testify at U.S. Department of Education Hearings on proposed regulations for the Protection of Pupil Rights Amendment.

More than 1,300 pages of testimony were recorded by court reporters as parents, public school teachers, and interested citizens spelled out their eye-witness accounts of the psychological abuse of children in the public schools. They related how classroom courses have confused schoolchildren about life, about standards of behavior, about moral choices, about religious loyalties, and about relationships with parents and with peers.

There is no good way to summarize the anger and disappointment expressed by these grieving parents about what is going on inside public schools today. Each testimony should be read itself to learn the specific facts of what has actually happened—and to hear the authentic expressions of parental love overlaid with indignation at what is being done "in the name of education."

The testimonies, however, could be excerpted to a readable length — and that is what we have done in this book — always using the actual words of each witness. This book gives the highlights of the actual testimonies at the seven Hearings conducted in March 1984 by the U.S. Department of Education.

These Hearings explain why the American people are so dissatisfied with schools today. These Hearings explain *why* we have 23 million adult illiterates who graduated from public schools, and *why* young people are experiencing high rates of teenage suicide, loneliness, premarital sex, and pregnancies.

These Hearings explain *how* schools have alienated children from their parents, from traditional morality such as the Ten Commandments, and from our American heritage. These Hearings explain *why* children are so emotionally and morally confused and *why,* in the apt colloquialism, they need to "search for their identity."

These Hearings explain *what* children have been doing in their classrooms instead of learning to read, write, spell, add, subtract, and the essentials of history, geography, and civics. These Hearings explain how children learn in school to be "sexually active," take illegal drugs, repudiate their parents, and rationalize immoral and anti-social conduct when it "feels" good in a particular "situation."

These Hearings speak with the thunderous voice of hundreds of parents who are angry at how their children have been emotionally, morally, and intellectually abused by psychological and behavioral experiments during classroom hours when the parents *thought* their children were being taught basic knowledge and skills. Parents are indignant at the way that educator "change agents," spending federal tax dollars, have used children as guinea pigs for fads and experiments that have been substituted for real learning.

EDUCATION AS "THERAPY" These Hearings provide page after page of documentation for the foresightedness of former educator and U.S. Senator Samuel I. Hayakawa, who warned the Senate in 1978 that the schools have become vehicles for a "heresy that rejects the idea of education as the acquisition of knowledge and skills" and instead "regards the fundamental task in education as therapy." He said that such inquiring into attitudes, beliefs, and psychic and emotional problems is a "serious invasion of privacy."

This "heresy" is what has resulted in the schools replacing *cognitive* education (which addresses the child's intellect, and teaches knowledge and skills) with *affective* education (which addresses the child's feelings and attitudes, and spends classroom time on psychological games and probing personal questionnaires).

In practice, this "therapy" education is a system of changing the child's values by techniques such as attitude questionnaires which dig into the privacy of the child and his family, psychological games in the classroom, and forcing the child to make adult decisions about such matters as suicide and murder, marriage and divorce, abortion and adoption.

"Therapy" techniques used in the classroom include violent and disturbing books and films; materials dealing with parental conflict, death, drugs, mental illness, despair, and anger; literature that is mostly negative and depressing; requiring the child to engage in the role-playing of death, pregnancy, abortion, divorce, hate, anger and suicide; personal attitude surveys and games (such as Magic Circle) which invade the private thoughts of the child and his family; psychological games which force the child to decide who should be killed (such as the Survival Game); explicit and pornographic instruction in sex acts (legal and illegal, moral and immoral); and a deliberate attempt to make the child reject the values of his parents and his religion.

The promoters of this strange "therapy" education speak in a jargon designed to prevent parents from understanding either the purpose or the methodology. It's a sort of Aesopian language which means one thing to the "therapy" professionals, but another to parents who don't suspect or understand what is happening.

The jargon includes "values clarification," "behavior modification" (mastery learning, etc.), "moral reasoning," "decision-making," "higher order critical thinking skills," and "humanism." These phrases identify "therapy" techniques which are generally integrated throughout the school curriculum, but are especially evident in courses such as "sex education," "death education," "drug education," "family living," "parenting," "citizenship and character education," "global education," and "talented and gifted programs."

The originators of "therapy" education began peddling their notions in the 1930s about the same time that the teaching of reading started its steep decline. This psychological experimentation existed only in spots here and there around the country until 1965 when federal funding through the Elementary and Secondary Education Act began to finance curriculum and teacher training for the entire country.

THE LAW AGAINST CLASSROOM "THERAPY" By 1978, the protests of parents about "therapy" in the classroom had reached the point that Congress amended the General Education Provisions Act by a section which was officially labelled the *Protection of Pupil Rights Amendment,* and became informally known as the *Hatch Amendment.* This statute provided that no student shall be required (under any federal program) — without prior written parental consent — to submit to psychiatric or psychological examination, testing, or treatment in which the primary purpose is to reveal information about

(1) political affiliations,

(2) mental and psychological problems potentially embarrassing to the student or his family,

(3) sex behavior and attitudes,

(4) illegal, anti-social, and self-incriminating behavior,

(5) critical appraisals of members of the child's family,

(6) legally privileged relationships, such as those of lawyers, physicians and ministers, or

(7) income (except to determine eligibility for

financial assistance).

This amendment was not controversial in either House of Congress. Probably no Senator or Congressman thought that anybody could object to providing schoolchildren with this mantle of protection against such classroom abuse of their personal rights or family privacy.

But after the Pupil Rights Amendment was passed, the Department of Education refused to issue regulations which provided for enforcement; or an opportunity, a procedure, or a place for citizens to file complaints; or a remedy for violations. Some Congressmen charged that the federal bureaucrats did not issue regulations because they did not like the statute and did not intend to enforce it.

Consequently, all citizens who were brave enough to try to file complaints when schools violated the Pupil Rights Amendment were given the royal run-around. Their attempts were futile and frustrating. Local schools denied that the law was relevant; they evaded and equivocated, stalled and stonewalled, harassed the parents who complained, retaliated against their children, and arrogantly continued psychological "therapy" in defiance of the parents.

Despite mounting evidence of widespread violations, no regulations were issued for five and a half years after the Pupil Rights Amendment was passed in 1978. Finally, in response to a crescendo of complaints from concerned citizens, including an organized effort by the national pro-family organization, Eagle Forum, the Department of Education published proposed regulations in the *Federal Register* on February 22, 1984, and announced that it would hold seven days of Hearings to receive public comments.

WHAT THIS BOOK INCLUDES The seven U.S. Department of Education Hearings took place in March 1984 as scheduled. Hundreds of parents, teachers, and concerned citizens testified about violations of the Pupil Rights Amendment. This book contains the highlights of their testimonies.

The testimonies at these Hearings were given by men and women who were, for the most part, total strangers to each other. Yet the message was the same from every part of the country. It came through loud and clear that child abuse in the classroom is a national disease carried to every state by the Typhoid Marys of federal funding.

It is significant how many of the testimonies in this book are from teachers or nurses, as well as parents. The teachers who have been forced to administer "psychological treatment" or "therapy" programs are victims as well as their pupils. Enforcement of the Pupil Rights Amendment is necessary so that teachers will again be able to follow their chosen profession and teach knowledge and skills to the children they love.

It was not easy to select portions of the 1,300 pages of Hearings to publish in a book of readable length because the entire record is so interesting and authentic. Two guidelines were used.

(1) We selected actual examples of how children were abused in the classroom rather than long explanations of the theory or purpose of "therapy" cur-

ricula. The latter is of great interest to the scholar, but parents and citizens are more concerned with first-hand proof of child abuse in the classroom — how to recognize it, prevent it, and stop it.

(2) We omitted most of the demands by witnesses for strong regulations and descriptions of what they should include. While it is very important for the record that almost every witness articulated a demand for strong regulations, (including their application to the National Institute of Education [NIE] and the National Center for Education Statistics [NCES]), the general reader does not need to read the same point a hundred times over.

In reading these excerpts, the reader might wonder, where are the testimonies from "the other side?" Did we exclude the testimony of parents and teachers who approve of "therapy" courses and activities in the classroom, or of teachers and school administrators who object to enforcement of the Protection of Pupil Rights Amendment?

The answer is NO, there was not a single such witness at any of the seven Hearings. No teacher, school principal, academic psychologist, or author of a "therapy" program came forth to defend the theory, the practice, or the purposes of these curricula. This book is, indeed, a fair, accurate, and balanced sampling of all the testimonies that were presented in the record of seven full days of Department of Education Hearings.

The National Education Association did not send any representative to testify at the Hearings even though the NEA is hysterically opposed to enforcement of the Protection of Pupil Rights Amendment. The NEA Newsletter of April 16, 1984, gave the reason *why* "the NEA is opposing the regulations":

"Enforced as currently written, the Reagan Administration's 'child privacy' regulations would mandate that all instructional material — including teachers' manuals, films, and tapes — must be made available for parental inspection."

But, why shouldn't all teaching materials be available for parental inspection? Who do the NEA officials think they are that they can deny parents the opportunity to inspect the materials being used on their own children?

Strangely, there was no media coverage of these seven days of Hearings even though they involved intensely controversial issues, dramatic presentations by hundreds of concerned parents, and documented accounts of child abuse in the classroom. The Department of Education issued appropriate news releases, and hundreds of citizens traveled hundreds of miles from faraway cities in order to speak at the Hearings. But, to our knowledge, there was no television coverage at all and fewer than half a dozen newspaper articles in the entire country.

REGULATIONS ISSUED AFTER SIX YEARS After the March Hearings were concluded, a great silence emanated from the U.S. Department of Education and from the media. Weeks passed, and both acted as though nothing had happened. Eagle Forum and many of the witnesses demanded that the Hearings record be published, but the Department of Education refused.

After months of silence, I published the Hearings myself — which I had the legal right to do since the typed transcript was a government document "in the public domain." This book, consisting of the edited record of the seven days of Hearings, was published August 13, 1984 under the title *Child Abuse in the Classroom.*

Three weeks later, on September 6, 1984, the Department of Education issued the strong regulations we had been demanding. On September 15, President Ronald Reagan told the annual national Eagle Forum Conference: "I'm happy to tell you today that new regulations to enforce the Protection of Pupil Rights Amendment, sometimes called the Hatch Amendment, have been completed by the Department of Education and were published in the *Federal Register* on September 6. Like you, I believe that parents' rights in education must be respected."

These new Pupil Rights Amendment Regulations went into effect on November 12, 1984. They are the strong Regulations which the witnesses in the March Hearings had demanded. Pages 9 and 10 of this book give the text.

These Regulations spell out pupils' rights NOT to be subjected — without the prior written consent of their parents — to "psychiatric or psychological examination or test," which means activities pertaining to "attitudes, habits, traits, opinions, beliefs or feelings"; or to "psychiatric or psychological treatment," which means activities or instruction "designed to affect behavioral, emotional, or attitudinal characteristics of an individual or group."

The final Regulations do apply to the National Institute of Education (NIE) and the National Center for Education Statistics (NCES), which had been omitted from the proposed Regulations as published in February. Most witnesses at the March Hearings had demanded their inclusion because the

NIE is the fountainhead of most of the federally-funded "therapy" masquerading as education. The NIE has spent millions of taxpayers' dollars on controversial, unnecessary, and objectionable programs in the sensitive areas of curriculum development and teacher training, which are *not* appropriate areas for the Federal Government at all.

The American people do not want federal agencies to develop textbooks and curricula for local schools; *that* kind of federal thought control is simply not consistent with a free society. We are much better off if private publishing houses offer their wares, and then local school boards make their own selections of textbooks and curricula from a wide selection without pressure to use federally-written or "federally-approved" materials.

The Regulations provide for voluntary compliance at the local level, and, if this is unsatisfactory, for the filing of complaints about violations with the Department of Education. After investigation and other procedural requirements, the Department is authorized to withdraw federal funds from a school system or other contractor in violation of the law.

The National Education Association, which fought the Act and the Regulations all the way, began publishing hysterical attacks on the Regulations as soon as they became final. The NEA Newsletter of December 3, 1984 proclaimed in oversized type: "The Hatch Act Could Change The Way You Teach—FOREVER!" The NEA position is that the schools should be able to teach whatever they want to the schoolchildren—and that the schools should not be accountable to the parents for anything. That's what they call "academic freedom."

As more and more parents read this book, more and more parents question their children about what is going on in the classroom. In many cases, they find that their children have been subjected to violations of this law for years, but that fact had been concealed from the parents who did not suspect that classroom time was devoted to psychological "therapy" instead of to traditional basics.

All over the country, armed with this book, parents are starting to assert their parents' and pupils' rights under the Pupil Rights Amendment. This book gives them the tools because it provides the first-hand experiences of other parents all over the country.

Parents who demand compliance with the Pupil Rights Amendment and its Regulations are *not* demanding that any materials be removed or censored. Parents are demanding only that the schools obey the law which requires them to obtain written parental consent before children are subjected to any of the materials or activities covered by the Pupil Rights Amendment. The primary burden is on the schools to comply with the law, and then the parents can file a complaint if the schools disobey the law.

The Regulations should be distributed to all principals and teachers, and published in the regulations handbook of all public schools and of any private schools which are recipients of public funds, directly or indirectly. A copy of the handbook should be available in the library of each school for the information of all pupils and parents.

The Protection of Pupil Rights Amendment, its regulations, and a clear statement of the procedure for filing complaints, should be posted in every school in a prominent place alongside of the mandatory "equal opportunity" postings. The complaint procedure should be incorporated into the students' rights and responsibilities statements, and copies made available to all pupils and teachers.

When a teacher intends to use materials or classroom practices covered by the Protection of Pupil Rights Amendment, the materials and a description of the practices should be available for parental inspection in accessible places for at least a month before their intended use. The parental consent form should contain a specific description of the materials and practices, and should make it clear that they are to be used in the classroom (so that the parent is not misled into thinking that it is individual counseling). This will assure that the prior consent of a parent is *informed* consent.

Such written approval should be placed in and remain in the school file at least until the end of the academic year. Such record-keeping is for the protection of pupils, parents, teachers, and schools.

Children whose parents do not give consent for participation in such programs should be provided with an alternative academic educational program. They must not be punished, harassed, embarrassed, have their grades reduced or their work load increased, because of their parents' decision.

Parents should not be intimidated by accusations that they are "censors" or "enemies of public schools." The Protection of Pupil Rights Amendment does not stop any federal funding or prohibit any program — it merely requires parental consent before objectionable programs are used. How could anyone object to that?

Parents should not be intimidated by accusations that enforcement of the Pupil Rights Amendment will increase federal control over local schools. That is false. The Regulations merely force those using federally-funded programs to obey the law with respect to those materials.

Parents should not be intimidated by a claim that the objectionable course is not subject to the Pupil Rights Amendment because it does not use federal funding. Since most psychological curricula and teacher training were either developed with the use of federal funding, or appear on lists of federally-approved programs, or the teachers were trained how to use them in workshops financed with federal funds, **the burden of proof is on the school** to prove that any given program has *no* federal funding involved. The NEA Newsletter of December 3, 1984 states that, "The Hatch Act now covers every classroom teacher, every teaching method, and all classroom materials."

One should not assume that private schools are safe from the "therapy" programs described in this book. They may be subject to the Pupil Rights Amendment if they use curricula developed in whole or in part by federal funding. In addition, many private schools have adopted very similar programs. It is up to the parents to find out what their children are doing during classroom hours and assert parental rights.

The time has come for parents to assert their rightful authority over the education of their children. This book gives parents the tools to protect their children against child abuse in the classroom. This is *the* civil rights issue of the 1980s.

Phyllis Schlafly

I.

Excerpts _from_

Official Transcript of Proceedings

BEFORE THE

U.S. DEPARTMENT OF EDUCATION

In the Matter of:

PROPOSED REGULATIONS TO IMPLEMENT
THE PROTECTION OF PUPIL RIGHTS AMENDMENT
SECTION 439 OF THE GEPA
ALSO KNOWN AS THE HATCH AMENDMENT

DATE: MARCH 13, 1984

PLACE: SEATTLE, WASHINGTON

Archie Brooks

I want to address the issue of Values Education through a program called Preventive Guidance and Counseling used this past year in Lincoln County School, Lincoln County, Oregon.

In October, 1982, a group of Lincoln County parents discovered their children returning home from school in a greatly agitated manner on certain evenings. Upon closer investigation, parents discovered the children were most stressful on the days when the Guidance Counselor was in the classrooms. As parents became more concerned, they investigated the Guidance Counseling Program through questioning their children. They discovered a number of interesting points:

The parents did not know their children were even in a Guidance Counseling Program. The parents did not know what a Guidance Counseling Program consisted of. They were not sure they had given permission for their children to be in the Preventive Guidance Counseling class.

The questions often used by the teacher were personal, probing questions dealing with personal feelings, values, and private family matters. Most children interviewed were bored with the class, but went along with it because they felt compelled. The principal confessed to having no knowledge of what exactly the Guidance Counselor was doing.

Children had been threatened with a pink slip, a disciplinary action, if they did not cooperate. The Preventive Guidance Counseling Program was in all the grade schools in North Lincoln County, using the same counselor, and the same materials.

The Oregon State Standards and Guidelines states that instructors may utilize only commercially prepared materials, and use only activities which have been reviewed and approved by the principal. Yet the counselor was using "original" material not approved by the principal or school district.

As parents at Delake School educated themselves in the matter, they found the permission slip they had signed at enrollment at the beginning of the year was a single-page, all-inclusive permission slip covering five areas: (1) Permission to allow a child to be involved in Speech Therapy, if needed. A detailed account of the step-by-step procedures was affixed to this slip. (2) Permission for fluoride treatments. (3) Permission to participate on field trips. (4) Permission to have their picture put in the paper, if needed. (5) Guidance Counseling. There was no explanation of what this was, what the procedure was, no description of the class, or any hints as to the purpose of the class. In fact, most parents did not know it had a classroom format, feeling that counseling was on an individual basis.

Parents also became aware that students who did

not have parental permission would have to leave their classroom during the sessions and go to another room or library. Having to leave made these students feel uncomfortable.

Once parents began to realize that there was a Guidance Counseling Program and permission was required, and that they could have their children removed, then they began to remove their children.

As time passed and parents further educated themselves, they became aware of the terms Values Education, Values Clarification, Humanism, Social Change Agents, and so forth. The questions being asked students in a classroom setting, all together, included:

Do you have a close relationship with either your mother or father?

Have you taught a Sunday School class or otherwise taken an active part in your church?

Do you believe in a God who answers prayers?

Do you believe that tithing — giving one-tenth of one's earning to the church — is one's duty to God?

Do you pray about your problems?

Do you read the Bible or other religious writings regularly?

Do you love your parents?

Do you believe God created man in His own image?

If you ask God for forgiveness, are your sins forgiven?

Have you ever had problems so bad you wished you could die so you would not have to face them?

Would you rather live with someone else?

Would you like to have different parents?

What chores do you have at home on a regular basis?

What do you fear—real or imagined?

If you could change one thing in your home, or school, what would you change and why?

Why did your parents get married?

Do your parents ever lie to you?

In regard to these questions, many parents were upset due to an invasion of student and family privacy. A strong emphasis was placed upon the student's "feelings." In some cases, children were being alienated from their parents through expressions of moodiness, rebellion, self-centeredness, and so forth.

Many of these young and immature students did not know how they felt about certain complex issues. Their reasoning ability had not fully developed and, therefore, their responses could not always be explained clearly. This left them open to depending upon the group for an answer that was acceptable among the peer group. They felt frustrated and confused. Parents also asked themselves *why* these questions dealing with religion were asked when public schools are to avoid religious conversations and issues, especially questions of a personal nature, as these were.

Upon approaching the District officials, both hired and elected, and asking for an accounting, the parents were met with ridicule, arrogance, stonewalling, contempt, shifting of blame, direct and implied threats, pleas of ignorance, and lack of knowledge.

With the passage of time, parents realized the Preventive Guidance Counseling Program was simply manipulating the values, feelings, emotions, and attitudes of the individual students. So they began to pull children out of the class. Eventually, four school levies failed to pass, not because parents did not want to pay higher taxes, but because the School Administration and the School Board were unresponsive and unwilling to dismantle the Preventive Guidance Counseling Program as it was, or to modify it to be more acceptable to parents.

Parents tried on many occasions to explain that it is not the responsibility of the school to actively guide value information or to suggest in any way to a child that he has a right to develop his own value system. No child develops his own value system. Values are learned "someplace," and that primary "someplace" should be the home.

Here is a letter which one parent wrote to the editor of the local newspaper.

"I am writing this letter concerning the classroom counseling—as you will notice, I said classroom counseling. I have nothing against one-to-one counseling with parental consent, group counseling with children who all share the same problems, with parental consent, or a child or group who wants to talk to a counselor or even a teacher for a reason. There are times when a child or group may wish to go and talk to someone.

"I did not know they had group counseling or classroom counseling when my daughter was in 5th grade. I now understand her feelings back then when I would meet her for Camp Fire meetings on Mondays. She always seemed depressed, upset, did not want to go to the Camp Fire meetings, and looked like she had been crying sometimes. When I asked what was wrong, she told me nothing.

"Well! I found out this year that she was told not to tell anyone about what was said in the group. She kept her word, no matter how much I asked last year. I do not like anyone telling my child not to tell me anything. I also do not believe a teacher or counselor has the right to allow other children to badger, make fun of, or make that child or another one cry in a group and lay a guilt trip on them.

"I never gave permission for my daughter or son to be in group counseling or classroom counseling. If I feel one of my children needs to see a counselor, it will be one of my choosing, *not* that of the school's.

"Mr. Stempel told me none of this would be happening if Values Clarification had not been used. I told him I was glad it happened, otherwise I would not have known what was going on. I do not like to be in the dark about what my children are being taught, and I was in the dark about this.

"Parents are 'untrained and unskilled,' according to the books I have read which are used as references in the Preventive Guidance and Counseling Program. By whose standards are they saying parents are 'untrained and unskilled' to handle their own children's problems? And whose standards are they using to teach our children morals and values? Whose? Is it the Church? Hell's Angels? James Jones of the Jonestown massacre? Theirs?

"It is my responsibility as a parent to teach my children right from wrong, their morals and values, help them know the consequences of what will happen on decisions they make, to let them know I will be there to help and stand by them. Trust is taught between child and parent the day you bring them home from the hospital. They learn who to trust starting at a very early age.

"Children can very easily be led to think and act differently as they grow up and enter school. They do not have a concept that what is being asked—such as 'Do your folks smoke?' 'What do you do around the house?' 'Do your folks steal?' —is an invasion of their privacy or that of their parents. Whose business is it if you do smoke? No one's. You hear people complain about violence. You should read some of the activities in the books used as references in the Preventive Guidance and Counseling Program. Some of the activities that could be used would really make you stop and think, and maybe make your hair stand on end. There are other ways to teach besides using Values Clarification and Humanism. We do not need to use violence to get a child to think.

"Our children are out of the classroom counseling and will stay out, and God help anyone who tries to come between our children and us.

"Larry and Betty Grahn."

In addition to this mother's report, let me share examples of abuse in the Preventive Guidance Counseling Program.

One child, an 11-year-old girl, was placed in front of her counseling class to tell her "feelings" when she found her father dead. Upon disclosing this information, she was later hassled by classmates with teasing questions.

A second child was forced, under threat of a pink slip—a disciplining action—to stand in front of a class and tell all the "feelings" and experiences of parents going through a divorce. She was asked specifically what it felt like, and then which parent she now wished to live with.

A third child was answering a questionnaire and said, "Daddy spanks me, and sometimes pulls down my pants to spank me." Dad was then taken to the police station.

Each of these examples took place in the Lincoln County School District, and each relates the problems caused by the Preventive Guidance Counseling

Program.

In conclusion, the District Administration and curriculum planners now use much the same material that reflects Values Education and Values Clarification in the New Health Education Program. This program, for grades 1 through 8, includes "peer influence on safe practices," "different and unique individuals," "a child's role in the family"—all for Grade 1.

Grade 2 has "communicating feelings and dealing with hostility and aggression." Grade 3 has "self-regulation, biofeedback, and coping with peer pressure." In Grade 4, there is "predicting counsequences of behavior." Grade 5 teaches "coping with distress, biofeedback."

Grade 7 has "biofeedback, coping with personal loss, and techniques for resolving conflicts." Grade 8 includes "coping skills for dating and sexuality-contraceptives." In Grade 7, "coping with personal loss," is the same basic program as Perspective on Loss Through Death and Divorce which caused so many problems for children in the 1982-83 school year in the Preventive Guidance Counseling Program.

The basis of the above topics is again Values Education and Values Clarification. They contain the same basic subject matter and questions as the old program which parents fought to have eliminated. The Preventive Guidance Counseling Program was one class twice a week. The new Health Education Program, which again uses no set curriculum, but only a loose-leaf notebook filled with ideas teachers can choose to implement, will be taught throughout each day scattered in several different classroom subjects.

In reading through the Standard Guidelines for Guidance and Counseling and Elementary School Guidance and Counseling from the Oregon Department of Education, I did not find one mention of requiring or seeking parental permission.

TESTIMONY OF
Janet Brossard

I got into this because my child in the fall of 1982 was in the 8th grade of one of the junior high schools in Bellevue, Washington, and I heard that she was in Health. Now, we didn't sign her into Health. It hadn't bevn made a required course the year before, and in the Bellevue School District, you sign for the children's elective courses. They have a form that comes home that these are the choices that your child has made, and do you approve of that, so you only sign for the electives. The required courses are just given to them.

I asked what she was going to be having in that, and I wrote a note to the teacher, and sex education was listed as one of the things. So I asked if I could see the sex education program.

In the meantime, we had gone to an open house. At the open house, the room was filled with parents and the teacher had the textbook on the table or on each desk. And she said, "This is the text we use." Flipping through that, I could see that it was very innocent. It was fine, but then, I decided to ask the teacher if I could go and see all the materials. She showed them to me, I was very concerned because some of them were very much of the decision-making style, and I said, "Well, do you teach morals?" and she said, "No, we don't get into morals."

I said, "How can you teach decision making without getting into morals?" And she said, "We do, but we just don't teach morals."

She didn't understand my question, so we just talked it over with the principal, who brought in the Director of Curriculum, for my husband and me to speak with. We are pro-life, and we decided after talking with him that they were using an awful lot from Planned Parenthood. In fact, this teacher was having the National Abortion Rights Action League come in one day, and Planned Parenthood for three days, and a Right-to-Life speaker for one day. I felt that was just a little bit too much in favor of abortion, and so we decided that our child would not go to the class. We told her that, and she said, "I want to go because what will happen if I'm taken out is that I'll have to go every day to the class to get checked in, and then I will have to get up and walk out of the class when the teacher tells me and go to the library and sit all by myself."

And she said, "Besides that, I have friends in my class, so I'll find out what's going on in there anyway." So, I said, "All right, you can go and I'm going with you." So that's why I attended the sex education classes for three weeks in the fall of 1982.

After I attended them, whatever there was, well, I felt that the teacher, if she had done her own job would have been all right, but the District gave directions. The District had her give lessons in activities. They were supposed to be activity-oriented classes. Most parents wouldn't know what these "activities" are. You wouldn't understand. The "activities" that occurred included giving the students "Dear Mabel" letters. Three or four children in one group would go into the "Dear Mabel" letters. Last fall, they came out with a book of these lessons and activities.

Consequently, anyone can go and find out about these letters. Here is a sample:

"Dear Mabel: I'm 15 and having sex with my boyfriend. Sometimes he uses birth control, but sometimes he doesn't feel like using anything. I'm afraid to use anything myself. I'm a little worried about getting pregnant, but I figure it's not likely to happen at my age. What do you think I should do about my boyfriend?"

Then, you have four or five kids making a response to one of these letters. Other letters were about problems of pregnancy, girls who are pregnant, and what shall I do? I felt that this was having the children teach each other about morals.

Well, I wrote a three-page letter to the Director of Curriculum. He did not answer me by mail, but he called up and thanked me for my letter and said he would share it with the Health Education Advisory Council, which was responsible for the health program.

So I asked the teacher who was on that Council afterwards, the next year, if she had seen my letter, and she had not. He had not shared it with the Council at all. I was really just ignored. So, we ended up forming a group called the Concerned Citizens of Bellevue.

I would like to read a questionnaire which was given to 13-year-olds in the 8th grade:

"Adolescent sexual behavior instructions. Indicate in the space provided the minimum age at which each of the behaviors listed is considered appropriate or acceptable in your value system. In other words, when is it okay to engage in _____. [The child is supposed to fill in the number for the following 25 items]:

"Holding hands; kissing; French kissing; petting; masturbation; petting but not all the way; love making with a person of the same sex; staying out all night with a sex partner; talking with the opposite sex about sex; talking with parents about sex; smoking tobacco; smoking marijuana; drinking booze; getting drunk or stoned; using swear words; seeing explicit sex in movies; seeing violence in movies; having intercourse; having a variety of sexual partners; living together; getting married; creating a pregnancy; having an abortion; taking birth control pills; becoming sterilized."

Then the instructions to the teacher are that,

after they have done that, they are to section off the room—"Is it okay before 14 or after 14"—and the children are to physically get up from their seats and go over to these sections and indicate which of these, or how, they answered the questions.

In another class, there are activities where the kids have to actively get out of their seats and go. One instruction says:

> "Have all the students stand on the center line. Make a center line down the center of the room. Have all the students stand on the center line and tell them that you are going to read a series of statements. If they feel the statement is true, they take one giant step to the right. If they feel it is false, they take one giant step to the left. Students who choose to pass can sit on the line."

And here are the statements:

> "All sex education should take place at home.
> "There should be sex education in the schools.
> "Guys would prefer to marry virgins.
> "Girls would prefer to marry virgins.
> "If two people are engaged, it's okay to have sex before marriage.
> "If two people are in love, it's okay to have sex before marriage.
> "You should have sex only with someone you love.
> "Sex should be romantic.
> "Sex should be spontaneous, just happen when you feel like it.

"Our society puts too much emphasis on sex.

"Young people today have a healthier attitude about sex than their parents.

"I would want my son to be a virgin when he got married.

"I would want my daughter to be a virgin when she got married.

"Men have more sexual partners than women do."

Then, to the teacher, the instructions are:

"If you feel the climate at your school and in your class would allow, do the voting a second and perhaps a third time. On the subsequent votes ask the students to vote as they feel their parents would vote, then as their grandparents might vote. Discuss reasons for differences."

After attending the class and looking at this book, I felt that they are really trying to get children away from their parents' opinion. They never mention religious beliefs; it is just never mentioned. They are trying to get them to form their own opinions, which I feel is humanism, and I don't think that this has a place in the school, either.

Here is another example. The teacher is instructed to present an overhead transparency, uncovering one at a time, from the top to the bottom. On the left side of these overhead transparencies are the words: "Nose," "Leg," "Elbow," "Breast," "Penis," "Vagina," and "Intercourse." On the right-hand side, the teacher is supposed to write the slang. Instructions to the teacher are:

"Ask the students to write down any slang word they know of for that word. When the list is all uncovered, go back and ask for voluntary oral responses. Be prepared to offer some yourself when the students are reluctant to respond."

After that, the instruction to the teacher goes:

"Ask the students to write down ways they learned what they know about sex. Then go over the list and put a plus by the source if it is a positive message and a minus sign if it was a negative. Then discuss. Ask teachers to list the things that they feel an 8th grade student should know about sex. Review list and put a P if parents should teach, an S if school, and F if friend, and O if other."

The program lacks dignity. Here is another example, for which the teacher needs butcher paper and felt markers. It says that she uses this activity—

"if you feel your group to be able to deal with it halfway maturely. Divide class into small groups, segregated by sex this time. Ask the boys to draw the outline of a female figure and the girls to draw the outline of a male. Give each group a list of the names of the parts of the reproductive system, males to girls and vice versa. And ask them to draw them in on their body pictures. Allow about five minutes. When finished, tape them to the wall. Ask the boys to correct the girls' drawings and the girls to correct the boys'. Teacher checks them all."

I see no reason to embarrass children in that manner. It's ridiculous. The whole program never mentions marriage as a prerequisite for sex. Never. The whole program goes on the assumption that everybody is doing it. Here is a sample of that. This is an exercise in regard to the sexually transmitted diseases:

"Rank these situations from the least to most distressing one:

"One, you discovered you have STD and you have had intercourse with only a steady boy or girl friend.

"Two, your best friend tells you that he or she has STD and it came from your boy or girl friend.

"Three, you discover you caught STD from a stranger that you met at a party. Now you have to tell your boy or girl friend that he or she may have it.

"Four, you are scheduled for a regular physical examination with your family doctor. This morning you notice some small sores on your genital region. You are sure the doctor will see them and tell your parents.

"Five, right before sexual intercourse, your partner reveals that he or she has STD."

All of this, I feel, is just telling the kids that, "Gee, everybody is doing it." Of course, they constantly reminded the children to go to Planned Parenthood for their birth control.

The parents have no idea the kids are being

asked these things and that they are discussing these types of things. There is one teacher in Bellevue who has all the boys say "vagina"; he calls them individually and they have to all say this out loud in class. The boys say "vagina" and the girls all say "penis." One girl told me that she was so embarrassed that she could hardly bring out the word "penis" because all these boys were sitting in the class. It just embarrassed her so. So he made her get up in front of the class and very loudly say it ten times. This just embarrasses the children.

I feel what they are accomplishing is to embarrass them, to break down their natural sense of modesty, to just break down their barriers, and they are not gaining anything by this. They say that they don't want the kids to have sex, but if they break down their natural defenses, those kids are going to have sex more easily. Having them sitting in the classroom and discussing these types of things is just going to make it so much easier for them to have sex.

So, consequently, I really feel that parents should be told.

TESTIMONY OF_____
Carrie Brooks

In January of 1982, I became aware of the Title IX-funded Sex Equity Program, or the Women's Educational Equity Act Program called WEEA, in Lincoln County, Oregon, one of five counties chosen in the United States as a test site to change the thinking patterns of America's children. I became aware something was going on when my 3rd grade daughter came home singing a song she had memorized from a record bought with Title IX funds, and monies from the sale of that record went to "Ms. Foundation." My daughter sang:

"I hate housework. It is just no fun. Ladies on TV are paid to smile."

While I was trying to teach my daughters the joys of keeping a home clean, the blessings you give and receive from a well-cared-for home, my daughter was being brainwashed by Marlo Thomas and Carol Channing on this record. I then began to investigate what was going on, having no idea the years of groundwork women activists had given to their pet project, funded by the Federal Government.

The ACLU Handbook says parents have the right to all instructional material used on their children, yet I was denied materials I wanted to see. What they did finally give me was too general or not applicable. Teachers were allowed to use their own information, so each school's system was different in teaching sex equity, or as it really should be called, gender equity.

I went to a demonstration site where teachers from all over the United States came to see how Lincoln County implemented Title IX. One of the demonstrations was in a 1st grade room. The students each had two naked paper dolls, one male, the other female. They were asked to dress the dolls in work clothing to show that both genders could work at any job.

The thing I found interesting was there were no dresses. All clothing was male oriented. Then the teacher had the students sit in a circle while she pulled out objects from a sack, like a pancake turner or a tape measure. She asked, "Who uses this, mom or dad?"

If the students did not answer the way she had wanted, she would say, "Well, who else uses this?" Finally, one little boy raised his hand and said, "I don't care. Men ought to be doctors, and ladies nurses."

The teacher then asked how many of the students agreed with him. By the tone of her voice, they knew no one should raise a hand, so no one did. The little boy was so humiliated by the peer pressure and class manipulation by the teacher that he started to cry. This is classic of the type of discrimination, bias, stereotyping, and harassment that this program has included.

After a couple of months of investigation, I was branded the "Moral Majority" by an interstaff letter in one of our schools. In this letter, the teachers were advised not to give out any information to parents asking questions about Sex Equity or the Preventive Guidance Counseling Program. All pupils inquiring were to be sent to the principal, who told them they could only temporarily be exempt from a teaching to which they objected.

As I reviewed different manuals that teachers

were using in the schools, I discovered many class activities that would be illegal under the Hatch Amendment. I know that there were no permission slips given out to parents for these activities, yet questions on family values, self-analysis, opposite role-playing, unisex ideas, discussion of family roles in students' homes, and sex-role values were discussed. One book said, "Students are no longer to be called helpers, or boys and girls, or students, but WORKERS." That is socialist language, and definitely against my wishes as a parent.

Another book showed *only* pictures of opposites to traditional roles, such as the father feeding baby, or mother holding a firehose in her "fireperson" job. The children didn't realize they were being fed only one side of the social picture.

To show *only* the opposite role is discrimination toward men and women in traditional roles. To be fair, both types of roles should be shown to the unsuspecting student who believes whatever the teacher says. Otherwise, resocialization takes place, or brainwashing.

Title IX was originated to dispel discrimination, but I was called biased for my belief in traditional roles, and was stereotyped into an extreme position I do not hold. I was put down and discriminated against by faculty and administration officials. The children were being taught to be non-judgmental, and to go against family teachings. I believe this is illegal, but where do we go for help if not to the Hatch Amendment?

Our school district received federal funds to

teach "Sex Equity." I believe there are no funds coming now, but the teaching is firmly intact in the system after five years of funding. Teachers are required to attend sex equity workshops sponsored by Northwest Regional Laboratory in Portland, which received federal funds. They provide resource materials and teachers.

I discovered there was no set curriculum. Teachers chose what to teach from several manuals. They were to integrate the teaching into the entire day's classes. Women were really exalted in all the material I viewed, while male minorities were almost ignored. The goal of the Sex Equity program was to eliminate traditional roles of male and female.

After talking to a principal, assistant school superintendent, equity program coordinators, and teachers, I was told that news had been given out in county newsletters about the equity program for some time. Yet, I have talked to over a hundred women in the county at different speaking engagements, and only two knew of the Sex Equity or Preventive Guidance Counseling Programs, and those two were teachers. Sex Equity was not publicized enough. My daughter was being taught things I did not want her to hear, before I knew of the teachings.

I was told by the principal of the school my children were attending that "there were no real differences between male and female except a 'slight' physical difference."

Males and females have differences in talents, strengths, abilities, and are not the same physically or emotionally. I want my daughters to be proud they are female, and not just second-class males, as the androgyny teaching promotes. Our home values are in direct conflict with what is taught in the public school. This conflict created tension, lack of respect for authority, and inhibited our goals for our daughters. My rights as a parent have been violated by our school district. The Hatch Amendment implemented would protect our family from teachings we may not agree with.

As the law is now, there are no penalties for violations of parent rights. We firmly believe that men are men, women are women, and children should be taught to enhance and enjoy their male or female identity.

Title IX was a pet project of women's rights groups that received millions of taxpayers' dollars to brainwash our precious children. It left them no identities, no absolutes, no role models, and no satisfaction or fulfillment.

When the schools decide what to teach our children without our knowledge, or when the teaching conflicts with the beliefs of the family, something must be done.

For the sake of parents who no longer want their children used as guinea pigs of resocialization, please do something to make the Hatch Amendment really law.

TESTIMONY OF——————————————————
Marcella Warila
————————————————————————

I am a housewife from Portland, Oregon, the mother of four children, and a former teacher.

My testimony concerns violations of parents' and students' rights that I personally have observed in workshops for high school students in the Talented and Gifted Program in Area I Portland Public Schools. Candidates for this program are chosen from the top three percent of the national school population.

In December of 1979, in what was called a "Risk-Taking Workshop," a professional communications consultant made statements to 50 students, aged 14 and up, that would tend to alienate them from their parents' control and influence:

> "Your parents' values are different from yours. They grew up at a different time and have a different field of experience."

She told them that they are beginning to take risks, that is, make decisions that their parents might not approve, that they are running into conflicts with their parents, and that up to now, their parents have "got away with" directing or controlling them. Every mention of parents was negative.

She told them that, in making decisions, one of the things they need to evaluate is loss of support of people who are close to them. She said that, when their beliefs are bombarded by a sufficient number of opposing beliefs, their entire set of values will be shifted and be replaced by a new set of values.

This is the strategy of Values Clarification and of sensitivity training. The deliberate and methodical changing of a person's values and personality is called brainwashing.

In January, 1980, I attended a problem-solving, decision-making workshop called "Effecting Change." It was put on by two men—one from the Oregon Department of Education, the other a young teacher who was a highly-skilled sensitivity facilitator. He quickly established rapport with the students by telling them how smart they were and how much they could teach others. Then in a Values Clarification session, he encouraged them to air their gripes and discuss myths—meaning the restraints and restrictions that parents and society placed on them.

They were left with the impression that they are smart enough to make *all* their own decisions without parental interference.

They told those receptive teenagers that there are *no* objective standards of morality, and that truth is relative and can mean anything they want it to mean. When I interjected that truth does not change, and that morals do not change, it is attitudes toward morals that change, he replied, "Yeah, on one level I think I hear what you are saying, but I have a real difficult time with that, because my truths change from day to day."

The State Board man said, "One of the things we can be sure of is that there are different ways in which things are interpreted." To prove that even in math there is no absolute truth, he had the students add a column of seven numbers, putting them first on the overhead, then reading them orally.

Referring to me, he said, "She says that truth is always truth. In some areas *perhaps* that is true. In math, when you add these numbers up, it usually comes out one way, 4,100. The majority says 5,000. Your eyes played a trick on you."

Doing it right in "problem solving" means consulting the people you are working with — determination by the whole group. That left the impression that whatever is arrived at by group consensus is true and right. They did not distinguish moral from non-moral issues.

When I took my complaints to the Assistant Superintendent of Curriculum of the Portland Schools, he said, "If they are doing these things, it would be wrong," and he made an appointment for me with the coordinator of the Talented and Gifted Program.

I met with three coordinators, who insisted that sensitivity training was not used in the workshops, and that they were neither anti-parent nor humanist. They ended up saying that society is humanist and we have to work with that. They gave me an incorrect date for the next workshop, saying that, since our son was not participating, I had no interest in it.

But when I showed up at the Futures workshop anyway, one of the coordinators, a teacher at our son's school, treated me insultingly and tried to bluff me into leaving. The vice-principal of our school and head TAG coordinator had told me, prior to the first workshop to which one of our sons had been invited, that parents were welcome to attend. This teacher asked who I was and said that I didn't have clearance to attend; that she didn't know what my intentions were—I might be bringing in drugs! (I should have asked them if they have a lot of trouble with mothers bringing in drugs.)

She said that they couldn't let people come in off the street. She knew very well who I was, and I was the only mother there. I was unable to summarize the Futures conference because, although I am a college graduate, I couldn't understand much of the rantings of the two speakers. However, the gist was that society has always been controlled by an elite, and that these students are destined to be the elite who will control the future lives of all of us.

Parents are notified before students participate in these programs, but it is not an informed permission. Most parents whose children are recommended for the TAG program think that they are going to be given advanced academic education. They don't know that, in these workshops, attempts will be made to alienate their children from them and from moral values, or that their children will be taught to substitute the judgment and will of the group for that of individual judgment and responsibility. They don't realize that unelected planners are manipulating their bright teenagers to serve as conduits of their planned change.

These programs, which are funded with hundreds of thousands of dollars of taxpayers' money, are in violation of Oregon's Revised Statute 336.067, which says that special emphasis shall be given to instruction in honesty, morality and respect for parents and the home.

These programs are immoral and should be held unconstitutional. District Court Judge Noel Fox expressed it very well in a 1978 ruling in the Federal District Court of Western Michigan. He said:

> "Parental authority is plenary. It prevails over claims of the state, other outsiders and the children themselves. There must be some compelling reason for interference. It needs no further discussion to conclude that the right of parents to the care, custody and nurture of their children is of such a character that it cannot be denied without violating these fundamental principles of liberty and justice which lie at the base of all our civil and political institutions. Parents' rights in the case are guaranteed by the First, Fifth, Ninth and Fourteenth Amendments to the Constitution."

TESTIMONY OF_____

Joanne Lisac

I am a housewife from Milwaukie, Oregon. I am here to submit testimony about a guidance and counseling curriculum used in the North Clackamas School District #12, Milwaukie, Oregon.

There are federal funds involved in this program, although our district has been unwilling to produce the total cost. The District has not provided specified instructional materials and teacher's manuals we have requested. This 14-pound mass of material is an ideal example of why we need strong regulations for the Protection of Pupil Rights Amendment.

This curriculum begins in kindergarten and continues through the 12th grade. It has been integrated into all subjects.

My son participated in this curriculum for two years without our knowledge or consent. He was administered pre- and post-evaluations to determine attitude changes. He participated in Sidney Simon's Values Clarification, role-playing, and a myriad of group activities. One of these was to sit in a Magic Circle holding hands and divulge personal information about his thoughts, feelings, values, and beliefs.

He was placed in moral dilemmas via Lawrence Kohlberg and came home one day very confused as to the rightness or wrongness of stealing from a store.

He was put through transactional analysis via Alvyn Freed and, as a result, applied the principle of "playing stupid" at home whenever his Dad or I gave him a chore to do. It caused a lot of dissension in our home. We realize some of these things are typical of children, but it takes on a totally different connotation when you see it written down and find out your son has, indeed, been taught this in school. I got this page from my District, and my son recognized it as an example he was taught. My son was given questionnaires that he didn't even know how to respond to. Let me read this from Decision Categories:

"We all make decisions daily. Some are more important than others. Some require thought and study before making, and others are almost made automatically. The following decisions are faced by many people today. Read them and decide which decision category applies to each. Write the number code in the blank after the decisions to tell how much thought you put into each one.

   0 - Not under my control
   1 - Automatic—no thought
   2 - Sometimes think about it
   3 - Think about, but do not study
   4 - Study a little bit
   5 - Study a lot.

Typical Decisions

1. To get up in the morning
2. What to eat and when
3. To tell the truth
4. To criticize a friend behind his back
5. To drink alcohol
6. To work a job
7. To use drugs besides alcohol
8. To smoke
9. To follow school rules
10. To vandalize
11. To go to school
12. To lie to your parents
13. To believe in God

14. Where to dispose of paper and wrappers
15. What movie to see."

The invasions of privacy in this curriculum are endless.

"Do you have your own bedroom?

Are you going to practice religion just like your parents?

Who has the last word in your family?

Draw a picture of your house and family occupants; write what each one is saying.

Draw what your parents wear at home, at work.

What tools do they use at home, at work?

What is your parents' income?

How much time do your parents spend watching TV?"

And on and on. The young children are expected to fill in sentences such as, "The trouble with being honest is _____." They are asked, what would be the hardest thing for you to do: "steal, cheat or lie"?

This question was included for group discussion in 3rd grade: "How many of you ever wanted to beat up your parents?" Is this education?

There is virtually no way to control some of these processes such as Magic Circle and other sensitivity and encounter-type group techniques. Who knows what a child will bring out in these activities? How qualified are educators when handling an incident with a seriously disturbed child? What effect would it have on the rest of the class if a child came apart during one of these sessions? These encounter-type techniques are risky at best, and impossible to determine ahead of time.

We know of children who have divulged personal information about themselves or their families in these group activities. The class is sensitized to the exposed child's problem but, unfortunately, things don't always end there.

A classmate may get angry with that child and flaunt the disclosure to other children on the playground or elsewhere. Then what? Does the educator sensitize the whole school? What happens to the devastated child who learns, too late, that he shouldn't disclose personal information? The damage is done.

We do not send our children to school to have their morals, values, ethics, beliefs, thoughts, and feelings questioned, scrutinized, prioritized, and rearranged by the group. We do not abdicate our rights to raise our children according to our own moral, cultural, and ethical beliefs when we send them off to school every day. We do not send them to school to have those rights challenged and undermined by pseudo-psychiatrists posing as educators.

We do not send them to school to be taught "all points of view," but facts. Schools have become psychological playgrounds which are defended as "academic freedom." These processes are neither academic nor do they allow freedom. They are a deliberate attempt to manipulate and indoctrinate our children into a philosophical belief that morals and ethics are relative. Here is a critique of Values Clarification made by Professor Alan L. Lockwood:

> "Any values curriculum which rules out debate on the propriety or defensibility of moral value decisions is susceptible to charges of promoting ethical relativism. . . .
>
> Moral judgments require sound justifications, not simple expressions of personal taste. If not, how could we fairly and rationally oppose the views and practices of Hitlers, Mansons, Watergaters and the like?"

I'd also like to quote William J. Bennett and Edwin J. Delattre from an article entitled "Moral Education in the Schools." They stated:

> "Both Simon and Kohlberg also fail to avoid indoctrination. Both of their programs offer indoctrination in the 'values' they take to be important—the celebration of wants and desires, the exhortation to self-gratification, and a particular ideology of rights and 'special justice.' Although they both claim to disavow traditional moral education because it indoctrinates, Simon and Kohlberg clearly do not oppose indoctrination per se, but the indoctrination of traditional values."

It's a sad thing education has come to this point today. Parents pay taxes to support this system, whether federal, state or local level. We need some assurance that our children are being provided proven quality education instead of using our children as guinea pigs to promote psychological theories and someone's philosophical beliefs.

*TESTIMONY OF*_____

Michael Lisac

My name is Mike Lisac, and I am here in a dual capacity, one to represent the views of a father of four children who have gone through North Clackamas school system, and in the capacity of an Advisory Board member for North Clackamas Elementary School, which is a part of our North Clackamas School District.

Here are examples of two courses which caused parents to file complaints: MACOS (MAN: A Course of Study) and TA for Teens.

MACOS was a very subtle way of teaching our children genocide, homosexuality, euthanasia. It goes through, in story form, the Eskimo culture in Alaska.

TA for Teens is Transactional Analysis, which devastates the relationship between parents and children, and not only the parents and children, but all authority. It leaves our children thinking they can be autonomous, and autonomy means the children's own rules and regulations.

To give you an example of that in TA for Teens, one of the things it does is to tell the children how to bring out the "parent" in people. For example, they could do this by destroying things of value (that is vandalism — and we wonder why vandalism is on the rise!). The middle finger in the air is an excellent way to bring parents down on you. Spilling things consistently, over and over and over, is another example of bringing out the "parent."

TA for Teens is not an exceptional program; it is one of the philosophies used to implement the worksheets in the curriculum.

Something else that is really important is how they implemented the overall program. Whether it's Sidney Simon or situation ethics or Transactional Analysis or role-playing or Magic Circle, they are inflicting their philosophy on children. How did they do it? Well, they do it through a very simple technique called Home Rules. At McLaughlin Junior High, every class that our children attends has Home Rule signs, and what they say is "What I think." There are no right and wrong answers. When the child comes out, I'll guarantee you, he will be autonomous, will not respect any authority except the child's own authority. So he could kill, he could push drugs, he could rape and murder, and there are no right and wrong answers.

When my wife asked my son, "What does that mean?" he said, "You know, what we share at school is confidential." She said, "Well, what about Mom and Dad, can you tell us?" and he said, "No, I don't think so."

That's the thing. They just keep it a secret.

*TESTIMONY OF*_____
Larry Johnson
_____

I am a resident of the City of Milwaukie, Oregon. I am affiliated with the schools of North Clackamas School District in the way of an Advisory Committee member via the Gilchrist Elementary School.

I am happy to be an Oregonian; I was born and raised in Oregon. I graduated from the school system that we presently send five of our children to.

About May 27, 1982, our District implemented the so-called Guidance and Counseling — I say "so-called" because the goal of it is not guidance and counseling. When I went to my first school board meeting, I said, "Why would there be any controversy over guidance and counseling?" And they said, "Oh, well, there are some people who believe in absolutes."

I just sort of dismissed it, but then, as I got into this Advisory Committee, they asked me to review it. There are a few things in there that do surprise you. When they start questioning your children, you do get a little bit concerned. And here are some examples. They ask open-end questions such as:

> "What do your parents do?"
> "Sometimes I lie when _____." There is the assumption in the question that sometimes lying is acceptable.
> "I hate it when _____." That's just planting the seeds of hate.

Here's a "What's Important to You" worksheet.

"Number 5: Which would be the hardest for you to —

_____ steal a toy from another child's desk?

_____ cheat by looking at another child's paper?

_____ tell a lie to the teacher?"

So the problem is pretty obvious.

Here are other specific examples. We have a daughter, Brooke, who is in the 9th grade. On February 15, at Clackamas High School, they showed two movies in the so-called Health class. One was called "The Right To Live, Who Decides?" This movie showed actual actors playing out the "lifeboat situation," where you have the lifeboat that's got too many people on it and it is going to sink, so therefore, you have to throw somebody over, so the boat will float and you save some of the people.

So they go through the values. They say, "Well, this one's a doctor, and this one's handicapped, this one's a youth, this one's a parent, this one's an attorney." They go through the process of placing a value on each person. I totally object to that type of situation. Everybody has a tremendous value in our entire country. Nobody has more or less value.

What they are planting here is the assumption that you are more or less valuable because of your contribution, or whatever. Well, that's not what we believe in, and I don't like that type of teaching. The people would be screaming as they were being thrown over and killed. One might refer to this teaching of killing and murder as rather dramatic, but it's happening, and it's right here in our schools. When it's your school and your kids, you get sort of directly involved.

That whole situation was also in our Talented and Gifted Program (TAG) last year when our daughter was in the 4th grade. They had the TAG kids enact this thing. One was a housewife and one was a child, and one was a teacher, and one was an engineer, or whatever. As a group they had to decide who lived, and the one they decided to throw out first was the mother. It just rubs me the wrong way that the mother would have the least value in that whole setup.

Then there was another movie called "Parents—Who Needs Them?" The notes are Brooke's actual notes from the day. We didn't know they were going to have a movie, and we didn't ask her to take notes. The teacher asked questions and put them on the board: "What good are parents? What will they do? Are they very important?"

She puts answers like "they take care of you, they teach you things, they provide entertainment." And then, in the movie they showed parents and children fighting. Do we need that? There is so much negative in the world as it is without having to plant more and more. I have a real problem with that sort of thing.

TESTIMONY OF_____

Susan Simonson

I am chairman of a Committee for Quality School Textbooks in Corvallis, Oregon. I come before you as a public school teacher who has witnessed the tragic academic decline of the last 20 years.

Most importantly, I come before you as a mother of seven who has tried very hard to instill high moral values in her children, and who has had to withdraw them from public school to ensure that they will keep those values. I am now footing the bill for two children in college, three in private school and one who is home taught for whom I have purchased the curriculum, and another who in four years will enter a private school. At the same time, I support the public school with my taxes.

I could testify of repeated attempts on every one of my school-age children to change my children's values, including the 6-year-old twins, who were too young to resist, and they were too little to understand a lot of what was going on. In the interest of time, I will concentrate on my son, Jon, and his Family Life class, which was last spring.

Toward the end of this course last spring, my son told me what was happening in class. Mr. Davis, the teacher, would bring up a controversial moral issue, such as premarital sex or homosexuality, and call on members of the class to defend their positions on the issue. He would call upon those with opposite moral beliefs from Jon, thus exerting peer pressure on Jon to change his moral values. Jon was consistently called on up to 23 times per class session to defend his values before his friends with opposing views. When Jon mentioned to Mr. Davis that he was calling on him more than anyone else, Mr. Davis just said, "Oh," and continued calling on him.

For a teacher to attempt to change the home-taught values of a student is very wrong. The child does not belong to the school. The school has neither the right nor the parental mandate to tamper with high moral, religiously-held values. My son's morals are a part of his Christian beliefs. For a teacher to attempt to change them violates his First Amendment rights under the Free Exercise clause.

Secondly, since federal funds were involved in this class, the Hatch Amendment was violated when my son's sexual attitudes and beliefs were questioned. After careful consideration, I decided to pursue this matter, and I contacted the Superintendent of District 509J, Thomas Wogaman. He denied that this type of sexual-attitude questioning was a violation of the Hatch Amendment.

I sent a copy of my letter to Superintendent Wogaman plus a cover letter asking for help to Senator Mark Hatfield, the Corvallis High School principal, Senator Orrin Hatch, Verne Duncan — the State Superintendent of Public Instruction, Rep. Denny Smith, and the 509J School Board.

As a result, Senator Hatfield wrote a letter to our State Superintendent of Public Instruction. The Corvallis High School Principal was rude and denied a violation of the Hatch Amendment.

Senator Orrin Hatch wrote a letter to Superintendent Wogaman saying that what happened to Jon would clearly be a violation of the Hatch Amendment if any federal funds were involved — and they were. Senator Hatch also sent Superintendent Wogaman a copy of the *Congressional Record* regarding the intent of the Amendment. Wogaman still denied a violation.

Verne Duncan, Oregon State Superintendent of Public Instruction, replied that he saw no violation of the Hatch Amendment. Rep. Denny Smith wrote to Superintendent Wogaman and asked for a full accounting of the situation. The School Board did not reply. I contacted the teacher, who had been out of town. He denied a violation of the Hatch Amendment.

Then I sent a copy of Senator Orrin Hatch's letter and the *Congressional Record* testimony to Verne Duncan, State Superintendent, and the School Board.

I then wrote a letter back to Superintendent Wogaman pointing out that Senator Hatch, the author of the bill, felt my son's treatment was a violation of the Hatch Amendment. He replied with proof that federal funds were involved, but said that he still felt the Hatch Amendment was not violated. Next I wrote to Secretary of Education Terrel Bell and I received no reply. If this has not worn you out listening to it, it has surely worn me out writing all those letters.

I would like to see Hatch Amendment regulations written so that, if any federal funds are used in a school, failure to comply with the Hatch Amendment in any class, federally funded or not, would result in the loss of all federal funds until compliance was met. We need strong, definitive regulations to enforce the Hatch Amendment.

TESTIMONY OF
Cris Shardelman

North Kitsap has course goals that were developed out of the Tri-County Course Goals of the Northwest Regional Lab. These goals spell out the use of Values Clarification on students, including taxonomy or classification, particularly in Language Arts, although it has been in Home Economics and all the other subjects.

Students were subjected to numerous requirements concerning death-related subjects, including students writing their own epitaphs. Our teachers have been well trained in Sidney Simon's Values Clarification methods for years, and documentation is available to prove questioning of the student concerning values, beliefs, etc., of himself and the family.

In the introduction to *Schooling for a Global Age*, Professor John Goodlad stated:

"Parents and the general public must be reached also (taught a global perspective). Otherwise, children and youth enrolled in globally oriented programs may find themselves in conflict with values assumed in the home. And then the educational institution frequently comes under scrutiny and must pull back."

Kitsap County Schools involved in the Gifted Student Project LIFE find the concept is "developing a new global philosophy" centered "around futurism," and that they are supposed to use "the higher levels of thinking," and students agreed "that they look at the world differently from their peers." Parents should have been apprised of this result, and of the fact that the training exercises will be built on Bloom's taxonomy or classification. The citizens are not told that this program is developing leaders of a particular world view (globalism) and away from loyalty to their country.

Dungeons and Dragons is a game played in many classes, especially the Gifted, but in others in Washington state as well. This game has been named as the reason for several suicides in the United States.

Another Washington State program that flagrantly violates the Hatch Amendment is the Ethical Quest in a Democratic Society developed in Tacoma, which uses the Delphi method of pre- and post-testing, states that it measures students' growth, monitors them and that it puts humanism in every subject. The proposal stated that it would be used in all Tacoma schools, with nationwide dissemination. The proposal stated that it had its own value system, one opposed to those of the McGuffey Readers, and that it had a final orientation toward universal ethical principles.

We have the Scott Foresman Spectra Series for Social Studies. The teacher's manual states this:

"Some of the items have more than one 'right' answer, and students should be alerted to this fact. Such items are included for their value in testing critical thinking and values clarification.

"A classroom discussion following students' completion of each test will reveal to students points of view and insights that may not have occurred to each student individually, and it will reveal to the teacher those areas that gave students difficulty and that, therefore, require reteaching."

It is obvious that the student is being swayed by reteaching.

North Kitsap just adopted another social studies project called REACH, developed in Arlington School District with ESEA funds under Title IV. This is a series of four small books concerning Indians, Asians, Blacks and Mexicans. Each one is very derogatory to the Caucasian. In particular, the Indian book is most controversial; the source seems to be mostly Indian activist writings. Students have been asked to go home and ask their parents about their beliefs about Indians, a definite violation of the Hatch Amendment.

During this year, the Washington State Legislature was asked to fund the Here's Looking At You Two drug education program, and Governor Spellman tried to have it mandated in all classrooms. This program had 13 years of game playing, role-playing, questionnaires, and so forth, for evaluating student/parent beliefs and attitudes. Fortunately, so many people protested that it became voluntary. Under the guise of Mental Health, a program called WOW was developed at the Northwest Regional Laboratory. This program would have had the primary children exploring their attitudes, beliefs and values concerning such things as double standards, sexual exploitation, guilt and embarrassment about sexual activity, masturbation, homosexuality, and recognition of such words as stud and prostitute. There was an uproar in Oregon over this program. I believe this is a part of the Tri-County Goals that I mentioned earlier which North Kitsap has adopted. This project required taxonomy. I believe that at least one suicide was the result of the implementation of the suicide section of the mental health program.

Although I could cite many more violations, I believe the above will give a sufficient need for the regulations to be adopted—with teeth in them.

TESTIMONY OF
Dianna Storey

The necessity for regulations for the Protection of Pupil Rights Amendment can be demonstrated from an alcohol, tobacco, and drug program entitled Here's Looking at You Two. It was authored and developed by Clay Roberts of the Seattle area in

1972. It is designed for K through 12 and has been designated as a model youth program by the Health and Human Services Department. It is presently used in 44 states and in 45% of the schools in Washington State. Mr. Roberts told me that he received federal funds to help him in his development.

I have chosen two examples from his program which I believe demonstrate the invasion of the students' privacy by requiring students to reveal information concerning sexual behavior and attitudes and to make a critical appraisal of other individuals with whom students have close family relationships.

The first example is taken from Plan A, 7th to 9th grades, and it is titled Risk Taking. The preface in the teacher's manual states that the assumption is that, if students can take risks for the gain of high sensations, then risk taking itself may be that substitute abuse. The introduction to the teacher clearly establishes that this program is based on assumptions and hypotheses. In essence, this program is an experimental program and an invasion of students' privacy.

The lesson calls for a game of risk which includes the following instructions: Risk or game cards are distributed to students who are arranged into small groups. Each student rolls dice to determine his or her category.

The categories on cards include: One, two, physical; three, economic; four, personal, social; five, drugs; and six, choice of the other four categories.

I have chosen several situations from personal

and social categories. They are:

One, swimming in the nude at private beach with friends;

Two, not telling your parents the truth as to where you are going and what you will be doing;

Three, having sexual intercourse with your boy or girlfriend;

Four, cheating on an exam.

Remember, now, that this is supposed to be a drug prevention curriculum.

The students then take the above topics and apply the remaining instructions, which are:

B. Determine by your standards whether the activity is a low, medium, or high level of risk.

C. Determine the level of gains one can expect from engaging in this activity.

D. Explain circumstances that might alter your response. For example, with regard to the intercourse, the level of risk could be altered if the problem pregnancy could be resolved.

E. Game is complete when each student has had five turns.

F. Students record response on the worksheet as they play.

G. Students should listen actively and participate in discussion with other players of their group.

Examples of risk taking regarding the drug category include:

One, drinking alcohol and consuming some pep pills at the same time.

Two, buying marijuana from someone you don't know.

Three, drinking three to four glasses of beer.

Four, being asked to sell part of your marijuana.

These are only a few examples.

The ultimate goal throughout the game of Risk Taking is to train the student in the art of responsible decision making; however, teachers are instructed that students are never to be told that any decisions are right or wrong.

Sidney Simon's situation ethics and Lawrence Kohlberg's moral reasoning, which are both grounded on the assertion that there are no absolutes, governs the learning process of decision making, in which the students are asked to discuss their parents' attitudes in light of influencing their decisions.

The situation that is presented the 6th grade is as follows:

"While at a friend's house, instead of drinking pop, you decide to try some beer. You have both drunk a can and are popping the top of another one when your friend's parents walk in unexpectedly and see you with a beer. The teacher then shows some photoboards revealing a variety of expressions that might have been on the faces of the parents. The students then discuss this and decide individually which photoboard corresponds most closely to the expression they would expect to see on their parents' faces.

"As a class, students are directed to discuss how they would think their own parents would react and whether they would agree. Students are asked to suggest how they wish their own parents would react and why.

"Students are asked how they would react if they themselves were the parents. An activity follows with students role-playing the part of the parents and what rules they would have. They are asked to name other situations in which children's and parents' views may conflict."

I feel strongly that this 6th grade assignment and the 7th and 9th grade Risk Taking game clearly violate the intention of the Hatch Amendment by probing into the student's personal values as well as personal relationships with family members.

*TESTIMONY OF*_____
Nancy Hutchinson

I am a mother of two children. Up until seven months ago, I had a complete trust in our public schools and the leadership of them. My local school district has recently implemented a curriculum which has caused me to change my attitude of trust and confidence in the public schools.

A curriculum entitled Transition was developed in 1979, authored by Henry and Christine Dupont, and edited by Bonnie Goldsmith with the American Guidance Service, Inc. This curriculum is used at the secondary level. I find this material to be an invasion of my child's privacy as well as our family's privacy.

Transition features encounter groups. It involves psychological games which have no academic significance whatsoever. It contains pre- and post-testing of attitudinal changes. It deals with controversial subject matter as the teacher deems appropriate.

Another important part of this curriculum is role-playing. Permit me to read excerpts from the teacher's manual for the 7th grade; these are 13-year-old students.

Item: "Transition" features many small group activities in which students share thoughts, feelings and opinions.

Item: Observe what students are thinking and feeling.

Item: The questions provided for class discussion are usually inductive and open-ended so the students' responses need not be judged right or wrong. Examples of questions: Should students our age be allowed to read any books and see any movies we want? Should students our age have the right to refuse to go to school?

Item: Feel free to add or substitute questions based on students' interests and your own preferences.

Item: "Transition" is intended to foster openness and self-acceptance, not harmful self-disclosure.

Item: "Transition" features two kinds of role-playing. One asks students to act out what they think or feel. Another asks them to assume roles or points of view other than their own.

Item: "Transition" provides an excellent format for the discussion of controversial issues, since it stresses the acceptance of all ideas and feelings.

Item: Teacher explains what values are. After students name some, the class discusses how values develop. Then students list and rate five of their own values for review at the end of the unit.

Item: Ask students to observe how people listen in hallways and stores, at parties, and so forth for a specific period of time. Tell them they will report their findings to the class, leaving out the names of the people they observed.

Item: Groups of students play a card game called Exchange of Personal Information. Then they discuss how they felt during the game. The objective is that students will feel more comfortable when sharing personal information. After the game the teacher asks, "Were you a little uneasy the first time you were asked a personal question? Did you become more comfortable as the game went on?"

Item: Students share their lifelines with their class. The objective is that students feel comfortable sharing their lifelines with their classmates and will continue to develop intimacy and trust. After seeing their teacher's lifeline, they are more willing to share information about themselves. Suggest that Michael include his parents' near breakup because he was sure they would not mind. Students present their lifelines to the class. If students resist activity or do not take it seriously, their behavior could suggest distrust or poor self-esteem. You may want to discuss with the entire class the reasons for these feelings and perhaps repeat some of the earlier activities.

Item: If you feel that a student needs help with personal problems, arrange for her or him to work individually with the school psychologist, counselor or social worker. If several students need special attention, you might conduct small group Transition sessions for them with the assistance of a psychologist or counselor. (No mention of a mother's or father's involvement is made.)

In conclusion, I would like to say that we no longer have a school system which puts credence in parental input. In my view, educators have taken an all-knowing attitude displacing parental concerns, objections and insights. To prove my point, I quote from the NEA's 1982 Freedom of Inquiry under the '82-83 Resolution D-1, titled "Selection of Materials and Teaching Techniques":

> "The NEA believes that decisions on school learning, experiences and teaching techniques are best made by a teacher who knows the learner. Teachers and librarians or media specialists must select instructional or library materials without censorship."

Ruthellen Herzberg

I'm a wife and mother of two boys. They are enrolled in the 4th and 5th grades at Willamina Grade School in Oregon, which has approximately 600 students in kindergarten through 8th grade. My experience at the school has been both as a parent and as a substitute teacher. I'm a certified teacher in the State of Oregon, having less than 20 hours of psychology out of the 200-plus hours required for graduation with a B.S. in Education.

Although I'm aware there is a certain amount of informal counseling every teacher does in his or her daily routine, I'm in no way qualified to collect information for counseling purposes and certainly do not feel qualified to deal with psychologically-based situations that might arise as a result of questioning students about personal problems. I feel counseling should be done in a sensitive and private manner by specially trained people.

As a substitute in the 7th and 8th grades, I was expected to teach exercises in Values Clarification. Some of these exercises were in the form of a questionnaire. These tended to be very probing, making the student think about situations he might not have encountered before. All were about the students' feelings, eliciting personal information. Some of the exercises were in the form of classroom discussions. These discussions would sometimes follow a story I read. Students would then be given a few minutes to discuss in small groups and come up with a solution. There were no guidelines; all solutions were acceptable.

Accompanying the story which I was to read orally, there were teacher instructions indicating that I was just to read the story. I was in no way to influence the children's discussion and their conclusions about the story at all. This story is called Alligator River. It has an X-rated version and a G-rated version; it is the G-rated version I will read to you now. By the way, X and G were put there by the author of this book, not by me.

"Once there was a girl named Abigail who was in love with a boy named Gregory. Gregory had an unfortunate mishap and broke his glasses. Abigail, being a true friend, volunteered to take them to be repaired. But the repair shop was across the river and, during the flash flood, the bridge was washed away. Poor Gregory could see nothing without his glasses, so Abigail was desperate to get across the river to the repair shop.

"While she was standing forlornly on the bank of the river, clutching the broken glasses in her hands, a boy named Sinbad glided by in a rowboat. She asked Sinbad if he would take her across. He agreed to on condition that, while she was having the glasses repaired, she would go to a nearby store and steal a transistor radio that he had been wanting. Abigail refused to do this and went to see a friend named Ivan, who had a boat.

"When Abigail told Ivan her problem, he said he was too busy to help her out and didn't want to be involved.

"Abigail, feeling that she had no other choice, returned to Sinbad and told him she would agree to his plan. When Abigail returned the repaired glasses to Gregory, she told him what she had had to do. Gregory was appalled at what she had done and told her he never wanted to see her again.

"Abigail was upset and turned to Slug with her tale of woe. Slug was so sorry for Abigail that he promised her he would get even with Gregory. They went to the school playground where Greg was playing ball and Abigail watched happily while Slug beat Gregory up and broke his glasses again." End of story.

With that, the 7th and 8th grade children were to discuss and rate the characters in the story. There were five characters, and they were to rank them from the most offensive character to the least objectionable character.

There was one boy in the group who said, "I can't do that. All of the characters were bad; they have all done something bad. I just can't do that. How do I decide?"

The boy who said that is a rather unpopular boy, which I consider a self-esteem problem anyway. The rest of the class really got on his case and just came really down on him, and I am sure it didn't help his self-esteem at all.

I will now read to you the X-rated version of the story. You are not going to hear dirty words, but anyway, it's called X-rated.

"Once upon a time there was a woman named Abigail who was in love with a man named Gregory. Gregory lived on the shore of the river. Abigail lived on the opposite shore of the river. The river which separated the two lovers was teeming with man-eating alligators. Abigail wanted to cross the river to be with Gregory. Unfortunately, the bridge had been washed out so she went to Sinbad, a riverboat captain, to take her across. He said he'd be glad to if she would consent to go to bed with him preceding the voyage.

"She promptly refused and went to a friend named Ivan to explain her plight. Ivan did not want to be involved with the situation. Abigail felt her only alternative was to accept Sinbad's terms.

"Sinbad fulfilled his promise to Abigail and delivered her into the arms of Gregory. When she told Gregory about her amorous escapade in order to cross the river, Gregory cast her aside with disdain.

"Heartsick and dejected, Abigail turned to Slug with her tale of woe. Slug, feeling compassion for Abigail, sought out Gregory and beat him brutally. Abigail was overjoyed at the sight of Gregory getting his due. As the sun set on the horizon, we hear Abigail laughing at Gregory."

The same instructions go along with this story, also. As the teacher, I was instructed not to give any value clues. This left the students confused and it left me angry, as I considered it pointless teaching.

My instructions were to collect all the students' papers. I have since found out that these papers are put in files and used by the counselor and teachers.

As a parent I have had several dealings with the school that have made me feel I have no right to information about my child.

One such incident happened when I was meeting with the principal to discuss my son's classroom for the following year. I asked to see his cumulative folder. The principal told me I'd have to make another appointment to see it, which I did. I have reason to believe there was information removed from the folder before it was shown to me. Why I had to make another appointment was not clear, as the files were kept in the next room.

My 5th grader earlier this year came home from school telling me of their new classroom activity called Magic Circle. I asked what they did. He told me they sit in a circle and tell each other positive and negative things about each other. Again, the teacher is not a trained psychologist, and this type of group therapy can be harmful to a child if done improperly.

I also resent the probing questions asked by the teacher in this setting:

"How many of you have unemployed parents?"

"How many of you have divorced parents?"

"If any of you are abused sexually, I want you to tell me, because by law I have to report it."

These questions should never be asked to a group of children. It's insensitive and a direct invasion of privacy. Often children feel compelled to share in an intimate setting such as this, and share things that are not really significant — or are made to seem insignificant. Teachers should not be privy to this information unless it is directly affecting the academic progress of the child. Then and only then should the school need this information.

I consider this curriculum an invasion of family privacy, a subtle effort to erode all authority and undermine the traditional values that have made this nation great, in spite of our errors.

But more importantly, it's an invasion of the rights of the child, his right to his own mind. Under the guise of "letting the child choose and define his own values," this curriculum does just the opposite. The naive child is subtly programmed to think a certain way. He's made to question every belief and truism much before he is emotionally capable of assessing what he believes.

Everything in which the child has found security is psychologically exorcized. By the time a child is a young adult, he's got "Me," but no faith, no values, no authority. Little wonder the suicide rate for teenagers has quadrupled in the last 20 years. We need the tools to get our schools back to teaching the basics and away from the frills and fluff.

TESTIMONY OF_____

Rev. Ronald Watson

I am an ordained minister of Evangelical Church of North America. I have been a pastor in Lincoln City, Oregon, since August of 1975. I have three children attending public school in Lincoln County School District. My wife is a teacher's aide in the same school, and I am active on the Parents' Advisory Council.

In my son's 5th grade Health class, all questions were answered without regard to a moral right or wrong. Homosexuality was presented as an alternative lifestyle. Sexual activity among 5th graders was not discouraged, since it was feared that the students might be embarrassed and not ask additional questions.

I was present when a plastic model of female genitalia with a tampon insert was passed around to the boys so they might understand how tampons fit. Birth control pills were also passed around and explained. Anal intercourse was described. At no time was there any mention of abstinence as a desirable alternative for 5th graders. The morality that was taught in the classroom that day was complete promiscuity.

As a result of this kind of education without morality, we are experiencing pregnancy among 13-year-olds with resulting abortions. Our district's answer to pregnancies among young people, too young to raise and support their children, is to supply more information on birth control and abortions.

I believe that parents ought to be helped in their efforts to teach their children responsibility for their actions.

Last Friday I sat in on a Health class that taught the supposed benefits of alcohol. The reasoning is that, if it were taught that alcohol is hurting the children, an abusive parent might be offended and embarrassed.

My son is scheduled to be instructed in the ideal age to start having sexual intercourse when he takes grade 8. In Mental Health next year, he will be required to complete the sentence: "In my value system the ideal age to start having intercourse is _____." Age is not the question in the traditional moral Christian system—marriage is the criterion. By leading the student to assume that age is the criterion, atheistic humanism is being taught.

We parents have a right to protect our children from this godless "religion" and the irresponsibility it promotes. As a pastor, I help people whose marriages need strengthening to realize that God, our Creator, has established moral laws just as valid and relevant as the physical laws of gravity and nuclear physics which He also established. These people then abandon their irresponsible lifestyle, with the help of God, and build a solid marriage of mutual respect and God-given love.

Our schools teach an irresponsible sexual behavior such as is found with dogs and cats. The humanism our children are being taught is actually subhumanism. The schools refrain from teaching morals in order not to embarrass the parent who is immoral. The next step is for the schools to refrain from teaching that stealing is wrong in order not to embarrass the parent who is a thief. Our children need to be protected against such teaching.

TESTIMONY OF_____
William Dean Seaman

I am from Eddyville, Oregon, Lincoln County School District. I have three children who attend Lincoln County Schools and have myself been a teacher for over 16 years.

I have attended the majority of the Lincoln County School Board meetings since October, 1982, through December, 1983, and I attended the Rose Lodge School Committee meeting of January 11, 1983, during which several complaints concerning issues of Values Clarification—psychological probing and counseling on sensitive areas, with no parental permission prior to psychological experimentation with the students, in connection with violations of the Hatch Amendment—were aired and resolutions sought.

I witnessed with my own ears and recorded on tape the requests of each and every parent on the committee to have the Preventive Guidance Counseling Program and the Perspectives on Loss Program dropped. Specific complaints against the programs were:

No parental review of the materials was allowed prior to implementation, and even when the material was allowed to be reviewed, parents noted that certain pages of the curriculum had been held back from parent review.

No parental permission was acquired before involving students in this program, which LCSD admitted was an error on their part, and even after much discussion on the parental permission issue, the final report/decision by LCSD was that students would be in the program automatically, unless they had parental requests to be withdrawn — totally adverse to the unanimous desires of the entire parental aspect of the committee.

Instead of listening to and heeding the recommendations of the parents on the committee, the Lincoln County School District officials asserted their own set of recommendations, allowing for the program to operate under the Lincoln County School District ground rules, instead of having the programs stopped immediately and reviewed for all legal and improper aspects.

Parents of the committee addressed their concern that Guidance and Counseling programs such as these, and the associated Perspectives on Loss, can be taught and counseled on a one-to-one basis or in small groups with parental permission, and the requirement of Oregon State Law would be met, on the basis of availability of a counselor and counseling program.

Lincoln County School District refused even to consider this possibility, even though in the next election, the entire Rose Lodge School area voted against all school measures as an apparent registering of dissatisfaction with it.

Research on the counseling program in Lincoln County School District shows that it is an experimental psychological program (this was admitted by Dr. Force, Superintendent, on the December 28, 1982, KNPT, Newport, Oregon, Talk Show) and that it had been going on nearly two years of the three-year trial when the parents of the District even discovered it was going on. Materials and information concerning the program were refused to parents until the Concerned Parents of Rose Lodge Committee formed. By the time the program was finally discussed at School Committee level, there was less than a year left until the experiment was complete.

Lincoln County School District, in the January 11, 1983, Rose Lodge meeting, did admit that this controversial material was all allowed to go into the classroom without School Board review or approval.

Jim Roberts testified at the January 11, 1983, meeting that his daughter had been punished for being removed from this program. Emotionally, she was openly chided and ridiculed by other kids in the school, without intervention from her teachers; physically, she was detained and threatened with a pink slip if she did not attend, causing her to lose "free" time during school, unlike the students who attended the programs.

What we are concerned about here is much, much more, and deeper than the laws that have been violated and overlooked here. The underlying attitude and philosophy of this and all its related programs — and the way they are conducted in secrecy from the parents — is an instrument of undermining proper upbringing of children according to the beliefs and ideals of the parents.

Discussions centering around divorce, sexual activity, homosexual and lesbian lifestyle, death and dying, abortion, and so forth, when introduced in the primary grades and led through discussion into liberal attitudes, can only serve to break down the morals of the students involved — if not then and there in the classroom, then to set them up for breaking and deviating from them in their shortly-arriving adolescent years.

Aside from students being placed under doctor's care directly from these programs, the Lincoln County School District and others in the area have run up quite a tally of social maladies in recent years.

While the actual Pilot Project experimental curriculum didn't begin until about three and a half years ago, the unwritten curriculum and philosophy has been taught in certain segments for many years, undergoing refinements and finesse in its approach and secrecy all these years.

While no one could accurately paint all social maladies as having been the direct cause of such counseling programs, a close look at the curricula and methodology we warned about, and sought protection from in the Hatch Amendment, reveal some interesting trends.

Teaching liberal attitudes in sexual behavior as acceptable behavior, as alternative lifestyles, are "everyone does it anyway" attitudes that only breed immorality in society, a degeneration that has led to the downfall of many nations in history, and a condition that even a prostitute would not wish on her child.

Teaching liberal attitudes on divorce, and opening the sores of divorce experiences for group discussions with preadolescents, lead to a geometric progression in the divorce rate where taught as such, and bring extreme social and psychological trauma in too young, too immature minds.

Teaching death as an ultimate end glorious in itself—degrading life and placing values on the "how much, whose," and so forth, and not the "how"—breeds dishonesty and selfishness in a definite secular movement.

Indicative of the teachings of such programs as we are discussing here, are increasing teen pregnancies, abortions, live-in arrangements, divorces, etc., even to the point of suicides.

The rate of pregnancy at Eddyville High School among its students and teen graduates, coupled with live-in arrangements, abortions, etc., has approached the 75% level out of wedlock, not counting divorces and annulments.

While Eddyville School of Lincoln County School District is not a very large school, let us not assume that it is atypical from most other schools of the district or any district counseling under such philosophy.

However, the shock of the community came this past year when one of our Lincoln County School District recent graduates took his own life. He had had trouble getting a job and training; he wasn't especially popular with the girls, but had plenty of friends who were close; he had parents who loved him dearly; and had even done alright in school for what he wanted out of it and put into it.

But his friends' attitudes on excessiveness of drugs and alcohol, and what he'd been taught — not necessarily in class, but through underlying philosophies surfacing in disciplinary measures, reward systems, and so forth, in school about drugs and alcohol not really being bad, or just being a cycle everyone passes through — he described in the warnings he wrote to all his friends and parents, and then he killed himself.

As I indicated before, I'm not saying that Lincoln County School District caused these pregnancies, or Billy's death, but I am saying that the attitudes pressed and impressed on students involved in such Preventive Guidance and Perspectives on Loss counseling programs inevitably lead to such tragedies.

*TESTIMONY OF*_____
Sandra Maynard

I'm from Willamina, Oregon, and I have two children enrolled in the Willamina grade school. I have a 5th grader and a 7th grader. I've always been very supportive of the school; in fact, I have donated many of my hours to teaching art and extra-curricular activities for the children. But I've come 275 miles because of my deep concern for my children's welfare.

The Values Clarification curriculum was brought to my attention by a friend only weeks ago, who ran across it in her substitute teaching in the junior high section of the school.

Subsequently, I asked my 7th grader about his homeroom activities. He told me of different stories that were read to him, oral discussions and papers the students were given to fill out and return to the teacher. Though he was urged by his teacher to turn them in, I asked him to start bringing them home for my viewing.

After reading a few, I made a visit to the school counselor, and she told me that it was her fault the parents were not aware of the program. She hadn't had time to inform them.

I also discovered that these papers were kept by the teachers in a file and could be used in counseling the students.

I have a few examples of questions just asked lately.

One paper was titled "How Well Do You Like Yourself?" on which children were asked to number from four to zero how true they thought was each of the following statements:

There aren't very many things about myself I'm ashamed of.

If I could live my life over again, there isn't much I'd change.

I don't have any regrets about my life.

If there really was a heaven, I'd go there if I die.

Nothing is too good for me.

I like where I live.

By the way, the title "Values Clarification" at the top of each of these pages had been carefully removed from the copies given to the students.

Another sheet of multiple choice included such questions as:

Which of these would you want most as a neighbor? A young blind person; A young crippled person; An old person.

With whom would you rather spend your vacation? A friend; A teacher; Your family.

To whom would you tell a secret? Your friend; Your teacher; Your parent.

Which would you hate most? Getting a spanking; Going to the doctor for a shot; Losing a five dollar bill.

How would you rather have your mother punish you? By spanking you; By taking away your favorite toy; or by talking to you.

Which would be the hardest for you to do? Steal a toy from another child's desk; Cheat by looking at another child's paper; Tell a lie to a teacher.

The questions I chose might not sound particularly harmful; however, the counselor said that she chose questions that were less controversial to use in class.

I don't like leaving the decision to the discretion of a person whose values may be far removed from mine and may choose to use all the questions at some time from the Values Clarification Handbook.

I have another example. I have the book right here — and it comes from Strategy No. 8, which is the chapter "Values Continuum." The purpose of "Values Continuum" serves to open up the range of alternatives possible on any given issue. Students begin to realize that on most issues there are many shades of gray, and they are more likely to move away from either/or black-and-white thinking which often occurs when controversial issues are discussed in the classroom. I will just read two or three examples of what was on the page:

"How do you feel about school? Are you a 'Dynamite Dan' — you think students would be better off if the school were blown to bits? Or just 'Stowaway Steve' — who loves school so much the janitor has to drive him out of the school each night before locking up?"

Here is one of the questions that the teacher decided to leave out:

"How do you feel about premarital sex? Are you a 'Virginal Virginia,' who wears white gloves every day? or a 'Mattress Millie,' who wears a mattress strapped on her back?"

I would not like that used for my children. This could leave my child very confused, at a time and age when he is especially vulnerable, by encouraging him to question his parents' values and even his own self worth.

Why are so much time and money spent on this program when it can better be used on academic curriculum? Also, I feel that these questions are an invasion of the child's and his parents' privacy.

The school should inform parents and request written permission from parents before using this curriculum. We need to protect parents' rights as well as our children's rights.

TESTIMONY OF _____
Sandra Youngblood

I am a parent of five school age children, three of my own and two stepchildren. I find that this Values Clarification in any form in the school system is invasion of our privacy, by trying to get at our children and dig out bits of information about them and other family members to be used as a tool against them.

I don't believe any parent wants home life brought up for discussion or acted out in class. This is not only humiliating, it is degrading to the student.

There is such a wide range of questions that are asked of students: questions about family life, sex, drugs, divorce, death, and even writing your own obituary, to how many shoes you have and who bought them for you.

I think that the innermost thoughts that a child has should not be put up for the whole school to see and discuss. I don't want the school to create situations among children, that normally would not be discussed for some time to come in the future, until they are adults and can make their own logical decisions. They should not be forced into a decision when they are not sure of what the subject matter is or even don't understand.

Values Clarification is trying to make these children make these decisions *now* instead of when they are adults. I believe our tax money should be put to better use to teach them how to read and write.

I went to the school and asked them about this program and if the parents were informed. They had no answer. They just seemed to forget. Oh, they forgot to inform the parents. They just slipped this program into the homeroom for extra work but didn't inform the parents, and, when asked for the papers that the children have filled out, they seem to disappear. They don't know what happened to them. They say that the kids have taken them home, but the kids haven't.

*TESTIMONY OF*_____

James Robert

I am from Lincoln County School District. The following happenings to students and parents in Lincoln County, Oregon, School System the past year will bear out the need for the Hatch Amendment to be enforced and expanded.

My daughter, in the spring of '81, came home from school and told of a student telling in class of his parents having a fight. This student was then tantalized by other students during recess, lunch time, and on the school bus. The other students were saying that his family was bad.

I told my daughter not to be involved in such actions if they were happening. I though at that time it was a one-time happening. I also wondered why, if it bothered the student, that the student didn't confer with his teacher or counselor in private on a one-to-one basis. I did not understand that this was done in a classroom situation.

In October, 1982, the next school year, my daughter came home from school in tears. When I asked her what was wrong, she didn't want to talk about it. Later at dinner time she wasn't hungry. At that time I realized that there was a serious problem because that's not her normal behavior.

I sat down with her and told her the only way mom and dad could help was to talk it out. My daughter told of a counselor who that day had singled her out in class to answer a questionnaire, "Perspectives on Loss," dealing with divorce and Values Clarification. This questionnaire, in answering, became personal and private and embarrassing to herself and her family.

I then told my daughter to tell the counselor that this questioning and probing bothered her. As I listened, it began to bother me. My daughter said that she had asked the counselor if she had to answer these questions in the classroom session. The counselor answered that she did. Again my daughter asked if she had to participate. The counselor answered, "Yes, and if you don't, you will get a pink slip or a loss of recess," both of which are reprimands.

My younger daughter, in the 4th grade, then spoke up and started telling the happenings in her room with the same counselor.

These happenings included role-playing, Circle Times, and secret Circle Times, in which my daughter was instructed not to tell anyone what was said or done, not even parents.

At this point I was still questioning what I was being told by my children. I went to the Rose Lodge school principal with the information my children had told me. I was told by the principal, Cal Parrish, that the school district didn't have any such program and didn't conduct classes in any such manner.

I discussed this again with my children. I also talked to other parents who, in turn, discussed it with their children. Through these discussions, we found that what the children were telling was true.

I then scheduled a meeting with the principal,

counselor, and my daughter and myself. The counselor started questioning my daughter by telling her "Don't you remember, it was voluntary?" My daughter answered, "No." The counselor moved closer to my daughter, saying again, "It was voluntary." My daughter answered, "No."

The counselor, moving even closer, and looking directly in her eyes, said, "Don't you remember, it was voluntary?" My daughter answered, "You made me do it."

I then excused my daughter and asked to see the material used. I was told that it was unavailable, that there was only one copy, and it was not in school. The next three weeks I requested the material repeatedly and was always told the material was not available. I finally gave the school a date and told them to have the material or I was going to get a court order. The material then became available, and the school personnel told the parents that they only used one page, page 95, out of 100 and some. The children went through this material and picked out several more pages that were used.

This was just the beginning of what we were put through. We went to a local school committee November 16, 1982, and told the committee what was happening to our children. The parents did not know what was going on in the classrooms. The local school committee acknowledged the problem but didn't seem overly concerned.

The Director of Elementary Education said that he would look into it. He also stated that we had to follow a complaint system, 6144, of Lincoln County.

We started doing this by filling out complaints, which were turned in to Principal Cal Parrish. The school system accepted part of the written complaints and a review committee was formed with nine out of close to 50 complainants, and several school personnel, and Director of Elementary Education, William Stemple.

When parents asked questions, we would get answers such as, "We are not talking about that. We will get back to it later." Later never came.

I have, as evidence, a January 11, 1983, presentation to Lincoln County School Board, in line with the 6144 complaint procedure. This particular material was eventually removed, but was replaced by other of the same sort under a different name. As of now, this type of questioning is still continuing in our schools in many forms. Our children hesitate to relax and enjoy school as they once did.

My daughter has had to receive medical treatment because of this form of tension. The use of Values Clarification in its many forms causes problems where problems never existed.

I believe that the schools should be for education only, and that parents should once again be allowed to have the right to handle their children's emotional problems and teach their values in their own home and not the school.

We have children in the 2nd grade. Their counselor puts puppets on her hands, and here are the questions she asks these youngsters in the 2nd grade puppet show:

"Do your parents steal?

"Do your parents lie to you?
"Do your parents hit you?
"Why did they get married?"

And all kinds of other personal questions. The Hatch Amendment must be implemented in its entirety, because children are being damaged, intimidated and harassed.

*TESTIMONY OF*_____
Mary Cole

I am from Corvallis, Oregon. When my son was in the 6th grade two years ago, a great deal of questioning and prying took place in the classroom. They were asked questions dealing with emotions and feelings concerning family and self. Examples are:

"If I had a gun, I would _____.
"When my parents leave me alone, I feel _____."

Some other questions seemed nonsensical. Others dealt with siblings or parents, even teachers. It appeared that much of the class time was spent on these "fun activities," to the extent of neglecting academics.

When my husband and I started asking questions, we were met with a defensive attitude, if not hostility.

Upon requesting that our son be transferred to another class, we met a great deal of resistance from the teacher and the administration. It was shortly after the administration sensed our anger that they transferred our son, but it was agreed to only if I came in for a conference with the teacher and the vice principal. It didn't make any difference that I had already talked to the teacher. I spent 45 minutes being told what a good teacher she was and that nothing had taken place in the classroom that was against the law.

At the end of the session, I felt my son was dishonest and in need of counseling. The final word from the vice principal came in an admonishing tone to the effect of, "Now, you don't want to leave here and talk about this. After all, you wouldn't want to have your name on the troublemaker list."

After I left, I realized that I had been threatened.

Other examples of such questioning are found in the 6th and 7th grade Health classes. The 7th grade requires a private journal to be kept by the student on his feelings. Some subjects written about were on religion and moral ethics. I was embarrassed by some of my son's comments on religion because, in his young mind, he had given an unbalanced picture. No efforts were made to correct grammar, punctuation, sentence structure or continuity of thought. What a waste of school time!

I appeal to you, as one parent out of many, please help us. We are defenseless against this invasion of our privacy and the right to raise our children by our values. This type of question not only infringes upon the rights of parents, it is emotionally upsetting for the child.

II.

Excerpts from

Official Transcript of Proceedings

BEFORE THE

U.S. DEPARTMENT OF EDUCATION

In the Matter of:

PROPOSED REGULATIONS TO IMPLEMENT
THE PROTECTION OF PUPIL RIGHTS AMENDMENT
SECTION 439 OF THE GEPA
ALSO KNOWN AS THE HATCH AMENDMENT

DATE: MARCH 16, 1984

PLACE: PITTSBURGH, PENNSYLVANIA

Bettye Lewis

I'm from Flushing, Michigan. I am currently the President of Michigan Alliance of Families, Inc., a pro-family organization that was founded for the purpose of researching, evaluating and informing and educating the public on any and all issues that are a threat to the traditional family unit.

The necessity for the Hatch Amendment was evidenced by the fact that Congress voted unanimously to pass this in 1978. The critical need for such legislation was apparent from the testimony from parents, lawyers, teachers, doctors and psychologists nationwide.

The testing and evaluation in all of the areas addressed in the Hatch Amendment is, and has been, taking place since 1970; in the area of health, all areas of sex behavior and attitudes, as well as family, mental and emotional well-being, are questioned. The student is also tested to make certain that he/she knows his/her rights to contraception, counseling, drug overdose and venereal treatment — all without parental knowledge or consent.

He is also tested on his knowledge of all social agencies that will offer all of these services to him/her without financial obligation on the part of the minor child. They are to know all of the health agencies at the local, state, national and international levels. Our children are actually being programmed to assume complete responsibility for their bodies while becoming totally dependent on social services and the government to meet their needs, rather than dependent on those who love them most—their families.

Our State Department of Education is actually declaring that individual students will continually need to appraise their own value system to coincide with our changing society.

Testing in the area of social studies discloses the students' attitudinal changes in many areas. Only the feminist point of view is acceptable; all women must work. Children are tested on the traditional family concept, religion, prayer in the schools, desegregation, racism, ethnic background and heritage, capital punishment, etc. These areas of testing are a means of determining if the objectives of multicultural, global, law related, and comprehensive health programs have been accomplished.

If the schools can't reinforce the values of the home, the schools do not have the right to deliberately destroy them. This is the contributing factor—the probing of children's attitudes, values, beliefs and emotions—that caused the tremendous outcry and protest that brought about the need for just such legislation as the Hatch Amendment.

The Hatch Amendment is the lifeboat that has been provided for parents to protect their children from psychological probing and testing, to guard them from the grasp of the change agent and the learning clinicians now in control of the sea of education.

Theresa Bak

Being an informed and concerned parent of a 19-, 16-, and 5-year old, I can truly say that the quality and direction of education has drastically changed within the past 10 to 15 years.

Parents are downgraded and passed over as ignorant or not important in any decision a student would make in his/her life. The word "values" is stressed repeatedly, but what values are they talking about? Certainly not the parents' or the students' religious convictions. Stressed over and over is the phrase, "your value," with nothing concrete to base it on; meaning, there is no right or wrong, just do your own thing.

Theory practices such as Kohlberg's moral reasoning development and Sidney Simon's Values Clarification are taught as a moral and concrete way of choosing your own values over any other form of reasoning, leaving the student to feel that the Ten Commandments and one's own parents' feelings and sacrifices do not enter the picture.

The attack upon the traditional family and parents is blatant and sad. Not only is it confusing for the student, but parents are at a loss as to what to do.

Instead of teaching the fundamental basics to students, schools and teachers are taking the roles of psychologists and psychiatrists and using the classroom for exposing family problems of a personal and private nature. Questions along these lines are asked of the students almost daily. Journals are mandated with no motive of having the sentence structure or grammar corrected, but only to invade the sanctuary of the students' mind, heart and home.

Role-playing and brainstorming are two of the Values Clarification techniques used in the 5th grade book, *Good Health For You*, by Laidlaw Publishers. Chapter One stresses feelings; the teacher has the children role-play a family situation such as mom gets a job, or a conflict situation involving adolescents and siblings. The chapter invades privacy of home rights by discussing rights and privileges that children would like to have but are not yet allowed to have. The invasion is further extended by discussing dating rules.

Sexually explicit material is being shown in audio-visuals or recommended for outside reading. Statements such as, "Sex outside of marriage is now socially acceptable," which is stated in the Butterick publication of *Marriage and Parenthood*, continue to erode the home values. "No longer a single moral code is acceptable. What is right for you is objective for you. You determine your own value, what parents did may or may not work out for you. Decisions are yours." This quote from the Butterick publication on dating is a sample of the remarks which permeate the filmstrips and films shown to our youth.

There was a parent who wrote to the teacher and asked her child to be excused from any Values Clarification, moral dilemmas, role-playing, sensitivity training, group therapy, or survival games. This parent received a letter from the school which I would like to give as testimony:

Dear Mrs. Gould:

"Following our conference with Paul's teachers on October 13th, 1983, two teachers have contacted me. They are concerned by your statement, September 1st, 1982, regarding testing of basic academic skills only for Paul.

"They are also concerned regarding the notification you wish if 'techniques known as values clarification, moral dilemmas, role-playing, sensitivity training, group therapy, survival games' etc., are employed.

"Please be advised that although class activities may not be labeled as such, interpretations, values, conclusions and judgments are integrated in all courses. If you wish to know more specific details, I suggest that you contact the assistant superintendent.

"The course content, classroom activities and testing of all classes has been reviewed and approved by the curriculum committee. Teachers must follow the approved format and will not be deviating from it.

"I thank you for your participation and concern for your son Paul's education."

I've reviewed the chapters on drugs in the 5th and 6th grade health books and critiqued them carefully. The 5th grade drug text is very unhealthy; it is a poor approach to teaching about drugs. It is not firm at all on the serious consequences of taking drugs, yet it tells a child he is responsible for his own health and decisions but does not make clear what to base those decisions on.

I implore you to please form some concrete laws and regulations to protect the basic rights of our children and their families from the intrusion of the school and its teachers into the private and personal lives of the student, family and home.

TESTIMONY OF_____ _____
Marcy Meenan

I am a cluster chairperson for parent representatives in the Pittsburgh Public Schools. I also serve proudly as the First Vice President for People Concerned for the Unborn Child, a Southwestern Pennsylvania grassroots organization with over ten thousand members.

Let's talk about privacy. Children are keeping diaries which teachers read daily and comment on. Teachers are being asked to use this holistic approach under the misconception that diaries are kept to check grammar and punctuation. A mother called me to complain about her daughter's diary. The child had written that she was angry with her mother and that she wanted to kill her. The teacher responded in red ink to this child's remark in the diary, saying: "Don't kill her, just punch her out."

Other parents are complaining that children are taking tests that ask very personal questions about family matters. Still other children are told to enter such information into computers.

Open-ended sentences pry into the personal area of the child's beliefs. Questions are asked with *no* correct answer provided, implanting dishonest values. For example, one test that I recently saw said: "A child is asked what he would do if he had only one dollar and his mother's gift cost four dollars. Would he: (a) Steal the gift; (b) Borrow three dollars from a stranger; (c) Change the price tag to read one dollar?"

Survival games are played. Children are made to decide who can live and who must die. Abortion is presented as though it is a contraceptive, and contraceptives are presented as something you must use when you reach the 5th or the 6th grade.

Plays presented to students with actors dancing on the United States Flag are not uncommon and were a big problem here in Pittsburgh. Kids are definitely being programmed to accept a new global perspective

Parents don't have a leg to stand on without seriously enacted regulations. What would you tell a mother whose daughter was told she was a "racist" because in class, in front of her mates, she would not discuss whether she would date a black man or not?

And each day until she did, she was asked to leave the class five minutes earlier than the rest of her class. The teacher worked on her until she broke down and admitted she was probably a racist but would now consider the date.

This is the form of therapy to promote social change. There are change agents in the schools, let us face the facts.

*TESTIMONY OF*_____
Marian Darr

I have come from Tonawanda, New York. The use of role-playing and psycho-drama (the most powerful tool to bring about attitudinal and value change) in global/multi-cultural programs is clearly a violation of the Hatch Amendment. Role-playing is psychological treatment.

The whole problem came about when schools started becoming more concerned with children's attitudes, beliefs and emotions, rather than providing them with a basic education. What we have today is a situation where dramatically fewer children, young children, can read, write or count, but who have become worldly wise to stories about sex, drugs and violence.

This does not speak well for the long-term emotional stability of the child. Such implicit value changes which attend teaching very young children about drugs or sex, or which challenge their faith in their parents, constitute the most vile threat to the American family unit.

In conclusion, I would like to point out that in the last 10 to 15 years the moral standard of our country and our schools has so degenerated that it leaves our children completely bewildered. They are taught about sex with absolutely no moral guidance whatsoever.

TESTIMONY OF
Evelyn Bonk

In the schools across America today the sacred rights of parents and the civil rights of students are being violated. The innermost thoughts, values and convictions of students are being probed and examined by any certified teacher for any reason whatsoever. In my child's Marriage and Family Living Class at Hill McCloy High School in Montrose, Michigan, the students get pages of questions examining their most personal feelings about premarital sex, marriage, etc. Enraged over this invasion of my child's conscience, I brought this to the attention of the School Board.

Because of the present form of the Hatch Amendment, a lawyer determined the questions to be illegal, and they were dropped from the course. However, some of the questions were later printed on another type of paper with a different heading, and that was permitted. Some of the most offensive questions are as follows:

#1. What am I really looking for in a close relationship? Choices were, among 26: Someone with whom you want to establish an exclusive or long-lasting sexual intimacy; and, Someone with whom sexual intimacy would be only one of many varying experiences.

#2. In my opinion, sex is? (a) love itself; (b) a way of expressing feelings of love; (c) an enduring personal commitment; (d) a casual pleasure with no strings attached; (e) a prelude to marriage. [A child who believes sex is just for marriage would have to write the answer in himself.]

#3. In a love relationship with someone of the opposite sex, I believe that the following factors are most important, on a scale of one to ten. Among choices is included sexual skills.

#4. Am I ready for mature love?

#5. At this point in my life I would prefer (a) a sexual relationship with someone, not involving any lasting commitments; (b) an affectionate relationship with someone not involving sexual commitments; (c) several varying kinds of relationships with no exclusive commitments; (d) a single long-lasting committed relationship, both physical and affectionate.

#6. One of the least important reasons for considering sexual intimacy with someone is so you would be considered popular?

    #7. A person should be sexually experienced before getting married?

    #8. Sometimes it might be appropriate for a girl who is not married to decide to bear and raise a child?

    #9. Living together unmarried is one possible option in your future?

I feel these questions were an invasion of my child's civil rights, but I was also very incensed by the "no right or wrong" message put across in these questions.

In the Health & First Aid Class in the same school, students were asked to discuss such personal things as:

    #1. Ask students to discuss their fears. Do they think that many of their fears have been instilled by parents or friends? Ask students to describe physical symptoms they have felt during anxiety.

    #2. Ask students to give their own definition of love. Ask students to explain the difference between jealousy and envy. How do they feel about these feelings? What can be done to alleviate these feelings? Ask students to think about whether envy can be a desirable emotion. What would be some desirable outcomes of envy—accomplishment, success, competition, etc.? Can resentment be used for constructive means? Ask students to discuss this question and give examples from own experience whenever possible.

If adults could take the place of children in these classrooms, I am certain this invasion of privacy would soon cease, as adults would soon refuse to allow this. However, children in the classroom are very vulnerable. And even if warned by the parents to not answer personal questions or take part in these discussions, few would have the courage to stand apart in the classroom.

TESTIMONY OF——————————————————
Alice Leidich

I would like to take a quote from Senator Orrin Hatch's testimony, August 23, 1978, before the Senate during consideration of the Education Amendments of 1978:

> "Simply stated, our amendment requires that before any elementary or secondary age child is subjected to psychiatric, behavior probing or other nonscholastic and nonaptitude testing, that there must first be obtained the written consent of the respective child's parent or guardian. This whole problem came about when schools started becoming more concerned with children's attitudes, beliefs and emotions, rather than providing them with basic education. And what we have today is a situation where dramatically fewer young children can read,

write or count; but who have become worldly-wise to stories about sex, drugs and violence. This does not speak well for the long-term emotional stability of the child. Such explicit value changes, which attend teaching very young children about drugs or sex, or which challenge their faith in their parents, constitute the most vile threat to the American family unit. The techniques used to change your child's attitudes and values are an invasion of privacy in the first degree."

My position is that the public schools are, though perhaps unknowingly, promoting the religion of secular humanism. Permit me to take a quote from the *Humanist*, November/December 1978 issue and let them say it for me:

"For some time now moral-education programs have been conducted in the public schools, but not without vigorous opposition. Many religionists who reject moral education programs in the schools maintain that secular humanism is being introduced and that this constitutes a violation of the separation of church and state. Earlier objections to sex education and the teaching of a theory of evolution drew similar criticism. In spite of strong opposition, moral education and Values Clarification programs are making rapid progress in school curricula."

I would like to take a quote from a paragraph

from the *Humanist* magazine, dated January/February 1983, entitled, "A Religion for a New Age":

> "I am convinced that the battle for humankind's future must be waged and won in the public school classroom by teachers who correctly perceive their role as the proselytizers of a new faith: a religion of humanity that recognizes and respects the spark of what theologians call divinity in every human being.

> "These teachers must embody the same selfless dedication as the most rabid fundamentalist preachers, for they will be ministers of another sort, utilizing a classroom instead of a pulpit to convey humanist values in whatever subjects they teach, regardless of the education level — preschool day care or large state university.

> "The classroom must and will become an arena of conflict between the old and the new — the rotting corpse of Christianity, together with all its adjacent evils and misery, and the new faith of Humanism, resplendent in its promise of a world in which the never-realized Christian ideal of 'love thy neighbor' will finally be achieved."

TESTIMONY OF_____

John Forrest

Here is a book by a teacher entitled, *Using Role Playing in the Classroom*. It gives all the information on how you should do it. There is a large section on the dangers of the problems that you get into in delving deep into the emotions of the children in having to act these things out. And it warns that teachers should be constantly on the alert for the emotions that will evolve into the situations where physical damage is done to the students when they get into fights.

Here is a book by Dr. Rhoda Lorand. She is a psychoanalyst. Her book points out the dangers of untrained teachers in attempting to do in classrooms what is normally considered in psychoanalysis as a form of medicine.

We had three particular cases while I was on the Board of Education. But each of them, under certain circumstances, could have caused the teachers to be sued. Even if nothing was collected, it still would be an awful hassle for the teacher to have to go through.

In one case, a young girl obviously had emotional problems. She was early in her high school years at the time this happened. She would get disturbed at school: the parents weren't sure why, but she would come home on certain occasions very badly disturbed, and the next day usually didn't feel like going to school. One day she shot herself. After considerable checking, the coroner decided that, because she did not leave a suicide note, it must have been an accident; she had slipped on the living room floor and the gun had discharged and practically blew her head off.

While I was on the School Board, we also had a case of a boy who went into the superintendent's private office. The school said he stole the sum of around $80 from one of the classroom accounts. This boy was in the 5th grade, and it turned out that the reason he had done this was because the "value" he had picked up was that he wasn't making friends in school. He had started in that school that fall, and he really was having difficulty fitting in socially. The way it was discovered that he took the money was that he went out and bought candy, pop and other goodies for his friends, and that very excitement gave him a group of friends.

Had a classroom teacher, through Values Clarification procedures, been partly responsible for this change in his life, wherein he felt stealing was a moral thing for him to do, considering the purpose he had in mind, she very well might have been in line for a lawsuit.

The last case happened after I was off the School Board. A young boy, whom nobody knew had been on drugs, was in his senior year. On the last day of school, they went to school only part of the day. The rest of the day they went to Nelson's Lodge nearby, where there are very high caves, ledges, and so forth. And as they were driving along, they almost stopped the car, and he opened the door to jump out. He decided he could fly, ran from the car, leaped off the top of one of the ledges, and flapped his arms and fell and was killed. Up to that time, they didn't realize that the boy was even using drugs.

The two drug programs that I have just recently gone through and have in my possession now, both teach that the student should decide on the basis of the harm, the physical harm, that the drug could do against the "values" that he might accrue from using the drug. The student must decide on his own whether or not he ought to use drugs. Now, had this last tragedy occurred after the student had been in a class like that, I am sure the parents could have filed suit.

TESTIMONY OF
Vandola Stevens

As a result of spending my time in a parochial school, by the 11th grade I already had all my required credits, so I was forced to take electives. My senior year at Okamos Heights High School, which is a public high school, I was forced to take all freshman courses, because those were the electives.

In one class, our Future Class, we had a panel of kids to decide which unborn child should receive a special drug designed to raise the IQ level of a retarded child based on race, social status and need. The teacher asked my opinion, which children should receive the drug, and I questioned his ethics in using this assignment.

In my Family Living Class I was asked to fill out papers asking about my family life, my parents' lives, mainly their relationship with each other. Class discussions were held on our parents' arguments: what they did right, what they did wrong in arguing; and also their private sex lives—how their sex life affected our perception of things, the amount of closeness in our family.

We were taught that marriage was a promise, not a commitment or even a vow; that you should date as many people as possible and establish as many relationships as possible, but that is because relationships are not binding. They are only binding as long as both parties are content.

Divorce was not only possible but probable according to statistics. Children are a great responsibility, so if you choose a career, abortion is the quickest, surest and easiest way to solve that problem.

By Christmas of my senior year I sat down with my mother and started crying. I was severely depressed. I didn't know what I believed about myself. I didn't know who I was or anything. Even things I was positive about earlier, I just didn't know. I had to learn to know myself all over again. I had to learn what I believed all over again, using all the sources that the school taught me were outdated, such as my mom and dad, my pastor and my Bible. I had to learn to make decisions again, the hardest part of all, and one that now, four years later, I am still having problems with.

*TESTIMONY OF*_____

Gloria Lentz

As a newspaper woman, lecturer and the author of two books on schools and the changing values of our children, I have witnessed first-hand the disease that was thrust upon minor children attending government schools, and I recorded over a 20-year period its effects and spinoffs.

Wilhelm von Humboldt, a nineteenth century scientist and explorer, who described himself as a humanist and a liberal, wrote something that is very relevant throughout history and certainly is relevant to these hearings. Whatever we wish to see, he said, introduced into a life or a nation, must first be introduced into its schools.

In the '60's our public schools, at first with trepidation and then with galloping boldness, introduced a sex education/population control experiment that was taught in a moral vacuum with a secular humanist philosophy that undermined God and parents. As these value-free, children-may-choose, social, sexual, population-control engineering programs escalated, it was inevitable that academic achievement would grind to a halt.

Approximately 20 years have elapsed since these experiments, with their host of social engineering counterparts, made their initial incursion into the nation's schools, being interwoven, in most cases, into many subjects from English to Home Economics. From the onset, parents raised objections — first, on the local level, then on the State Board of Education level, on through their legislative bodies and right into the courtrooms — failing always to make a dent in removing these experiments.

Saturated with defeat at every government level, hope sprang anew for parents when Senator Hatch introduced the Amendment we are discussing with you here today. But the Amendment was to languish for almost five and a half years without regulations, making it a worthless piece of paper. Looking back on all of the other governing bodies that turned a deaf ear to the cries of the parents, I am hard-pressed to believe that this delay was merely an oversight, considering the continual controversy that swirls around these experiments nationwide.

In order for this experiment in sex education/population control to be a success, two areas had to be diminished in the child's mind: parents and religion, both of which encompassed a matter of conscience, obedience and morals.

Time permits me to give only a few examples of the many that I have gathered from lecturing across the country to document my charge. A school test had this phrase dropped in — just like subliminal advertising: "It must be lonely to be God. Nobody loves a master." A recent letter that I received from a mother, after I spoke in Ohio, said students were told by their teacher: "If your parents told you there is a God and He made this world, they are lying to you."

Parents in New Jersey tried in vain to stop Values Clarification from infiltrating their school. In doing a written assessment of the program, they could not find, they said, in any of the hypothetical situations, a single portrayal of parents in a positive manner. Parents were shown to be overreaching, nagging, unfair, overcritical of their children's friends.

Senator Hatch cited an ESEA sponsored program which had elementary students collectively put their parents on trial, the end result being that the mother and father were always found guilty. He also cited a program publicly funded in part by ESEA entitled, Future Directions of Family Planning in Wisconsin, for grades K through 12, which provides all forms of contraception, pregnancy and abortion referral education information and services to persons as young as ten years of age without parental consent.

In a teacher's guidebook, under a chapter entitled, "Making Decisions," I found the following: "One, the way to prevent pregnancy; Two, deciding if you want to remain a virgin until you are married; Three, deciding if you will defy your parents."

It has become painfully obvious that schools can no longer turn out serious scholars or skilled craftsmen in meaningful numbers when the very basics of education are interspersed and thinned by these damaging experiments that preoccupy our children's minds. Even educationists are turning against these experiments.

A number of critical articles have begun to appear in in-house teacher's journals. All agree on one point: Sex education in the schools — and let's call it what it really is, a population-control experiment by the government — has done nothing, they said, to curtail sexual activity among students, but rather has stimulated promiscuity. A newsletter of the National Association of Secondary Schools Principals called on school administrators to: "Find sufficient courage to call a halt to the charade we have been playing with the public on this issue. To accept new monies for this," they said, "under the prevailing situation borders on educational fraud."

A resolution of the Arizona Chapter of the American Federation of Teachers, passed last year states that: "As professional educators we stand firmly opposed to inferior, radical experimental programs that use operant conditioning and are now being promoted in the United States under classroom management."

Every atrocity that has befallen our schools and our children can be traced directly back to the time when the schools veered away from the world of academia and skills and took on the role of experimenters with this sex education/population control obsession.

Before parents sign the parental consent paper, as the Hatch Amendment requires, I ask that the following words be clearly written on each and every consent form:

"Warning, these experimental programs may be dangerous to your child's and family's mental, physical, moral and religious health. Upon signing this consent form, you waive all rights guaranteed you under the Constitution of the United States pertaining to your child's and your family's right to privacy. Any medical, physical, moral or psychological damages to the child or family will not be pursued by you in any court of law. The undersigned fully comprehends that, upon completion of, or during the course of these experiments, the aforementioned minor child may become sexually promiscuous, have no concept of right or wrong in the traditional sense, and may become anti-God and anti-parent."

If you will put this wording in, then I think you will, at long last, have given the parents a slim but sporting chance.

As I lecture across the country I see the anger and frustration of parents as they have tried to fight the government on these issues; but more importantly, as I heard again today, I have heard the anguished cry of the children and the parents as they live through and recount the damages done to them through these experiments.

Sandra Tapasto

The National Diffusion Network has developed many controversial and experimental programs which were subsequently implemented in our state schools. Many of these programs are diametrically opposed to traditional moral and ethical values. The philosophy contained in many of these programs is based on Sidney Simon's Values Clarification and Professor Lawrence Kohlberg's moral reasoning.

These programs that are well thought out and planned to undermine love of God, country and family use change agents in the school to achieve their purpose. In their arrogance the perpetrators of these crimes against our children dare to presume to know what is best for them in defiance of parental authority — that authority which is God-given and belongs to them alone — when it comes into the delicate dimensions of sex education, family matters, and political and financial status.

It is apparent that one of the goals of these change agents is to destroy the student's faith, beliefs, and moral system. Another is to create tensions and conflicts between parents and their children by having the students regard parents as old-fashioned, unlearned in the ways of the modern world, and, therefore, unfit to guide and direct them. To disregard government's legitimate expectations from its younger citizens in the matter of loyalty, patriotism and defense is another goal.

MACOS: Man — A Course of Study, a program which indirectly teaches grade-school children relativism as they decide which members of a family should be left to die for the survival of the remainder, cost the taxpayers $7,000,000.

I will list programs currently in operation in our states, mostly in New York, which I find objectionable.

Facing History and Ourselves is both controversial and experimental, and is clearly designed to alter students' attitudes on political and social issues, and uses pre- and post-testing to evaluate student attitudinal outcome. The intent of the program is deceitful. Through psychological manipulations, frightening films, moral dilemmas, the use of Professor Kohlberg's moral reasoning, situation ethics, the use of the Milgrim "shock" experiment, role-playing, the use of personal journals, group criticism sessions, and so forth, 14-year old students are bound to be negatively influenced.

This course has been evaluated, and over one-half of the students' entries in their journals reflect on how guilty they feel, how fearful, desperate and confused after taking the course. One quotation reflects those of many other students:

> "I felt as though something I have had all my life has been taken away from me, something that can never be totally restored. . . . I almost feel I need it back because I feel so awful without it."

A second program is Preparing for Tomorrow's World. It contains much of Kohlberg's moral reasoning and Behavior Modification.

Third is Project Legal, Law Related Education, which also contains Kohlberg's moral reasoning and Behavior Modification.

Fourth is Talents Unlimited. Its objectionable elements are: forecasting, evaluation, pre- and post-testing, and creative thinking which may be controversial.

Fifth is TIPS, Teaching Individuals Positive Solutions, which could be dangerous because of its decision making (whose decisions?) role-playing, moral dilemmas (whose morals?), decoding (whose interpretations?), creative writing (probing?).

The sixth is the Me-Me Drug Prevention Program. Our objections are its pre- and post-testing, invasion of privacy, students making their own decisions, and making teachers aware that their own feelings affect how they respond to students, that is, they are not to impose their moral standards on the students.

There are many, many more financed by the student's parents' hard-earned tax dollars.

Let's hope the overwhelming majority of parents will refuse to feed the prurient curiosity of the intellectual Peeping Toms. To inquire into the sexual attitudes and beliefs of an eight-year old, said one Senator concerning Values Clarification in schools, and to probe into children's psychic and emotional problems real or imagined, rather than into the level of their intellectual achievements, this is certainly a serious invasion of privacy.

The schools are being used as places to promote contraception and to encourage abortions. And I feel that this should be stopped, that the classroom should not be used as a place of selling the idea of contraception.

I am a former Army nurse, and as I took care of the patients who fought in Vietnam, silently suffering in the hospitals in Japan and in Buffalo and in Hawaii, I think what a great injustice this is for them to have made all these sacrifices and to see their children go to school and be indoctrinated in the very things that they went to fight against.

Kirk Lewis

I have been a teacher for 32 years, a member of the School Board, a taxpayer.

As we strive to better the lives of the poor and the aged and the sick, John F. Kennedy once said, let us always remember to nurture the one institution on which these people depend the most: the family. A government that is the enemy of the family can never be the friend of Americans.

Has our own government actually become the enemy of the family through various programs and projects being federally-funded by various branches of the Department of Education?

The evidence seems to point in that direction when one discovers such projects as the Affective Test Development Project of the Lansing School District. This project was funded by the National Institute of Education. It is interesting to notice that, on the cover of this proposal, someone attempted to change the title of this project and marked out "Project" and wrote in the word "Research." So the title of the project now reads: "Research on Affective Test Development."

This is significant in that it is unlawful for the NIE to be involved in the development of curriculum or testing instruments. It is to be involved in research only. By eliminating and adding these words, this project which was actually a development project has become a research project. Now it can be declared that the Federal Government is not in the business of affective values test development.

This project was granted $24,007.13 by the NIE, which listed on the registration form, "NIE Grants Program, Essential Skills" as the approved category. Since when is affective or value testing one of the functions of the public schools regarding the essential skills of children in the government classrooms?

This project was to develop a self-report instrument which they deemed appropriate for measuring the effect of the affective value program serving in grades K through 2, and 3 through 6. This included pre- and post-testing, the collection of data, and the use of the instruments in a variety of affective values programs to determine the effectiveness of the instrument as a measure of change and finally assessment of the instrument as a measure of change produced by affective value programs.

The subjects of this project were 3rd, 4th, 5th and 6th-grade students in nine schools in the Lansing School District. Complete pre-test data were received for 595 students; 448 of these students had complete data for both pre-and post-testing for at least one of the subscales.

This document also states that in September of 1978, the test was administered to 750 students in the 3rd, 4th, 5th and 6th grades from buildings receiving counseling services. Only 79 of the 750 students had been identified as being in need of counseling services at the beginning of the year.

As a parent and taxpayer, I resent the fact that 750 students were being treated as if they were in need of counseling, all of them being treated as if they were mentally and emotionally ill.

The instrument used to measure change was the student self-report, a 35 question multiple choice questionnaire. The first group of questions on this questionnaire is about you, the next group asks about people you know in school, and the last group is on things you do in the classroom.

Classroom teaching is done by staff trained by the Office of Evaluation Services. The classroom teacher remains in the room. The tester introduces himself/herself and explains the reason for conducting the test and that the tests are confidential, and that teachers, parents and counselors would not see the students' answers, so "please be as honest as you can."

The student self-report is organized into three subscales: self-concept, getting along with others, and classroom behavior. Self-concept was defined as both self-image and an image of oneself as a person whom others like. Getting along with others was defined as a lack of belligerence, the presence of pro-social skills, a general attitude of regard and liking for others, and empathy for the problems of others. Finally, the classroom behavior subscale measured compliance issues, disobedience, talking out of turn and the lack of concern for work. All of the aforementioned information has been taken directly from the document called Affective Test Development Project.

Also included in this report is the following:

"The principal investigators for the grant have been immersed in the development issues for the last 18 months and have become intimately acquainted with the advantages and pitfalls of developing and using objective affective value instruments in a public school setting. A process has been developed which can be used to successfully produce measures of the specific behavior and affective value changes promoted by counseling services. Finally, an instrument has been developed which will provide an excellent starting point for a general measure for affective value programs in grades 3 through 6.

"The Lansing School District Office of the Evaluation Services has complete access to the school district's computer maintained student files. Thus, we can access a large data base of demographic and student activity information for students receiving counseling services.

"Computer packages are available in the Lansing School District's data processing system which permit the extensive analysis of the data collected on the instruments. One of these packages has capabilities of performing factor analysis, calculating scale reliabilities, and correlating the measures with other affective and scholastic achievement measures. A second package available to the district is the Easytrieve System. This is a file message and report writing facility which has permitted us to build a data base of achievement and demographic information and merge this with test score information from the counseling department."

Shocking, frightening, awesome, astounding, horrifying. Just what word can adequately describe the feeling that engulfs an individual as he reads of a project such as this. Students are all treated as in need or having problems. Children are being pre-tested, then subjected to an affective values program as treatment for the disturbed child; then the child is post-tested to see what measurement of change has been produced by the affective value program.

No parent has ever been notified, been allowed to view the materials, nor have they ever consented to psychological diagnosis or treatment by an unlicensed psychologist or a psychiatrist. The children have even been promised that their parents won't be allowed to see their answers, "so be honest."

If all this isn't shocking enough, we then learn that all this information that has been gathered on the behavior and values of children will be fed into computers to be kept in student files in a data bank — sophisticated data processing systems which build a data base of achievement and demographic information and merge this with test score information from the counseling instrument, the student self-report.

No wonder there is such mediocrity in our government schools when 750 elementary students were deprived of valuable educational time while being used as guinea pigs in a government funded project such as this.

TESTIMONY OF_____
Flora Rettig

I come from Center Line, Michigan, two miles north of Detroit.

I am the mother of eight children, seven of whom have graduated from Center Line High School, and my last child will be a senior next year. My husband is a retired postal clerk, and I have always been a full-time housewife and mother.

We have lived in Center Line for almost 50 years. We are Roman Catholics, and for the last 16 years we have chosen to send our children to the public school.

The course of study at Center Line High that is violating the students' rights and is a gross invasion of privacy is a course that is required for graduation. It is the Senior Semester Sociology, Psychology Course, and it was implemented for the first time last year. The book used in this class, *You Are Somebody Special*, by Charley Chase—he happens to be a minister—was purchased with Chapter I funds.

Much of the material used in this class, the questions and the Values Clarification techniques, deal with the personal and family life of the student and his social problems. Much of the material covered in the course concerns sexual activity, and many of the situations question parental authority. The whole course gives a humanistic approach to living and ignores the fact that probably most of the students are Christians.

The many papers that I am enclosing with this testimony are worksheets used with the book, *You Are Somebody Special*. Here are a few examples of questions asked in the course:

"Should Bill and I live together before marriage? Does religion have some meaning in my life or is it nothing more than a series of outmoded traditions and customs? My parents don't like the guy I am dating—should I listen to them or see him anyway? You and your boy/girl friend have decided to engage in premarital sex—who would you tell? Your father came home drunk last night and beat up on your mother—whose help or advice would you ask? To what people are you willing to tell what kinds of things? How much discipline should parents exercise in the homes—can there be too much discipline or not enough? How late should the son or daughter be allowed to stay out on weekends or week-nights? What should the policy be about the son or daughter using the family car? Should the son or daughter be expected to do any work around the house? Should they get an allowance or should they be expected to have a job after school or during the summer? Have you ever donated money to a charity or cause? Explain. Describe the time you really wasted money. Do you have a savings account? In what ways do you save? How do you feel about your saving habits? In Darlene's house, her mother has never worked outside the home; although there is never much talk about it; her father handles all the money and pays the bills. Her mother asks him for money whenever she needs it—what do you think of this? When Darlene marries, who do you suppose will handle the money? Do you think Darlene will plan on working at a career after marriage—why or why not?"

After listening to these few examples of questions asked of the students in our school today, there should be no doubt in your mind about the urgency for getting regulations for the Hatch Amendment.

Before I continue any further I feel that it is important for me to share with you how I became aware that humanism and Values Clarification were being taught in the schools. Two and a half years ago, I didn't even know what these terms meant. It was after a great tragedy in our family that my eyes were opened.

On Labor Day, September 7, 1981, our 22-year-old son, Joe, committed suicide. He had used marijuana since junior high and, about a month before he died, he told my husband that he had decided to give up smoking pot. He went into deep depression and took his own life by carbon monoxide poisoning. He left a note saying, "I did it because I couldn't think or nothing."

He was victim of a modern-day plague, pot smoking. We had known that Joe had used pot for a long time, and he sold it also; but we didn't realize to what extent until after his death. Then the other boys told us. Two weeks after his death, when we were going through his belongings, I found some English papers he had written four years earlier when he was a senior.

In all of them, he had written about using pot, and the teacher had corrected them with written comments in the margins. He must have been proud of them because he had good marks on them, and so he saved them in a small wallet box in a little cabinet next to his bed. At the time I wondered why the teacher hadn't called us to let us know of his great obsession with marijuana. A year later, when I found out that Values Clarification was used in his unit in the 8th grade physical education class, I knew then why she hadn't called us. The course objective stated: "We will attempt to teach the different categories of drugs, their effect and, hopefully, how to make a knowledgeable choice using your own individual value system."

A week later, when going through some more of his things, I found some more papers with notes taken in his psychology class. The notes were about psychic experiences: ESP, psychokinesis and astro-projection. I found a paper, too, with dream analysis and notes on suicide. I began to question what was being taught at Center Line High School.

I then asked my younger son, Greg, who had just graduated, what he learned in psychology class. In his notebook that he had saved, I found notes identical to Joe's. He also had notes on dream analysis and suicide. I then asked my daughter, Theresa, who was a junior, to bring home the psychology book from the school. It was *Psychology For You* by Sol

Gordon, the 1974 edition. Sol Gordon is a signer of the Second Humanist Manifesto.

As I looked through it, it seemed to be a "how to" manual to the occult world. It suggested devising an experiment with a Ouija board. Pages 234 to 239 explain how to do meditation and TM. And on page 313 and 314 it tells how to do yoga.

I went to the school with my findings and said that I didn't want Theresa in the psychology class the next year.

Just seven weeks ago our neighbor boy, also 22 years old like my son Joe, committed suicide. How many more families must suffer through this kind of anguish before you put a stop to this insidious cancer that is destroying our public educational system?

As a Roman Catholic I believe in God and that He creates all things. I believe in the Ten Commandments and not in situation ethics. I believe that the *Bible* is the word of God. I believe that Jesus is the way and the truth and the light. I believe Jesus when he says, "Without Me you could do nothing."

From all my research, in the past two years, I have discovered that the techniques used in our schools are those that are used to treat the mentally ill. I have come to the conclusion that our educators consider all the students mentally ill and that the schools have been turned into mental clinics, with the teachers as the psychiatrist and the psychologist.

TESTIMONY OF
Patricia Hartnagle

The Hatch Amendment is now nearing its sixth birthday. It has been one of the well-kept secrets of Washington. It has never been given any media attention, regulations or guidelines have been totally neglected, and there has never been any attempt to enforce it in any manner. For the most part, the public at large is ignorant of this legislation.

As a school board member whose sole responsibility lies in safeguarding and representing taxpayers', parents' and childrens' rights and welfare, I am very troubled that this tool of such importance has been denied them so long.

As James Kilpatrick, a columnist for the *Washington Star Syndicate*, so aptly put it, "Twenty or thirty years ago the Hatch Amendment would have been regarded as inconceivable. Even five or ten years ago few people, myself included, would ever have understood Behavior Modification in the public schools. But it is a measure of weird goings-on in public education that the Senate clearly understood what Orrin Hatch of Utah had in mind. The Senate was determined to crack down on the arrogant curiosity of a gaggle of crackpot psychologists who have invaded the public schools."

Questionnaires and situations are used extensively throughout all grade levels and all curricula. I consistently see and know of violations both with my own children and others. They are asked to do family trees, personal timelines, family portraits, "me boxes," diaries, participate in Magic Circle activities or Sanctuary, and a number of personal and psychological exercises.

When I really began to know and learn exactly what students were put through was when I found a sex education test paper my child had taken in a Family Living course which we had no idea would include sex education. We never received information nor did we give permission for his participation. That course was even in violation of the State Sex Education Act which stated that a district had to first decide to teach and then adopt a formal program with guidelines (which had not been done). Again we were dealing with a law for which we had no recourse if it was violated.

From that point on I became more aware of what was really going on in education, and I became more angry and disillusioned than I had thought possible. I, like so many other parents, had trusted teachers and education, and what I had learned did seem inconceivable.

Also inconceivable to me was that seemingly perfectly intelligent teachers and administrators had been retrained by our behaviorists into believing that this new way of teaching was necessary and innovative and would teach the students how to think and make good decisions.

Professor John Goodlad is more than anyone else responsible for the open-classroom, global education courses, "feel-good" education, and the retraining of our teachers until they don't know how to teach in the traditional sense of the word.

In the report of the President's Commission on School Finances, 1970, Mr. Goodlad said:

> "The use of conventional wisdom as a basis for decision making is a major impediment to education improvement. The majority of our youth still hold the same values as their parents and, if we don't resocialize, our system will decay."

In *Schooling for a Global Age*, John Goodlad says:

> "Parents and the general public must be taught a global perspective; otherwise, children and youth enrolled in globally-oriented programs may find themselves in conflict with values assumed in the home. Then the educational institution frequently comes under scrutiny and must pull back."

A close associate of Goodlad's, Dr. Benjamin Bloom, the father of mastery learning, in his recent book *All Our Children Learning* states: "The purpose of education is to change the thoughts, feelings and actions of students."

William Glasser and Sidney Simon have been heavily involved in developing such programs and psychotherapeutic strategies as values, role-playing, psycho-drama, socio-dramas, operant conditioning, Behavior Modification, "time-out" boxes, open ended questionnaires, surveys, and diaries. Teachers' manuals of these often state that these strategies are to change students' attitudes, values, and beliefs.

Such education abandons the cognitive, logical and rational approach to education. That a change of attitudes and values is the purpose of affective education programs and materials is a fact; this can be supported by documentation from leading educators, psychologists and so on. They are used to bring about political and religious indoctrination.

TESTIMONY OF_____

Barbara Powell

The following quotation is a suggested assignment for junior and senior high students throughout the State of Michigan:

"First ask the students to relax, feel comfortable and close their eyes. Then ask them to fantasize and design a form of birth control that they would enjoy using. If possible, they should include in their design how the contraceptive would work to prevent pregnancy, but this is not necessary."

"Next, ask students to share their designs out loud, noting differences and good ideas. The various designs may elicit much laughter.

"Finally, in discussion, elicit from students the criteria they consciously or unconsciously had in mind when they designed their methods of birth control. These may include factors such as ease of use, comfort, safety, effectiveness and reversibility. Ask students to apply these criteria to present contraceptives and rate them accordingly."

This assignment was taken from the manual, *Preparing Professionals for Family Life and Human Sexuality Education*, which was enabled to be printed and distributed at no charge by the United States Office of Education. This manual is a professional resource to be used by instructors in developing in-service and other training programs for teachers involved with sex education.

We parents do not want our tax dollars used to change the values of our children as demonstrated by this assignment, as well as many others, in this teacher-training manual. This assignment is a two-fold violation of parental rights. First, it teaches our children to be immoral; secondly, it teaches them to disobey the law.

The following exercise is also suggested in the manual, *Preparing Professionals for Family Life and Human Sexuality Education*:

"Divide into three groups representing: a) 8 or 9 year olds; b) 12 or 13 year olds; c) young adults. Each group should take 15 minutes to select one of the following topics and develop it into a values education dilemma, case study, or role-play and explain how it might work with the assigned age group. The topics are listed as follows: a teenage pregnancy, using contraceptives, boys and girls seeing one another naked, a teenager's abortion, an out-of-wedlock birth, a woman leaving her husband and child."

We parents do not want our children involved in moral dilemma exercises in the public schools because of the inherent force of public self-disclosure in such exercises. This is an invasion of privacy which is unlawful. Recently there has been much publicity in the media about our local, state and national governments' concern regarding child abuse. This is a righteous concern, but then I must ask: Why are our tax dollars being used to develop programs which invade the privacy of our children? This too is child abuse.

Likewise, we parents don't want our tax money used to involve our children in role-playing negative situations, as was also suggested by this exercise. This is a Behavior Modification technique which is a violation of parental rights. Another brazen example of an attempt at Behavior Modification can be found in the following exercise taken from the same federally-funded manual:

"Vocabulary Brainstorming:
(a) Divide the class into groups of five or six. Select one word or phrase and then have each group list as many synonyms as it can in three to five minutes. Use words such as penis, vagina, intercourse, breast."

(b) Now, rearrange the class in couples and ask that they engage in a conversation for three minutes, trying to use as many of the words on the list as possible."

We don't need federal funding to teach gutter-level language in the schools of Michigan.

*TESTIMONY OF*_____
Elaine Andreski

I am a mother of four children, a traditional Roman Catholic and Home School Chairman for Michigan Alliance of Families. Approximately 17 years ago I became involved in the educational process.

In the 1973/1974 school year, my two younger children were involved in an experiment in Behavior Modification. Hesse Elementary School in the Warren Consolidated School System was targeted to develop a program that would ultimately change the attitude, self-image, human relationships and self-control of the student involved. Not only were the desired changes to affect the student, but parents were not to escape it either. The behavioral changes would alter the parents' attitude through in-service programs.

This comprehensive behavioral modification experiment included a restructuring of the teacher's role in education. The teacher would now become a facilitator in the classroom, using techniques such as: team teaching, simulation games and other behaviorist-oriented methods for changing the attitudes and behavior of students.

I recognized this as the B-STEP Program designed to convert every classroom in America into a mental health clinic. Social change was the ultimate goal.

In this new approach to learning, one of the

teachers, a Mr. Wright, shaved in front of the class because some children don't get to see their daddy shave. This was termed a learning experience. The children were able to take home some of the whiskers to show their parents. Some wonder why we have functional illiterates today?

At the junior high level, in this same year, my oldest son, Jeff, was placed in an experimental Language Arts Class at Butcher Junior High School. Here he had to study gangs for six weeks. The selection of reading material for the class included many paperbacks which were filled with four-letter words. My son brought it to my attention. I then approached the teacher about the connection between language arts and gangs, hoodlums and bums.

We were later told that our son was placed in this experimental pilot program because he scored very high on some achievement test.

TESTIMONY OF————————————————
Lois Wolthuis

I am from Ionia, Michigan. It is harmful to our children when we, as parents, tell them one thing and the teachers or change agents tell them something different. The schools and the teachers put doubts into the minds of our children against their parents and against their belief in God.

My 3rd grade daughter was told that there was

no right or wrong, that she could do whatever she wanted to do. My child was told that we came from animals and the teacher did not even mention God or creation even as a theory that some people believe. This was very upsetting and disturbing to our 3rd grade child. When my child was told to write whatever she wanted to write in answer to questions about her home and family, the teacher promised that the answers to these questions would not be shown or told to her parents. What an invasion of privacy! These questions upset our child very much.

Educators, psychiatrists, psychologists and parents agree that these open-ended questionnaires, surveys, diaries, role-playing and other Values Clarification strategies are harmful to our children, and indeed a part of psychiatric and psychological examination, testing or treatment.

One of our other children was forced to keep a personal diary. Again, this is an invasion of a child's privacy and of the parents' privacy. You do not keep a personal diary of your innermost thoughts at school. At the end of the year they were to give away the diary to a friend or throw it away. They were not to take it home.

We spent several months working with our local School Board, but they refused to cooperate and help remove the objectionable material, books, films and classes from our school's curriculum.

Our children were harassed and physically harmed by some of the students who had parents that were in favor of secular humanism. Teachers had our children remain alone in the classroom, and they did not have an equal learning opportunity by having a different subject or a different class with a teacher to go to during those times when the objectionable material was being taught.

Some of the other children had to sit in the principal's office alone while the other children were using the objectionable materials. The children were being made fun of for being in the principal's office.

The Ionia public schools also hurt our children by holding back their earned report card grades. Our children are good students, and they had worked hard for their grades. We went to the School Board and asked that they be allowed to take their exams and their grades be given for the work that had been done, but the School Board refused.

TESTIMONY OF———————————————

Lynn Schmidt

In Ionia and Muir, Michigan, I as a parent, and others discovered our children were being subjected to psychiatric testing, role-playing, open-ended questions, diaries, survival games, programs such as Me-Me and Man: A Course of Study and *Values Clarification* by Sidney B. Simon who's a humanist professor at Amherst, Massachusetts, and Kohlberg's moral reasoning. There are also films such as "Future Shock" and "Lottery." One young woman who had viewed the film in her high school over 15 years ago put it this way:

"I remember very clearly the film 'Lottery' that was shown in our school. The film centered around an average family in a small town. The focus was mainly on the mother of the family and the preparations for a town picnic that was going to take place. Everyone was excited. The day of the picnic, everything went as you would expect the picnic to go, lots of laughing and games, and so on, until someone said that it was time that everyone be a part of a circle that was being formed. Numbers were drawn out and then a number was called out. The mother in the film had a terrified look on her face; the others started saying things to her and their faces were all distorted. They all circled around her and started to stone her to death, even her own family. I remember that after the film was over and the lights were turned on, there was complete silence in the room. No one understood the film or the reason for showing it. For quite a time afterwards, I had nightmares and the film seemed to haunt me. Even now, when I think of it, it leaves me cold."

When we found out about these films, we went to the School Board and we demanded a public showing of "Future Shock" and "Lottery." We had several parents there. When I saw that film, it just made me sick to my stomach. I was an adult, and I saw how it must affect our little children. In that film, a little boy stood there whose own mother was being stoned.

Somebody picked up a stone and handed it to the little boy for him to throw it at his mother, and he had such a shocked look on his face. The blood was coming down her forehead, and she was screaming.

So we went to the School Board about it and wanted the films taken out, and they told us, "No, that is censorship, you are censors." I found out later that my older daughter had seen it twice, and she had never come home and said anything. I think the reason she didn't was she was afraid mom would go down to the school, and, you know the peer pressure—they don't want mom or dad down there.

TESTIMONY OF————————————
John Tomicki

I do not wish to offend anyone's ears in this room or their sensitivity, but I am going to read a series of questions for the record. This is a current exam being given in Englewood, New Jersey, schools, in the 9th grade level. And this exam was given to a particular student, despite the fact that we have in New Jersey a mandated sex education program in which parents may excuse their child. The parents completed the necessary steps to have their child excused; nevertheless, the teacher directed the child to participate on the first day of class. Here are some of the questions:

"Things Adolescents Are Worried About. [You

are supposed to score from zero to three, whether you are worried a little or worried a lot.]

"How far to go sexually, are you worried about that a little or a lot?

"The size and appearance of your body, such as penis or breasts.

"How to avoid a pregnancy, are you worried about it a little or are you worried about it a lot?

"Are you worried about sexual orientation, about homosexuality?

"What influences you about sex—family, TV, movies, magazines?"

Dennis Cuddy is a Senior Associate with the National Institute of Education. In an article that he wrote to the *Newark Star Ledger*, a newspaper in New Jersey, on June 26, 1983, on page 55, he quotes from a National Education Association pamphlet, "Education for the Seventies": "Schools will become clinics whose purpose is to provide individualized psycho-social treatment for the student, and teachers must become psycho-social therapists. Children are to become the objects of experimentation." That was in the seventies. We are now sitting in 1984.

While we studied the sex education program, we looked at some films. One film was going to be used in the 7th grade in my local school district; it was to study "How Life Begins." That was the name of the film. It was subtitled "The Male Reproduction System." And it was not a moving film, it was 35 millimeter slides with a voice override. The first words were—we are going to study now how life begins. Guess what was on the picture? Guess what is being displayed?

It was a young boy and a young girl in the front seat of a convertible. I don't know where they found a convertible today, anymore, to take a picture of, but there they were in the front seat of the convertible in an embrace. Now, that was the message sent to those children: This is how life begins, in a front seat of a convertible.

I think that these purveyors of sexual information who transmit the joy of it, without the responsibility of it, must be held accountable.

TESTIMONY OF
Bryan Staff

I am from Manistee, Michigan. I am the father of three young boys and also the uncle of two teenagers, a boy and a girl, who are in the Manistee public school system.

I have in my written testimony "Are You Ready For Sex?" taken from the sex education curriculum at Manistee Junior High School in Manistee, Michigan. These questions are asked to 8th graders:

"One: Do you know why your parents and/or religion have taught that intercourse should wait until marriage? Do you accept these ideas? If so, then would you be creating a lot of inner turmoil to go against your own beliefs?

"Two: If you do not accept the beliefs you are taught, is it only at the intellectual level; Do you feel really comfortable and firm in your own beliefs? Try to imagine how you would feel about losing your virginity. Would it make you feel less valuable, less lovable, less good? If so, it is a bad bargain.

"Three: Are you yielding to group pressure from your friends against what you feel is right for you? Don't dismiss this question lightly; most people don't recognize the full extent of the influence exerted on them by peers. It is easy to feel you are hung up or abnormal when your way is against most of the people around you. Remember also that some friends may be giving the impression they are more sexually experienced than they actually are.

"Four: Are you expecting too much from intercourse? If you believe that intercourse will transport you to the stars, make you overnight into a real woman or a man or any other such overblown fantasy, it won't. Try to get your expectations down to earth before you decide.

"Five: What does intercourse mean to you—a permanent commitment for life, fidelity for both partners, love?

"Six: However you answered question five, does your current relationship meet these criteria? Does he or she understand what it means to you, and do you understand his/her feelings? If intercourse means commitment to you and a lark to him, that is trouble.

"Seven: Is your current relationship emotionally intimate and open? Could you tell him or her if you were scared or if something hurt? Could you tell each other if you never had intercourse before and were really nervous? You are much more likely to have a satisfying experience if the relationship is on that level before you have intercourse.

"Eight: Can you get effective contraception and will you both use it faithfully and correctly?

"Nine: Are you prepared to face a pregnancy should your contraception fail?

"Ten: Do you have the opportunity for uninterrupted privacy, free from fear of being heard or intruded upon?"

I have here a teacher's manual from the sex education course at the 9th grade level in Manistee High School. And I can open this manual anywhere, I don't care where, and I am going to find situation ethics, brainstorming, Values Clarification and humanist doctrines in general.

When the school boards are confronted by parents' objections, they say, "Well, your children have a choice." But when my sister-in-law's daughter, my niece, was told that she had to take sex education, she brought the consent form home to her mother. Her mother said, "No, you are not going to be part of this." So, they made the girl compile book report upon book report, an unreasonable amount of book reports, to be done each and every week. Not only that, she was separated from schoolmates and completely isolated and made a social outcast, until enough pressure was exerted on her that she exerted pressure upon her mother so that her mother finally consented for her to become part of this sex education program.

Is this not an attempt to change and subvert our children's way of thought and discredit parents who hold traditional values and beliefs?

TESTIMONY OF_____
Kay Fradeneck

I am married and the mother of three children. I reside in East Detroit, Michigan, a suburb of Detroit.

I have come here today to testify and inform you about two subjects offered at East Detroit High, 7140 10th grade Health and 1160 Composition. I have found practices in these courses that are prohibited by the Hatch Amendment as well as Michigan State Guidelines.

Please review the pamphlet entitled, *Teen Pregnancies: Decisions, Decisions*, author, Curriculum Innovations, Inc. The setting leaves the student with the impression that, if she were to become pregnant, her parents would be hysterical, irrational and incapable of helping her because they would look to their own needs to determine her best options.

It also describes or suggests her own inability to

bear her parents' anger and disappointment. The result is that we have a young, frightened and vulnerable teenage girl who, upon the suggestion of the author, feels she cannot approach her parents. Rather than encouraging her to seek the counsel of her parents, the author suggests that she seek out doctors, social workers, school counselors, ministers, and counselors at places like Planned Parenthood. Not only does this alienate the parent and child, it leaves the teenager grasping for help and advice from those persons or facilities who could encourage a decision which may have life-long adverse effects on the teen and her family.

Another publication used in 7140 Health is entitled, *Sexual Intercourse*, author, Curriculum Innovations, Inc. It is, in effect, a "do it yourself" manual. The student is taken through foreplay, erections, when to have intercourse, positions for intercourse, orgasm and how to act responsibly in regard to the needs and feelings of the partner. This is the description that the publication asks the reader to consider when deciding whether or not to engage in sexual activity:

> "There are two qualifications for joining in any kind of sexual activity — that an individual feels that it is right for him or her at that particular time with that particular person and that he or she is fully able to handle the sex, the love and the consequences."

This is clearly situation ethics. Notice that neither marriage nor chastity were mentioned in considering the decision to become sexually active?

This brings me to my next example. Based on the publication entitled, *A Glossary of Sexual Terms*, author Curriculum Innovations, Inc., chastity is defined as: "An old-fashioned word that means avoiding thoughts or acts resulting in intercourse." I find this to be inconsistent with the definition found in *Webster's Seventh New Collegiate Dictionary*, which states: "Chastity: (a) abstention from unlawful sexual intercourse; (b) abstention from all sexual intercourse; (c) purity in conduct and intention, etc."

Through the use of these and similar supplementary items, and in conjunction with the practices of psycho-drama and questionnaires, the student is caused to expose his or her attitudes and feelings about sex, abortion, pornography, as well as other related subjects. Since many of these publications mention the parents in relation to the materials, through class discussions, critical appraisals do arise. The result is a challenging of values of the student and his or her family.

With the use of Values Clarification, a psychological technique, the values can be determined through a variety of methods and then treated or "clarified" to what the public schools deem appropriate. Please note these examples that I found while browsing through my nephew's 1160 Composition textbook, entitled *Rhetoric 3*, authors, James K. Bell and Adrian A. Cohn. On page eight the text is discussing unity in paragraphs in the topic sentence. Here is the example the text uses: "4. Subject: Religion; Focus: I don't have much use for any kind of —"

You finish it yourself. Because the students of this class are required to keep journals and because this material is discussed in class, the students must reveal their attitudes toward sex, religion and anti-social behavior.

On page 77 the text is explaining how to organize a paragraph and specifically how to organize an argument. Here is the text example:

"*Playboy* should be sold on campus because—

"(a) *Playboy* features stories and articles by some of the best writers in America;

"(b) *Playboy* deals with important moral problems;

"(c) *Playboy* is concerned with contemporary social issues."

The text did not establish that *Playboy* is pornographic material which a student of 16 to 17 years of age cannot purchase legally in Michigan.

Also, on page 79 of the same chapter dealing with paragraph organization is the model paragraph: "Main idea: The typical teenager has three main characteristics: he is affluent, he is educated, and he is casual about sex."

This type of teaching has a dual effect: It teaches the student about composition, and it instills the values of the State that the State feels are appropriate.

On page 42 we find this example, in the chapter dealing with the development of the paragraph. An egghead is anyone who seems to be so absorbed in the pursuit of knowledge that he hardly sees the obvious pleasures of life—partying three times a week, getting wasted on Saturday night and lying to your parents about your reasons for staggering home at three in the morning when curfew is up at twelve sharp. Instead of living, the egghead thinks."

In closing, I have a personal testimony to share concerning Values Clarification and the effects it has on an individual, both short and long term. I was educated by the very system that I am here to testify about today.

As a result of the indoctrination that I received as a student, I began abusing drugs and became sexually promiscuous. As a result, I became pregnant twice, and twice aborted my babies, the effects of which are still evident with me today.

I was applauded by my teachers for my decision to abort and encouraged to share my experiences with my peers. When I was a senior in high school I was living with my boyfriend. Because of this, I was invited to speak to the Marriage Class at my school, and I discussed the personal and intimate details of that situation.

It was only after I had nearly ruined my life that I began to reconsider what I had been taught in the public schools. By the grace of my Lord, Jesus Christ, I started to make positive changes in my life.

Today, I have three children to raise, three children whom I wish to protect from the effects of this type of teaching. This is my personal mission for testifying before you today.

My suggestion, ladies and gentlemen, is that specific rules and penalties be adopted to prohibit this use of values-altering techniques practiced under the guise of education. Those rules should specifically name the techniques as Values Clarification, situation ethics, and methods used to accomplish their objectives. This should include such practices as role-playing, psycho-drama, questionnaires, journals, psycho-therapy, brainstorming, group dynamics, and other practices aimed at revealing the values of the student.

Please stop this horrendous crime against the minds of our young people and the family institution. Our future as a country depends on it.

Beth Skousen

I am Chairman of the Michigan Pro-Family Coalition.

Dr. Max Rafferty gave a marvelous speech in Washington, D.C. in 1981 on Basic Concepts for Basic Schools. And I would like to just put forth his seven basic concepts.

Number One: Organize in every school district in the land a Citizens for Basic Education Committee. Call on local school board members individually, one at a time with large numbers on your part, and tell them, unless they meet your demands, they will be defeated in the next election.

Two: Demand that at least one fundamental school be set up within a year in that district. Such a school would teach only organized, disciplined, systematic subject matter and essential skills. It will teach reading only by the phonics method. It will have strict discipline, report cards, examinations and regular homework.

Three: Insist all teachers take a nationally printed achievement test with the publishing company usually situated in Princeton, New Jersey, setting a minimum passing score. The same company should grade the scores, the testing forms, and not the faculty.

Four: Test the students the first day of school and the last day of school.

Five: Pay the most state money to the schools that improved the most each year. If a school got money on subject matter, knowledge and mastery of specific skills, don't you think that that would improve them?

Six: Take the top five percent of district teachers whose pupils improve the most during that year and give them each a $1,000 bonus.

Now, you say, where is the money going to come from? This is how, Dr. Max Rafferty said. Count the number of deputy superintendents, associate superintendents, assistant superintendents, administrators and assistant administrators, and supervisors and curriculum consultants; fire them all, and do not replace any of them. Remember that the typical private school which is in business for money hires only one headmaster and one secretary. Send the teachers back to summer school every year until they can pass the test. Don't fire them, educate them.

Seven: Work on state legislators. State legislators fund the state teacher colleges. Appoint a task force composed of parents, news media, and retired teachers of academic subjects, with full power to visit any of these teacher training institutions without any warning. Visit classes at random, ask to see the curriculum and lecture notes, quiz the professors, talk to the students, and then present an annual re-evaluation report to the state legislators.

Mrs. George Staples

Subtle interest in alcohol and tobacco may be encouraged through the 8th grade Social Studies book, *The Way Our People Lived*, by Woodward. On page 49 it says: "The ordination of a new minister always meant a tremendous drinking bout. The congregation drank six and a half barrels of cider, 25 gallons of wine, two gallons of brandy and four gallons of rum." It is interesting to note that the drinking bout involved a minister and not a mayor or doctor.

Drinking is listed under customs. I have other pages in which drinking is mentioned in that book and tobacco is discussed in 13 pages of the book. But there is no mention of other customs, like preserving fruit and vegetables, making jams and jellies or pickling meats, all of which was necessary in those days. One would wonder if such teaching increases curiosity in the pre-teen leading to the not uncommon very young alcoholic.

May I submit a book published by Barnes & Noble entitled *Educational Psychology*, part of a college outline series, and it is keyed to your textbooks. On page 101, and I quote:

> "The new education seeks to develop desirable attitudes, and the school environment must be so arranged that the way of life cultivated in school will continue outside the school—a new philosophy of life must be developed."

These philosophies and ways of life must be left to the parents. It is not the responsibility of the schools. Schools are places of learning reading, writing and arithmetic, not new philosophies of life.

As we have removed prayer and the Bible from our schools, yoga and transcendental meditation and other Eastern religions have crept into the classrooms and gymnasium, replacing the Judeo-Christian ethic. Mount Lebanon High School has a sign pointing the way to the yoga room.

I would like to tell you about our son who spent a year in Behavior Modification. He was diagnosed at age eight as hyperactive, learning disabled and having a behavior problem, none of which he is anymore.

It was recommended, and we wholeheartedly agreed, that smaller special-education classes with individual teaching would be helpful for him. We did not know that we were signing him into Behavior

Modification. The only rule in that classroom was, "Don't hurt anyone."

Like many of us who procrastinate over avoiding these things we don't like, he avoided work as much as possible. In this class he didn't have to work, a reinforcement that he is still trying to overcome. It did not take him long to pick up everyone else's idiosyncrasies. Within two months, this skinny boy became fat by gorging his lunch by 9 a.m. with another boy. He set fires with the ones who set fires; he stuffed toilets with the ones who stuffed toilets. He stabbed and punctured himself with pens and pencils with the ones who slashed his flesh. At the end of the year, we pulled him out and put him in a private school where, with much patience and perseverance, encouragement and discipline, he has slowly progressed. But it has taken seven years of constant attention.

TESTIMONY OF_____

Frances Reilly

The NEA's report, "Education for the Seventies," states: Schools will become clinics whose purpose is to provide individualized psycho-social treatment for the students, and teachers must become psycho-social therapists.

Examples of many offensive assignments given my 8th grade daughter bear this out. In one she was instructed to write a poem and tell a lie. This was repeated throughout the instructions. Another time she was instructed to write a paragraph in a private journal on the subject: It is okay to cheat. Her paragraph ended with the words: When you cheat and don't get caught, it feels good.

Psychological testing invades the child's privacy as well as the parents'. Through many multiple choice questions in this test, a morally good answer, such as: "No, I would not," is never one of the choices, even when the student is asked: "Would you shout down the speaker? Would you smoke marijuana? Would you throw rocks at someone?"

This type of education has produced young people whose way of life and actions are destructive to our society and to the human spirit.

TESTIMONY OF
Lawrence Dunegan, M.D.

There is great need to protect our students from being presented with inappropriate questions and classroom discussions relating to their personal beliefs, feelings and attitudes.

I want to relate just one incident which has contributed to my conviction that our children need to be protected from certain elements which have entered the educational system. In our high school recently, in what was called a Health class, 11th grade students were given a series of questions for each of which they were to choose one of two possible answers. They were then told to grade their own papers on a point system according to which answer was chosen. They were then told that this was a mental health index. They were told right there in the classroom that anybody scoring above a certain number of points had a serious mental health problem and was in need of psychiatric care. At that point, one girl burst into tears right in the middle of her classroom. Can you understand how devastating such an experience is for a child? If such a child does in fact need help, that is a cruel way to inform the child.

A boy whom I asked about the content of the questions would tell me only about one, concerning suicide. He was so disturbed by it that he could not completely say the word. He stammered, sui—, sui—, sui— several times, and then he stopped when I said that I knew what he was trying to say.

To me, that indicated a severe emotional impact was sustained even several days after the questions were presented.

No child should be confronted by the school system with material which is so disturbing to peace of mind. Those who prepare this kind of material for use in the schools are insensitive to the damage they are doing. The children and the parents who are responsible for the children need protection from insensitive educational authorities who have gained influence throughout our schools.

Sandra Bak

I am going to relate to you one experience that I have had that I feel is very significant because of how and why it occurred.

I played volleyball this past year and one evening our coach told us we would have a meeting instead of practice. I attended this meeting wondering what we were going to do for the hour and a half that it was supposed to last. At first we just talked about volleyball and our team, etc.

Then, she handed us a paper with questions on it. Some of these questions were: (a) My life will be successful if _____.; (b) I wish people would _____.; and (c) I am looking forward to _____. She told us to answer them and then we were to answer one out loud in front of our team and her. At this point, I kept wondering, why is she doing this, it has nothing to do with volleyball.

Next, she put us into two groups. One with four people, the other with three. She gave us a packet full of different shapes of construction paper. She told us that each one of us was to make a 9″ × 9″ square. We had six minutes to do it, and we couldn't talk.

At this point, I was getting upset. By looking at the pieces I knew there was no way of making the square. It was just something for her to observe us on. I felt like I was a mental case. Here I was on the floor trying to make a puzzle when there wasn't one to be made. I felt I was being manipulated and watched.

After this exercise we had to fill out a sheet with questions on what we had just done. Some of the questions were: "Rate your frustration while doing this exercise," and, "How did you feel towards the others around you when you were doing this exercise?" We also had to rate how valuable we thought the exercise was.

She tried to correlate this experience with volleyball by telling us that each person reacts differently in a situation. She said, "Two people may call the ball in a game, but each of them has different thoughts going through their mind." She said we were all individuals, but we had to work together as a team.

She collected the last papers we filled out. I still did not see what this had to do with volleyball. It seemed more to be some sort of psycho-therapy where she was trying to find out more about us. I could not believe how this was important to volleyball.

I left with a very weird feeling, like I gave away part of myself that I shouldn't have. I thought that how we played was more important than our personality; at least, that is all she should be concerned with.

As we were leaving, one of my teammates informed me that what we had just done was not uncommon to take place in her Critical Thinking class. Our coach is the teacher of that class. I don't understand what right or business they have to ask these questions about our personal thoughts, ideas, and feelings.

III.

Excerpts from

Official Transcript of Proceedings

BEFORE THE

U.S. DEPARTMENT OF EDUCATION

In the Matter of:

PROPOSED REGULATIONS TO IMPLEMENT
THE PROTECTION OF PUPIL RIGHTS AMENDMENT
SECTION 439 OF THE GEPA
ALSO KNOWN AS THE HATCH AMENDMENT

DATE: MARCH 19, 1984

PLACE: KANSAS CITY, MISSOURI

Myrtle Kelly

Outside the educational establishment, very few people are aware of the extensive psychological techniques used in public schools across the nation called Behavior Modification, moral education, or Values Clarification, funded by federal and state money, and introduced in the classrooms by those with little or no expertise in the use of such psychiatric and psychological strategies or the potential danger involved.

Briefly, Values Clarification uses Behavior Modification techniques to remove moral standards or restrictions instilled by parents or religion.

Professional men such as William Glasser, Lawrence Kohlberg and others are developers of these strategies. The students are taught role-playing and psychological games normally used under controlled conditions by licensed doctors.

Values Clarification is only one of numerous psychological techniques used in public schools. They all have the basic premise of removing all old values and replacing them with moral relativism.

All of the children in the class are subjected to these strategies. I would question whether a teacher with 80 to 100 students knows each child well enough to know the emotional needs of each one, or to be able to identify those with symptoms of value confusion as opposed to emotional confusion.

Those of us who worked with the Oklahoma State Legislature in 1980 passed our own version of the student protection bill. We found these psychological techniques to be most harmful to adopted children, children of divorced parents, and children with emotional or family problems. None of these children was excused from the classroom during these psychological sessions.

In one particular school where this material was used without parental knowledge, two of the children are now under permanent psychiatric care in clinics away from home. There were four known suicide attempts, and numerous unusual behavior problems. Can we say that these situations were the result of such programs? In two cases, yes.

Any child with a sense of insecurity who is forced to choose *which* member of the family — mother, father, sister, brother, or self — is to die in a cave, in a boat accident, or in a nuclear war, is going to have some extreme emotional problems and guilt feelings. Any child who is naturally assertive, overly confident or antagonistic toward authority, is going to increase those characteristics when spoon-fed a daily diet of "choose freely and do your own thing," especially when these ideas are promoted by psychological behavioral modification techniques.

TESTIMONY OF _____
Wilma Leftwich

I am from Broken Arrow, Oklahoma.

I would like to turn your attention to the blue section of the National Diffusion Network manual, page B-6.13, wherein a program called Preparing for Tomorrow's World is described.

Since this program is directly connected to Lawrence Kohlberg, and since Kohlberg tested students to determine whether or not they are operating at "higher moral capacity," the obvious questions which must be asked are the following: Who is Lawrence Kohlberg? What are his values? What is his definition of the word moral?

It is on the basis of my findings, after months of studying the man and his philosophy, that I am able to make the following observation. In his book *The Philosophy of Moral Developments*, Volume I, we learn that, through the decision making process, Kohlberg measures the degree of change in the student's moral levels. He does this by presenting moral dilemmas, which deliberately create an internal conflict within the student, making it virtually impossible for the child to resist the change.

However, these dilemmas are censored. They are biased and psychologically contrived. They do not (as is falsely claimed) present students all of the alternatives, pros and cons necessary to make a free choice. Instead they manipulate the student to grow in the desired Kohlberg direction. The message of such deceitful dilemmas is crystal clear and always the same: there are no rights or wrongs — no absolutes by which to live and act.

Kohlberg makes much of the need to develop an autonomous child. An autonomous decision maker, according to Kohlberg, should be free to define in his own terms what, if anything, is "right".

A Kohlberg convert thinks in this way: "To say one value is good and another bad is to imply that there is some moral authority in the universe outside of my own personal reason."

Kohlberg programs subject students to an endless barrage of pre- and post-tests which relentlessly probe the psyche. It is a widely accepted fact that, essential to the right of privacy, is our right to control the information about ourselves. As long as we are in control of the flow and direction of information to release about ourselves, we are exercising that right of privacy.

However, to measure the child's moral stages through Kohlberg's instruments means that the child must give information about himself but he cannot exercise control over the use and personal interpretation of that information.

It is here that the student's right to privacy stands every chance of being blatantly violated. On the subject of value neutrality, Kohlberg pulls no punches. He says on page 295: "The school is no more committed to value neutrality than is the government or the law."

He openly speaks of the fallacy of value neutrality. He states his position to "reject traditional stand-ards." Note that he does not say that his position re-mains neutral on *all* standards. I repeat his position: "Reject traditional standards."

Just what traditional standards does he reject? He shows hostility to parents on pages 73-74, to "ra-tional, ethical principles." This is an educator's gob-bledygook term for humanistic principles: "rational, ethical principles — not the values of parents or culture — are the final arbiters in defining educational aims. . . . Such principles do not warrant making parents the final judge."

He also suggests, on page 315, that "the fallacy involved in divine command theory is the fallacy that is a command of God, X is in the Bible, X is one of the Ten Commandments, X will be rewarded by God."

Kohlberg's material makes it abundantly clear that the Judeo-Christian view is disallowed, but only because he must make room for his own bogus religion.

TESTIMONY OF——————————————
Mary Jane Stanley

I am an educator, a parent, and a wife. There has been a growing trend in this country to produce what I would call "canned therapists." Though these people do not have the appropriate education or training to get a license to practice their art on one person at a time, they can practice on groups of unsuspecting children.

Educational groups have repeatedly echoed to the teacher trainees that they are to become psychosocial therapists. No public school is exempt from these therapists. They have been trained to practice using canned questions prepared by those trained in the field of psychology.

These canned questions are much like those used in personality tests of old, and many felt they were inappropriate. Martin L. Gross, a faculty member of the New School for Social Research found two objections to these personal personality tests. He said "they were inaccurate and they are immoral." They are one of the main thrusts against personal privacy and also the newest pseudo-scientific form of prejudice creating bias through unreliable scores indicating that someone is neurotic or maladjusted or introverted.

According to Mr. Gross, these tests are "inflicted upon unwary youngsters, and some are singled out for unauthorized guidance. Their scores often follow them throughout their academic years."

He said these things back in 1967 when these tests were answered on paper and the results kept confidential. This is not so today. With the canned therapists, the answers are no carefully guarded secret. In fact, they are on occasion answered verbally and discussed by the class.

I will agree that such tests may be used by trained people on individuals at their request. But the canned therapists practicing in today's schools are a far cry from that standard.

Just as no one is made a professional cook by knowing how to operate a can opener and turning on a burner, no one is made a professional psychologist or therapist by taking a few college courses in psychology and probing a class with canned psychological questions.

I might add that, as an educator, I have never found it necessary to ask my students psychological questions in the classroom.

TESTIMONY OF_____
Glenda Knowles

I am testifying as a parent with children in the public schools to demonstrate the need for strong Hatch Amendment regulations. Our public schools and the Federal Government have for years been involved in projects, programs and exercises challenging the student's moral and religious parental teachings.

Course Goal Publications for K through 12, funded by the U.S. Office of Education, are disseminated by the Northwest Regional Educational Laboratory in Portland, Oregon, which is an NIE laboratory. The price list states that 70,000 of these Course Goals are in use throughout the U.S. It further states how these goals were developed: "A classification of knowledge process and value attitude goals were developed after reviewing the theoretical work of Bloom and others."

What are Bloom's theories? Benjamin S. Bloom's system of mastery teaching incorporates teaching, testing and recycling the student until he achieves the desired objectives. Bloom's philosophy is preoccupied with developing, not just the intellect of the child, but developing the total child. Bloom co-authored a book entitled *Taxonomy of Educational Objectives Affective Domain* (which I shall refer to as *Taxonomy*).

This book gives instruction in testing students in far more than intellectual development. It states, "A variety of techniques, both of the disguised and direct types, is available for the measurement of attitudes, beliefs, and values, and can be used as models for measuring values considered to be outcomes of educational objectives."

To determine just how committed students are to the values, *Taxonomy* recommends that "matters are most conveniently appraised by means of detailed questionnaires and inventories."

Taxonomy further recommends "that students be engaged in sociodrama and psychodrama to test whether the students are committed to certain values." An exemplary test, according to *Taxonomy*, is described as yielding a profile of the student, which profile is said to consist of many values including home life, society, politics and religion.

Just how should our children measure up in these areas? *Taxonomy* answers: "Here is where the philosopher as well as the behavioral scientist must find ways of determining what changes are desirable and perhaps what changes are necessary."

Bloom defines good teaching as "challenging the students' fixed beliefs and states, "For example, the problem of honesty versus dishonesty versus white lies usually will result in a variety of acceptable solutions, each a function of the situation in which a concept arises." As reprehensible as this philosophy is to parents and taxpayers, our tax dollars are used to promote it as a result of the Federal Government's funding, promoting and disseminating Bloom's philosophy.

One objective in the area of reading and writing is that "the student shall defend or modify personal ideas when confronted with the ideas of others." Another objective is that "the student shall use appropriate skills in Value Clarification and the resolution of value conflicts." Still another, "student shall be aware that some people have and will have a need for a religious belief."

Indeed many of us as parents have seen such objectives being taught to our children in the classroom. For example, 3rd graders are being asked to give their name and address, personal family information and to list by name those they hate. The child is further required to criticize his family and answer the question, "One person in my family is often unfair. This is _____." The child must then expound on this incident by naming the specific person.

In other examples students are required to compare their religious beliefs as well as other values with those of their parents, and to discuss them.

These are precisely the reasons that I, as a parent and taxpayer, urge strong regulations to implement the Hatch Amendment to protect parents' right and responsibility to share our religious and moral values with our children without any challenge from any government institution.

TESTIMONY OF

Stephen Broady

I am a farmer currently engaged in the operation of over 1,000 acres of prime farm ground.

I became interested in education after my wife and I observed emotional changes in our daughter while she was attending a rural public school getting a federally approved project. The project name is Project Instruct. It was approved for nationwide use by the Joint Dissemination and Review Panel of the U.S. Office of Education on May 14, 1975.

Project Instruct is based upon the Exemplary Center for Reading Instruction, ECRI, the most widely used mastery learning educational project in the United States. These projects will be used in virtually every school district in the country. They use a type of teaching philosophy called Mastery Learning.

The mastery learning system is a type of psychological manipulation based on the Skinner ideology of rewards and punishments, wherein individual feelings are irrelevant.

Everybody knows who B. F. Skinner is, more commonly referred to as the author of Behavior Modification. The Skinner ideology, which is used in the teaching techniques of the mastery learning system, breaks down the process of learning to small bits of information, and actually codes any type of desired behavior into the learning process itself.

The real objective of these mastery learning systems with their Behavior Modifications is a deliberate attempt to make the child conform to an official environment, which is more suited to the thinking of the school's administration than to the needs of the children. These federally-funded mastery learning systems are used on young children. They have a highly-structured curriculum test and retest with the use of official criteria.

Stopwatches, direct eye contact, physical contact, psychological manipulation until the so-called mastery objective is achieved—these ideas and practices form a complex philosophy in which the authoritarian concept predominates. In the early part of 1983, I obtained the evaluation of Project Instruct from the superintendent's office of the Lincoln public schools.

At that time I was unaware of the so-called Behavior Modification based on Skinner's rewards and punishments, as used on my daughter.

It was only after a year of investigation, and reading and rereading the evaluation report, and contacting professionals within the educational establishment itself, that the full scope of this system became apparent.

The wholesale use of Behavior Modification is part of the Skinner psychology. As it was outlined in the evaluation, Project Instruct includes rewards and punishment not only for school children, but for anyone who comes in contact with the school system itself.

The rewards-and-punishment Behavior Modification system for an entire school system definitely raises a very interesting legal question. Anyone who tries to test the operation and practices of a school system using this school philosophy is punished in some manner. Those who report such operations favorably are rewarded. This reward system can be shown by looking at a school board president; not only his wife works in the school, but his mother-in-law works there as well.

Where I come from, these rewards are more often called bribes than they are rewards. Civil liberties are almost non-existent with people who use this so-called Behavior Modification on such a grand scale.

Project Instruct was a state-administered project using federal funds, ESEA Title III, section 306, to the tune of $710,000 federal bucks.

TESTIMONY OF_____

Anna Mayer

My husband and I have three children, eight grandchildren, 37 nieces and nephews. We have a big stake in the public schools and in the future of the country. I have been evaluating textbooks and teaching materials for approximately ten years.

Most of the parents I know send their children to school to learn to read and write, to spell, learn basic arithmetic and learn to love and appreciate our American heritage. They do not send their children to school to have their values and attitudes changed.

I have always been proud to be an American. Our system of government isn't perfect, but it has given the greatest amount of freedom and prosperity to more people than any other system on earth. It is very sad to evaluate textbooks and educational material pointing out all the faults of our system and comparing our country unfavorably to countries like Cuba or Russia. If the authors lived in one of those countries, they wouldn't have the right to criticize their government.

It is disturbing to read about all the poor Third World countries, and how greedy we are in America, and that we should divide our wealth equally. Nowhere do the authors recognize that we do have great wealth and freedom *because* of our American system based on freedom of religion, our constitutional government, and our system of free enterprise. The poor countries have natural resources like we do. They have the people. The only thing they don't have is a government that encourages them to produce. The textbook authors want us to give up what we have here, so we can all be miserable and poor.

The worst thing I find in the material is the godless philosophy that permeates much of the educational material our children use. I believe in God and I believe that God created the earth and everything therein. If some people think they evolved from some slime on a stagnant pond, that is their privilege, but I do not want that godless theory crammed into my children. Evolution hasn't been proved; it can't be proved, and many reputable scientists reject the theory.

We were very excited in Oklahoma when the Hatch Amendment was passed. We thought we had a tool to combat some of the Values Clarification strategies and other mind-bending techniques being used in the classroom. To our dismay, we found that there was no procedure to register a complaint. We were successful in passing a bill similar to the Hatch Amendment in Oklahoma, but soon found that many of the controversial programs to which we objected were financed by the Federal Government and that our state law did not apply. I am very happy that Hearings are finally in the process and regulations are being written to carry out the intent of the Hatch Amendment.

If the educators are really convinced that their programs are worthy, why are they afraid of the parents looking over the material?

I have a Future Studies publication, which was produced with the support of the National Institute of Education. The name of the publication is Future Studies in the Kindergarten through Twelve Curriculum authored by John D. Haas. The material is prepared for teachers to give them ideas. The preface suggests that the teachers infiltrate strategies into the curriculum. If this course has merit, why would a teacher be encouraged to sneak it into the curriculum? Topics suggested for study include: Fertility Control, Contraceptives, Abortion, Family Planning, Women's Liberation, Euthanasia, New Age Consciousness, Mysticism, ESP, New Religions, Changing Older Religions, Guaranteed Income, Nuclear War, and so on. To say the least, these above-mentioned topics are controversial and involve morals and value judgments. The text reveals that Values Clarification, creative problem solving, forecasting and predicting, bio-feedback, mood control, self-knowledge, and self-motivation will be among the learning objectives.

Some of the goals for changed behavior include developing great trust and respect for the diversity of people and lifestyles, global loyalty rather than competitive nationalism, and a willingness to share equally the world's resources.

Goals for skills to be learned include Values Clarification techniques and skills in conflict management. The students will probably use their conflict management skills in their own homes when their changed values conflict with their parents' values.

*TESTIMONY OF*_____

Donna Muldrew

I am from Lubbock, Texas. I am a former educator, with eleven years' teaching experience: five years in public schools and six years at the university level. I have a Master's Degree in Education, with a Major in Guidance and Counseling. My husband is a public school teacher of 20 years, and we are the parents of three children. It is with serious concern that I share with you my views regarding regulations for the Hatch Amendment.

For some time I have been alarmed over the increasing use of psychotherapeutic techniques and strategies in our public schools. Instruction in the use of Values Clarification, Behavior Modification, psycho-drama, role-playing, sensitivity training, encounter groups, open-ended questionnaires, surveys, and student journals is an important part of teacher and counselor education.

Teacher training, textbooks and programs have moved from the primary position of imparting knowledge and skills to the place of changing attitudes and values. In the January 1969 NEA publication, *Today's Education*, educators June and Harold Shane promoted the idea that in school, in the '70s, teachers would function as learning clinicians and that schools would become clinics to provide psycho-social treatment for the students. I would not have believed that statement had I not completed my graduate work in 1977 and personally experienced the change of direction that public education was taking.

Courses for counselors and teachers give instruction dealing in the affective domain, with the use of psychological techniques, strategies and testing. Changing attitudes and values is the purpose of many affective education programs and materials today. In one course, entitled "Group Techniques in Counseling," our class divided into two encounter groups for the duration of the summer session, to work through our problems, gain self-awareness, reveal inner feelings, and seek positive attitudes and behavior change. We experienced techniques that we would later use in classrooms and counseling sessions.

As a result of those experiences, I am convinced that such psychological treatment produces stress and clearly presents a risk of psychological damage, even for consenting adults, much less for children who are a captive audience in a compulsory classroom. It is relatively easy to see how such forms of sensitivity training, involving peer pressure, can result in the child exchanging individual values for group values and alienation of families.

Young people do not have fully developed value systems, nor do they have carefully defined reasons to support their beliefs and behaviors. The individual is vulnerable to the attack of the group that is supposedly helping him solve his problem. Criticism by the group of family, religion, attitudes and beliefs, produces disillusionment. These kinds of group activities can be incorporated into almost every classroom setting.

Many parents wonder why they lose their children to a whole new value system. Such psychological treatment could well be the reason. I do not want this for my children.

In a speech before the U.S. Senate, Senator Orrin Hatch said:

> "Our amendment simply holds that before young people, who in many cases have not learned to cross a street properly, become subjected to sensitivity training or some other variant of Walden Three, that we should first have a written O.K. of their parents or guardian. This whole problem came about when schools started becoming more concerned with children's attitudes, beliefs and emotions, rather than providing them with basic education."

Many of the developers of programs in question have received federal funding in support of their work. Sidney Simon, developer of the controversial Values Clarification, clearly admits his intention is to change values, attitudes and beliefs. A course entitled Understanding Human Sexuality, developed by Bellevue Public Schools, Bellevue, Washington, is a good example of the use of Values Clarification, and is also clearly an invasion of privacy. Simon's *Values Clarification* and Lawrence Kohlberg's moral reasoning, both based on situation ethics, are forms of psychological manipulation.

Here is a quotation from "Student Journal," a collection of diary entries written by students in response to the curriculum Facing History and Ourselves, which is very revealing. The student says:

"Life used to be so easy. There always seemed to be an answer to everything. Everything fit into place, getting up at 7:00 o'clock, going to school at 8:00, coming home at 4:00, doing homework at 8:00, and finally going to bed at 11:00. In my tightly scheduled life, I left no time to reflect. In these past four months, however, I have been forced to think. It hasn't been easy."

For responsible persons in authority to disturb the stability so well expressed in the first two sentences of the student's response is a serious matter.

Psychotherapeutic techniques should not be used in the classroom to bring about changes in political or religious views or to encourage students to reveal inner feelings and beliefs without parental knowledge or consent. The use of such techniques by psychologists, or psychiatrists, should always be at the discretion of the parent. The apparent intent of the U.S. Senate, in unanimously passing the Hatch Amendment, was expressed in Senator Hatch's statement when he said,

"The techniques used to change young children's attitudes and values are an invasion of privacy in the first degree, especially in some of the innovative testing questions, soliciting young children to pinpoint their father's or mother's faults. Again, what I am concerned with, as are my colleagues who have co-sponsored the Parental Consent Amendment, is not the monitoring of basic education, but of the behavior probing tests, games and surveys currently being conducted in many elementary and secondary schools."

Senator Sam Hayakawa, in his remarks to the U.S. Senate, so accurately and succinctly said,

"To inquire into the sexual attitudes and beliefs of 8-year olds, to probe into their psyche and emotional problems, real or imagined, rather than into the level of their intellectual achievements, these are serious invasions of privacy, and messing around with the psyches of young people does not stop with testing and inquiries. There are exercises in psycho-drama, role-playing, touch therapy, encounter groups, and other psychological games that have no academic significance whatsoever."

TESTIMONY OF_____
Jil Wilson

I am from Kenosha, Wisconsin. My husband is a pediatrician and a member of our elected public school board. We have four children: two in college, and two in junior high school. Our children have attended public, private, sectarian, and nonsectarian schools.

When I sent my first two children to school, I

thought my responsibility would be to be a good school helper, volunteering, baking, chaperoning, and encouraging my children. By the time my first two children had reached third grade, I realized something was wrong. The child I took to school in the morning was not the child I picked up after school in the afternoon. If this change had been a positive change, reflecting academic progress, I would have been delighted. However, the change I noticed was in their value system. They seemed to be desensitized to the morals I had been trying to instill in them as their mother, and I thought that I had failed.

As I investigated every possible influence on my children, I finally ended up in the principal's office at my children's school, and this is where I found out that I had failed as a parent. I failed because I had assumed the schools my children were attending were like the schools I had attended.

I found, instead, that the thrust of schools had turned from education to indoctrination. I found the values I instilled in my children were not reinforced, or respected, by the schools, but were very systematically challenged in the classroom. I also found many teachers, and other educators, delighted to find a mother who had had her eyes opened. These educators wanted to help to return schools to academic excellence.

My husband ran for School Board and was elected. And I founded an educational research group.

We now have four children and, as our family has grown, we have seen the schools become more manipulative. We have seen well-orchestrated plans developed to remove local control from the schools and, most of all, I have realized that the most important thing that I can do each school day is to take my children to school in the morning and reassure them that when they come out of school at 3:10, I will be waiting at school for them.

My real job begins at 3:10, when my children have returned to me and I can, if necessary, deprogram them from what has happened to them at school that day. The government has made me a deprogrammer because, under federal funding, these educational experiments were initiated, developed and disseminated. Now we have a proliferation of manipulative behaviorists, staffing and supplying our educational network, and leading us, as a nation, toward a future where our children will be functionally illiterate and easy to lead. Who will be their leaders and where do they plan to lead us?

I am presenting three programs to you today. First, I have a critique for you of the Planning, Programming, Budgeting System being introduced into our nation's schools. This is sold to the public as an accountability program, aimed at economic efficiency. In truth, it is a program where a child's value system can be manipulated and a student can be recycled or reprogrammed until his attitudes, feelings and behavior match the government's goals and objectives. My critique documents the validity of these statements.

The second program I am presenting to you is the Me-Me Drug Education Program, listed in the

1983 catalog prepared for the National Diffusion Network Division of the U.S. Department of Education called "Educational Programs That Work." Our school district tried to get materials on this program for use in our local schools. We were never able to get all the materials for review, even though I have copies of letters from a school board member, our local curriculum director, and one of our state legislators, who all tried to get the material from the project director. The material was withheld, by the way, in violation of Wisconsin law, because the project director would not release teacher-training material unless, prior to getting it, they would submit to training in the program. Before they would let you see what they proposed to do, you had to submit to their indoctrination, although it is, supposedly, a drug education program.

It is, in my opinion, in actuality, a values changing program, as evidenced by the pages I have copied for you from the program materials. In the teacher activity packages, Grades 2 through 6, page 2 of the Drug Information Book says:

> "The approach used in this program to the subject of drugs is prevention. This is a very small part of our program. Our program does not stress only factual information. Our program teaches factual information in conjunction with students learning about themselves, their values and how to make decisions. Teachers do not need to know extensive information about drugs to use this program."

What the teachers do use, instead of information about drugs, is Values Clarification, sensitivity training, encounter groups, role-playing, journal keeping, and the Kohlberg-style plan for moral development to challenge and direct the students' value systems.

Lawrence Kohlberg received a Ph.D. in Psychology from the University of Chicago in 1951. Kohlberg's method is a direct challenge to parents who based their child's moral development on religious, Biblical principles. For example, the Ten Commandments say that you shall not steal. Under Kohlberg, the teacher is not to directly teach moral development, but is to facilitate the transfer of the student from a lower stage to a higher stage by integrating moral dilemmas into the classroom.

These contrived moral dilemmas are put to the children in a situation where the reasoning of his present parent-instilled value system will be challenged. Students are confronted with an issue such as "Is it moral to steal?" Under the Kohlberg approach in the classroom, the teacher is not to be concerned with the student's conclusion. The reasoning process used by the students is the issue. Remember, the schools have peer pressure to work with them, and it can work against parents.

Kohlberg contends, "As they develop further, they elaborate more intrinsically justice-based reasons and use less religious reasons."

In our Wisconsin school, we could not get all the materials we wanted to review on this program prior to making a decision. I received a phone call from a parent in Texas, who wanted to share information on this program because her schools in Texas were using it as a model, with a different name. The importance of this is to let you know that, as these programs travel around this country, the name changes, but the intent and material remain the same. You must give parents a tool. We must have the right to give *informed written* consent before our children are subjected to these innovative programs.

Informed consent, prior to participation in a program, or activity, is of vital importance.

Recently, in my town, a lot of parents I know signed permission slips, so that their children could go to a school Leadership Council party on a Friday evening. The children were told there would be refreshments and games would be played. The "party" lasted from around 7:00 until 10:45 that night. It was held at the Teachers' Association headquarters, in their building and outside. My daughter had signed up for Leadership Council as an activity, but she has quickly learned that it is not to help lead those who wish to initiate and coordinate student activities. It is a question of leading those who wish to lead. One mother went early to pick up her daughter from the party. She was very upset by what she saw. Had she known ahead of time what was being planned for her daughter, she would not have signed that permission slip and let her go.

I have a statement from the girl who did participate and, also, the directions for the activities from the Leadership Council. The students at this party played boundary-breaking games, and they participated in a desensitizing program called The Special Olympics. The student wrote (and I have her testimony handwritten in my files):

"Then everyone joined hands and things were told by one person about different people in the dark, and they led us outside blindfolded and they separated us. [They left them in the parking lot like this, at 10:15 at night.] Then they started talking about leadership in voices that sounded like ghosts and ghouls. They finally brought us together and made us walk blindfolded in the dark, around 10:15, up and down hills, and over chairs.

"They put chairs in the parking lot and the students, of course, couldn't see them, but they were told, 'Step up and over.' Unless they did this, they would have stumbled. When this was all over, the students were told, 'This explains what leadership means.' "

In conclusion, I want to tell you that I feel our government has declared war on parental rights. The primary role of parents in the upbringing of their children was reaffirmed by the United States Supreme Court in 1972 in *Wisconsin v. Yoder*. We must have the right to informed consent on any program that involves our children and our schools. We must have our children back.

*TESTIMONY OF*_____

Joan Lauterbach

I am from Mexico, Missouri.

On September 3, 1981, I attended a parents' orientation for the Gifted and Talented Program for grades 3 through 6. The following are questions I asked concerning the curriculum. These points were mentioned in a letter that was sent to me; the letter stated that this is what they would be doing in this program. (The following year, they didn't list what they were going to be doing.)

No. 1: What is Values Clarification? The answer I received at that time was that the child is to consider what is important to himself, to teach the child self-awareness for decision-making and that there are no right or wrong answers.

No. 2: What is humanism? The answer was that the children are put in a situation. The children then discuss the situation and decide what to do. There are no right or wrong answers. One situation is where children have to counsel with another one who is considering suicide. By the way, our Gifted Program is geared for 3rd grade through 6th grade. We are talking about eight years through, probably eleven or twelve years of age.

No. 3: What is C.P.S.? The answer was Creative Problem Solving. These are group decisions, and there are no right answers.

No. 4: What is SCAMPER? I don't recall what they said the letters stand for, but it involves synthesis decision-making. Again, there are no right or wrong answers.

No. 5: What is the ME Center? The answer was that the object is to learn self-awareness, self-concepts, to learn about their own feelings, their own values, and to develop healthy and realistic attitudes toward self.

No. 6: What are relaxation techniques? The answer that I was given was, "We teach them yoga to attain peace, harmony and self-awareness." Also the teacher said, "I turn off the lights in the room and turn on moonlight, and then we just lie on the floor and talk and fantasize. We also play fantasy scenes, breathing exercises, and do the body scrunch, which is a yoga exercise. A set of cassette tapes, with giant-size postcard pictures are available, called Peace, Harmony and Awareness. Children are to meditate while looking at the pictures and imagine that they are there, on the mountain top, by the lake, and so on. They are told to remember how peaceful and restful they feel and that the next time they become angry or upset, they should remember how they feel right now."

To me, this is either a form of hypnosis, or guided imagery, or maybe both, but it is a psychological tool.

Astrology books for youth were also available at that time. Children were to write their own horoscopes and make their own astrological sign.

On September 4, 1981, I requested that our daughter *not* be included in this Gifted Program. A few weeks later, on October 2, 1981, we received a letter informing us that our daughter was participating in Project Challenge, another phase of the Gifted Program. We had not given our permission for her to be in this program. We did let her stay in for about two weeks until we could find out what was involved in the program.

Teachers, parents, and children who were participating in Project Challenge were invited to a Writing Workshop entitled, "Communal Writing, Discovery of Self." We attended this workshop. One activity was as follows: We were to write on a piece of paper, in this order: (1) the name of someone in our family, (2) an adjective that described that person, (3) three verbs describing scary or familiar things that he or she does (4) a thought about that person, and (5) the name of that person again or a synonym related to that person. The above could be considered a critical appraisal of a family member.

Also, parents, teachers and children were asked to close their eyes and pretend that they were going down the river with their child or parent, whichever the case might be. The scene was beautifully described and, after reaching the beach and parking the car, the parent and child walked hand-in-hand along the beach until they came to a boat. One of them had to get into the boat and might never return. The "boat," to me signifies death. At this point, we were to write about our feelings, as we remember the past feelings of our relationship and what we felt about the possibility of never seeing that person again.

Then we were given the opportunity to share with the group. One little girl, about ten or eleven years old, began to share what she felt and had written down. She became very emotional and cried as she said, "Mommy, Mommy, please don't leave. I don't know what I will do without you. Please, Mommy, don't go." The person conducting the seminar said, "Isn't that touching?"

On September 2, 1982, I met with a 6th grade teacher regarding a scene that was held in her classroom, pardon me, not a scene, a *seance*, that was held in her classroom. The children participating in Project Challenge chose five books from a book list. All these books were stories that include something in the realm of the supernatural. Even the students knew this, as they wrote an article describing the seance in the Project Challenge newspaper called "The Challenger." The students were given vocabulary words from the books and told to write sentences using the words. The children also had to role-play the main character in each book, such as a warlock, a spiritess, an exorcist, and a poltergeist.

Regarding the Career Education Program, 3rd grade children were asked to give a critical appraisal of themselves, to list things that they liked and disliked about themselves.

On November 25, 1981, an elementary counselor, or psychologist, demonstrated how she could control a metal washer hanging from a string. She showed them that she could, with concentration, make the washer sway in the direction in which she wanted it to go. She then gave the opportunity for the students to try it for themselves.

On February 22, 1983, I viewed a filmstrip that

has been shown to Kindergarten through 2nd grade children in our school system, Transactional Analysis for Tots. It discusses feelings, emotions and so on, and tells the children that parents are responsible for the child's bad feelings toward themselves. Parents are, for the most part, put down, and the children are encouraged to go to the psychologist, who will be their friend and listen to them if they are afraid to talk to their parents about their feelings.

Regarding Health Education Programs, in September 1983, the 8th Grade Health classes were given instructions to prepare an Attitude and Behavior Survey. The boys were to prepare surveys for the girls and the girls to prepare surveys for the boys. I guess this is one way of getting around not having the teacher be responsible for the questions that were asked. However, they were given a few examples of types of questions to ask, such as: How important is making-out with a girl? Smoking pot? Do you like girls who have had sexual experiences? Do you have sexual relations? Do you shave your legs? Do you have sexual relations with boys? Do you worry about getting pregnant? Do you think 8th grade girls should have sexual relations with boys? Do you think that 8th grade girls could care for and raise a baby?

These are just a few examples of psychological techniques and invasions of privacy that are taking place daily in our public schools. They are either directly, or indirectly, funded with federal dollars.

When I voiced my concerns to our local school administration, and to a school board member, I was told I should remove my children from the public schools since I did not like these programs and techniques being used.

I talked with the school administration, school board members, my state legislators, and the State Department of Education, about my concerns, and no action was taken by any of them. School administrators told me, at one time, that I would be unwelcome at the school because I had placed myself as an atypical parent.

TESTIMONY OF_____
Larry Rink

With the variety of programs that are available now, it is becoming increasingly difficult for parents to keep abreast of what is presented to their children in the classroom. In many cases, the programs made available are such that an individual teacher, or counselor, can acquire the program and implement the program, and use it in their classroom, on their own without the necessity of the school district's approval.

Many of the programs, as related to the regulations here, deal with areas that are nonacademic in nature, and deal instead with the morals and values and beliefs of the students. Some examples are programs such as Tribes, Quest, and New Model Me, which get into the area of Values Clarification, using exercises that give situations in which students are supposed to make judgments from a limited number of selected choices that present no absolute right or wrong answers; the students are supposed to choose which is the better of the two alternatives, without necessarily having all the information or all of the choices or other possibilities presented to them.

The National Diffusion Network lists a curriculum called Facing History and Ourselves. An evaluation of it by Professor Marcus Lieberman, Harvard Graduate School of Education, published in *Moral Education Forum* in 1981, Special Edition, states as follows:

"Furthermore, the effect of the program on students may not become apparent until considerable time after completion of the unit; nevertheless, experimental programs must be able to evaluate outcomes. This article summarizes the strategies we use to detect some of the effects of this controversial curriculum. During the first year of the Facing History and Ourselves program, we wanted to cast the widest possible net to capture changes in the students' moral ego and social development. Not too surprisingly, junior high students who took all these tests complained bitterly about the difficulty in answering the questions posed in the protocols. It became particularly difficult to persuade those students, who experienced a unit on resistance, to continue with the test. While the advantage of casting a wide net to capture any changes had seemed like a reasonable approach, the emotional response to what students perceived as a high level of abuse had been unanticipated."

The next few comments are quotes taken from the "Student Journal", which recorded excerpts written by students in response to the same curriculum, Facing History and Ourselves.

"The most meaningful parts of the book [Elie Wiesel's book entitled *Night*] to me were when the boy stopped believing in God, and when the father was dying. I think that, maybe, my faith is waning a little, just from reading about it. Unfortunately, this book will always be tucked in my memory."

Another student wrote in his journal,

"I'm conscious of having changed in the strength of my convictions on many of the ethical dilemmas we've confronted. But, in other ways, I'm less sure of myself and more introspective. Where do I draw the line between right and wrong?"

Another quotation is:

"We probed the questions that had no right or wrong answers and I became more and more confused as to how I stood on several issues."

And another child wrote:

"Seeing how other people think and express their opinions, I have learned that there is seldom a right or wrong, but rather a right or left."

From these, I would say it is apparent that the child's values, morals and beliefs were being affected and dealt with during the course of this curriculum. I don't believe it is the province of the school, or the teacher, to formulate or systematically venture into these areas of the student's privacy.

*TESTIMONY OF*_____
Robert Griggs

The following statement is my own personal experience. I testify against a trend that I have observed.

In the fall semester of the school year 1980-1981, in Hocker Grove Junior high in the Shawnee Mission public schools, there was a P.E. class that was for both male and female. They used a mandatory or compulsory course in yoga to teach the kids to meditate.

It was compulsory that the pupils get into positions for meditation, and go through several things including vocal repetition of words and language that really were not identified. A number of students (especially my ex-students who came back to me because they did not quite know who else to complain to) felt like they were being pushed into something that was against their beliefs.

I did a little checking out and I found that some of the parents felt this was a violation of their religious backgrounds because they firmly believed this was a type of occult practice and not just meditation.

I followed up with a call to the school and mentioned that I was a parent with three children in the Shawnee Mission district. To make it very brief and short, they did not receive my complaint at all.

That same semester in the fall of 1980-1981, they also had a course that was given as an elective, noncompulsory course. It was called D&D, or Dungeons and Dragons. They offered this as part of the curriculum. I do not know if you are familiar with this or not, but it is a role-playing fantasy course. The students who enrolled participated in imaginary life-and-death decisions, value decisions concerned with human worth, moral compromise, and extremely violent death-type experiences through their role-playing characters.

This elective was not discussed or defined to parents, to my knowledge. In fact, when I called to their attention that I felt that this was not a good course for students, again I had a rude reception.

In the school year 1981-1982, I had moved to Roeland Park School. The nurse asked to show a 6th grade movie about vitamins. I consented, supposing it was a nine- or ten-minute movie. The first three minutes of the footage was the actual birth of a baby.

It started out with a lady with her legs up and apart, and her feet in stirrups or something like that, with a doctor. It was very graphic and very detailed.

The children in the 6th grade witnessed three actual births. I sensed a state of shock in the little boys and girls that it was all new to them to see a man doing what a doctor does to deliver a baby. It was very graphic moving picture footage. The portion on vitamins was about two-thirds of the film, and that was pretty much just a film about vitamins. I did not see any correlation between the live births and the vitamins.

I asked the school nurse afterwards, and she said, "Well, someday they need to learn about these things." I made mention that, as a parent I would like to be informed when my children are going to be exposed to this sort of thing, and that maybe some of my students' parents would feel the same way. What I said was an unpopular stand with the nurse.

In the school year 1982-1983, I was in the Roeland Park Elementary Schools. People who are considered student counselors and social workers in the community were attached to the Shawnee Mission School District. I am not sure where their paycheck comes from; perhaps they were federally supported. Two ladies attached to the North district (I am not sure of the scope of their jobs) were invited a couple of times to my classroom and other classrooms in our elementary school.

They appeared to be junior high school counselors and senior high school counselors. The two counselors came and asked the teachers in grades 4 through 6 to take a long one-hour coffee break. I chose to stay for the presentation, just to see what it was.

After gathering the children, ages 8 through 10, of the 4th, 5th, and 6th grades into one large room, they numbered them off at random, one through five. They asked all those who were numbered one, three and five to remain standing, and invited the others to sit down. I could see that they were being forced into a kind of role-playing that they did not want. I found this very offensive. My kids kept looking at me, that is, the ones I was in charge of. I could tell they were saying, "Do we have to do this?"

Basically, they were saying to the children, *you* are the ones who will get into sex, drugs and alcohol abuse when you get into junior high.

The kids were shaking their heads, and some of them were trying to sit down, and they were being told to get back up and stand up. The children were told, *you* are the ones, but they were saying "no." Some were even speaking out saying, "No, not me. I am not going to do that." But the counselors were saying "We want you to know that, if you do this, it is not because you are bad kids; it is just that you need our counseling; and we want you to feel free to come to us so we will get you back on track."

I felt like that was really a poor way to present ideas to little kids, especially since three-fifths of the kids in our district at that time were into those three areas of moral decline. I felt it was wrong to literally tell the children than they would be tomorrow's generation of kids in trouble.

That same year 1982-1983, at Roeland Park Elementary School in Shawnee Mission public schools, student counselors and social workers from the Norris District made an unannounced visit. I had two types of visitation in my classroom.

I would be informed the social workers were coming and that they would like to have some time to work with the kids. I was for this the first time or two, but then I began to wonder. When they came I felt like they were trying to do some molding and shaping of moral values. The more they came, the more I felt that was what they really did, and I do not think that they are in line doing that.

The student counselors this time came and they announced they would like to have a 45-minute rap session with the class students. Again I was invited to take a 45-minute coffee break, which I declined.

They began this session by presenting a large chart, about a two and one-half by three foot rectangular chart, that had various pictures and writings on it. It was obvious that it was a Values Clarification chart. The different things on the chart were to be given to the children, valued by their size.

In other words the larger the thing on the chart, the more important it was. The smaller, the less important it was. A couple of the more obvious things were love, written in about ten-inch letters, and there was a house with a family inside; these were the big things on the chart.

But there were a number of other things on which they had to make some decisions about value standards. Two things caught the kids' eyes. One was a little tiny circle about three inches across on a large chart. The two smallest things on the chart were two circles, and they were not right together.

They were just stuck on there at random. One was a circle with a little red dot in it, and the other was a circle with a Jewish six-pointed star. These things were brought to the counselor's attention.

They lavishly complimented the kids who brought this to their attention and said, "You are very perceptive and have done a good job of discerning; what does that tell you?" They said, "They are real small."

The counselors commented, "That is good, What does it mean?" The children said, "Does that mean this is not very important?"

Of course, that is what the counselors were shooting at. And they said, "Yes, this is true. Christianity once served our country in a positive way, but now students today should seek other forms of religion to study and learn from."

Then the counselor suggested yoga and meditation, and some of the eastern mystic religions. I felt that that was an outright putdown of American values. It got into a religious context which should not have been brought up. Again these are little kids, up against a strong-speaking counselor. I just felt like the kids were taken advantage of unfairly.

In the year 1982-1983, in Roeland Park Elementary School, I had assigned reports to be written based on super-8 films and A.V. materials, available from the student film checkout section of our library. We had a number of these films that run about six minutes. They are on assorted subjects, and the kids can go freely and check out the films. They bring a little projector to the room; they can sit in a corner and view a silent film for six minutes and then write a report. It is an excellent motivator for short essays.

However I noticed one of the films that came into the classroom at the time. Again, I had trust in our library system until I began to see these kinds of things pop up. There were four very primitive films, and one was in such poor taste. Out of six minutes, there were three minutes of a spread crotch shot of a man exposing his business—private business, I will say. He was working on a tool or something, and it was a close-up shot, and that is what was on the screen for three minutes. You could see his hands working on something just above his male organs.

I do not think that there is a place in elementary school libraries for such material to be viewed by 9-and 10-year olds. Once I got wind of this particular film, I decided to check out the other A.V. materials, and I found three others.

I began to point out these things with my opinion that these were really not acceptable. I was told that I would not be at this school too long.

That is the kind of thing I have seen. I do not understand why there is such an emphasis on getting sex into grade schools in this way without parental approval or even informing parents. In the last couple of years, I have seen many books in our library that deal with the occult. It seems like there is a real increase in such books. I think there were at least 16 last year which I decided I did not want my 6th graders to read because they dealt with demons and witches.

These were supposedly real practicing witches.

Their dress was sometimes not at all modest. The female witch would wear a tunic-like garment that was open all the way down. You could tell that she was braless and exposed to some degree, and she was telling ways of putting a satanic curse against people that you are upset with.

The detail of these things surprised me; it was not an elementary-type book, but rather an introduction into the occult. I personally found these things offensive to my religious background, and I know that the bulk of the parents also would; if they understood the extent that this is going on and allowed in the schools.

I felt a lack of freedom to display our basic national heritage to our children. The main opposers seemed to be from within the school.

Two years ago, I did a Christmas poster for our school building at Roeland Park. We were informed by the superintendent of schools of the Shawnee Mission school district at that time that, even though the policy was that we could celebrate Christmas as an American tradition, it was strongly emphasized that we should use "holiday winter" instead of using the word Christmas or anything to do with Christ.

We were urged to refrain from any kind of recognition of Christmas as a religious holiday in any way. To go along with that, I made up a large bulletin board that was just stars in the sky, and the kids used their geometric tools to make a typical Christmas village, with stained glass windows, churches, and houses with wreaths.

I did not put on Merry Christmas or anything

that could be offensive. For the historical bit, I just put the star of Bethlehem at the top, and that was it. There was no Merry Christmas or anything else, and I presented it to the principal of the Roeland Park School. He said, "Well, I do not see where anybody would be offended by that." Before the day was out, he had left the building. Then I had three teacher colleagues come to me and tell me they were very personally offended that I would make a religious issue of Christmas.

I might mention that the teachers I have worked with do not seem to be personally offended by me or by my teaching methods, but in that particular building there seems to be a real thrust against any form of recognition of God in any way in that school. I protested and said, "I believe that Christmas is part of our American tradition, and that this poster is not breaking any rule or law; so we will leave it to the principal to decide it."

When he found that there were a few discontented, he ordered me to take it down. It just bothers me that we are losing a tradition in our public schools that we began with as a country. I think we are robbing our kids of some real American background.

For instance, the P.E. teacher would bring in contemporary music, with filthy lyrics, into the classroom. It hurt me that the kids I loved in my class, those girls and boys had to go in and do a routine to filthy music.

I am not talking about being against rock and roll. I mean that some of the singers today sing filth, and you would see them going through gymnastic routines to filth. The kids would come and say, "Can we bring our own music? We do not like this." I would ask the teacher, and he would be offended because he liked those filthy lyrics. That really bothers me because he was pushing something on kids that is immoral.

I even got in trouble last year for just teaching right out of a secular history book. It mentioned B.C. and A.D., and I had to "put fires out" because I brought out the dateline and told how history points the years before and after the coming of Christ. The fact that I would mention that brought the wrath down on me. This bothers me because it appears there is a structure there of some kind that is really fighting hard to develop an agnostic or atheist culture. It is hard to define where it is coming from, but I really see it.

Kids can get by singing about anything except God. I had a hard time on the playground, for instance, not allowing kids to cuss. Of course, when they found that out, they would not do it around me. But it is amazing what is allowed and what is attacked —when you bring in the moral issue, then you are an unwanted white knight.

IV.

Excerpts _from_

Official Transcript of Proceedings

BEFORE THE

U.S. DEPARTMENT OF EDUCATION

In the Matter of:

PROPOSED REGULATIONS TO IMPLEMENT
THE PROTECTION OF PUPIL RIGHTS AMENDMENT
SECTION 439 OF THE GEPA
ALSO KNOWN AS THE HATCH AMENDMENT

DATE: MARCH 20, 1984

PLACE: PHOENIX, ARIZONA

Theresa Todd

Project Charlie is a drug education program for elementary school children. Project Charlie and many of the programs the Hatch Amendment is intended to cover include Values Clarification strategies. You will note that 20 of the 21 questions on the first page are on anger. For example: "I get angry when my family _____," and then the child is to finish the sentence. "Someone in my family who really gets me angry is _____," and again, a blank.

How does the amateur psychologist, the teacher, deal with the emotional problems these questions may expose in the classroom? How can a teacher resolve this anger in 30 students at one time? Even a trained psychologist would find this difficult.

Page two reveals a further invasion of family privacy as well as a gross violation of the child's privacy, as follows:

"I think my parents _____.
The most important person in my family is _____.
The stupidist thing I've ever done is _____.
I feel ashamed when _____."

Values and Teaching by Raths, Harmin and Simon, contains the following statement. "Until a child feels emotionally secure, for instance, value-clarifying experiences are probably of little benefit and may even add to his disturbances." This statement reveals the potential for harm inherent in such courses; and this harm may not manifest itself immediately.

Consider this statement made by H. Michael Hartoonian of the Wisconsin Department of Public Instruction, in his paper, entitled "The Ethics of Our Profession: The Student and Schooling":

> "When students are coerced to reveal their 'inner feelings' in a classroom and when teachers play at being psychiatrists, psychologists, or therapists, we have a situation where the setting of 30 to 1, patients to therapists, and the lack of training of these therapists must raise ethical concerns about the invasion of privacy as well as competency."

It is essential that these proposed regulations prohibit teachers from playing psychologist or psychiatrist or therapist without a license while imposing "treatment" on children who are not sick.

The need for the Hatch Amendment is also evident from the "health education" program, better known as "sex education." One of the most objectionable sex questionnaires was published by the Department of H.E.W. in 1979. Consider some of the questions deemed to be appropriate for "all adolescents of junior high age or older," even though the materials claim that the questionnaires have been "pre-tested by different groups throughout the country." Parents are outraged by such questions as these on page 155:

"#12. How often do you normally masturbate (play with yourself sexually)?

#13. How often do you normally engage in light petting (playing with a girl's breasts)?

#14. How often do you normally engage in heavy petting (playing with a girl's vagina and the area around it)?"

Also, consider these questions on page 150 from the "Psychological Inventory":

"#112. I think sexual activities like hand stimulation and oral sex are pleasurable ways to enjoy sex and not worry about getting pregnant.

#119. For me, trying out different sexual activities is an important part of learning about what I enjoy."

These kinds of "health" programs must be regulated by the Hatch Amendment.

I recommend that there be a provision covering "biochemical" treatment. The January 1969 issue of *Today's Education*, an NEA journal, carries a feature that causes alarm. The feature "Forecast For The 70's," states on page 30:

"Biochemical and psychological mediation of learning is likely to increase. New drama will play on the educational stage as drugs are introduced experimentally to improve in the learner such qualities as personality, concentration, and memory. The application of biochemical research findings, heretofore centered in infra-human subjects, such as fish, could be a source of conspicuous controversy when children become the objects of experimentation."

TESTIMONY OF
Shirley Whitlock

I am the mother of eight children all of whom have been educated in the public schools. Their ages range from 15 years to 30 years. I have worked with children and youth of all ages in voluntary teaching positions for more than 25 years through my church affiliation, in Boy Scouts of America scouting programs, as a lecturer and debater of constitutional issues, and as a member of the Speakers Bureau of Arizonans For National Security.

When the time came for my children to enter school, beginning in 1959, I had the highest regard for public education; indeed, I had mentally put teachers on a pedestal and had implicit faith and trust in all aspects of public education from the teachers and administrators to textbooks and new experimental programs.

But as the years went by and I gained experience with all levels of the education process, I became more and more disturbed by the negatives which seemed to escalate with the passing of years. Negatives such as biased textbooks, declining test scores, lack of discipline, incompetent teachers, a multiplicity of experimental programs crowding out the basics, rising school costs without a corresponding rise in academic excellence and achievement, and so on.

But the most disturbing realization was the recognition of the fact that, no matter how hard I worked in parent teacher organizations, no matter how many times I attended school board meetings, no matter how often I consulted with teachers, school counselors and administrators, I as a parent and as a taxpayer had no control over my children's education. Not only that, but the people whom I elect to serve on local school boards have no real control over the local schools either. Education problems seem to be out of control.

In a truly free, vibrant, moral and constitutional society, education is controlled from the bottom up, that is, from the family up. But education in America today is controlled from the top down. As state and federal controls have tightened, freedom, excellence and real education have sharply declined.

As real education has declined more and more, social problems surface and at earlier and earlier ages; yet solutions to the problems are sought at the state and federal level, rather than at the local level, creating a vicious cycle of escalating and insolvable problems because the responsibility of the individual and the family is circumvented or abdicated.

Experimental teaching devices and techniques are being used to change attitudes and to expose feelings and beliefs of children. This is an invasion of privacy, and could either support and enhance the values taught in the child's home, or oppose, conflict and replace them with "new" values, depending upon the teacher and his or her own philosophy and ethical standards. Such values changing therapy has no place in public education where teachers have a captive audience of trusting children and unsuspecting parents.

An example of this which is gaining popularity all over the country is the assignment of daily "journal writing." Forcing students to write a journal is a major technique used in all the classroom courses in nuclear war, where it is obvious that the purpose of the device is to promote a philosophy of pacifism rather than to teach comprehensive and accurate facts relating to weapons and war.

Since the assignment of writing of journals may seem harmless and even educational, and indeed it could be used to improve writing skills, it is important to examine the "Student Guide to Writing a Journal" given to an 8th grade student in Phoenix, Arizona. This "Student Guide" makes it clear that the purpose of the journal is *not* to improve spelling, grammar usage, or penmanship skills. The instructions state, "Don't worry too much about style or correctness." The student is promised that the teacher who reads the journal will not criticize or even evaluate the writing.

If a child is writing a journal without regard to

style or correctness of vocabulary, spelling, grammar, punctuation, paragraphing, facts, etc., then student journals must have a purpose that has nothing to do with writing skills.

Guidelines stress over and over that it is important only for the child to reveal his feelings. He is to write about how he feels about other people, specific people in his life, and events that happen to him. The journal is not to be a description of his daily activities, according to the instructions, but how you "feel" about them.

The instructions give examples of what types of experiences and events he is to write about. All of the examples tell of depressing events and the child's unhappy reactions to them. Stressing negatives seems to be the emphasis.

Writing this kind of journal induces the child to remember and recall over and over again his negative and unpleasant experiences so they will not be forgotten but will remain vivid. This is a behavior psychology technique and puts the teacher in the position of a psycho-therapist. This can be psychologically damaging to some children. The writing of problems does not guarantee that the child has the maturity to deal with them. This psychotherapy technique is being used by amateurs, namely, teachers. This can create problems for the child where no solutions are offered.

Writing journals under such guidelines induces the child to nurture and build his own feelings of anger, fear, hate, guilt, revenge and frustration. It also encourages the child to share his innermost thoughts and feelings with some adult in the school administration (who is listed in the guidelines as a "correspondent" and to be thought of as "an extension of yourself"), rather than with his parents. This is a flagrant violation of the privacy of the home. It encourages the child to report events and attitudes within the home that are clearly none of the school's business.

TESTIMONY OF————————————————

Ada Thomas

The New Basic Skills Program serves as a cover-up for controversial subjects. The Arizona State Department of Education has evolved a generalized definition of basic skills, namely communication, computation and citizenship. These new definitions are the basis of a plan which provides model activity kits on basic skills instruction for all grades K through 12.

Arizona public school districts generally allow teaching controversial subjects except where the public objection is severe. School districts that elect to use the Arizona State Basic Skills Plan are able to integrate objectionable, controversial subjects into the plan and teach them without the public knowledge.

For example, the skill of citizenship is associated with what is called "the other three R's": rights, respect and responsibility. A controversial subject

can be integrated into citizenship using these three
R's and thus provide a basis for class discussion on
the chosen subject. Citizenship is not a "skill" per se,
but is a broad subject involving issues, many of
which are controversial. This was recognized and so
stated in the Controversial Issue Policy of the Scottsdale School District adopted January 7, 1975.

Some of the highly objectionable controversial issues that can be integrated in a broad topic such as
citizenship are sex education, Values Clarification,
death education, family life education, drug and
alcohol education, man's encounter with the supernatural, and self. These subjects tend to arouse
strong public objection and, for this reason, they are
often integrated into the basic skills subjects in order
to conceal them from public view.

The Arizona Department of Education, in 1979,
recognized three basic skills of which citizenship was
not one. These three basic skills so fundamental to
our society are the ability to read with understanding, write intelligently and with correct spelling, and
perform arithmetic calculations as required in our
present day economy.

The present "Basic Skills Plan" is improperly
conceived, it is diluted with topics *not* related to basic
skills, and it is an invitation to introduce and serve
as a cover-up for extraneous subjects which are often
highly objectionable. I want to read to you the Controversial Issue Policy of the Scottsdale schools
which is very similar to citizenship education in the
basic schools of our State:

"Training for effective citizenship is accepted as one of the major goals of our public schools. Our instructional program developed to achieve this purpose properly places great emphasis upon teaching about our American heritage, the rights and the privileges we enjoy as citizens, and citizenship responsibility which must be assumed in maintaining our American way of life.

"In training for effective citizenship it is frequently necessary for pupils to study issues that are controversial. In considering such issues, it shall be the purpose of our school to recognize the pupil's right, or obligation, to study any controversial issues concerning which at his level he should begin to have an opinion, to have free access to all relevant information, including the materials that circulate freely in the community, to study under competent instruction in an atmosphere of freedom from bias and prejudice, to form and express his own judgment on controversial issues without thereby jeopardizing his relation to the teacher or the school, and to recognize that reasonable compromise is often an important facet in decision-making in our society, and to respect minority opinion."

Here are several programs used in our schools: Let's Get Acquainted With Alcohol, Enjoy In Moderation, and How To Drink Responsibly.

These programs teach 2nd and 3rd graders that too much of anything, regardless of how much you enjoy it, can be harmful, and that alcohol is a liquid that comes from grains or fruit. These grains or fruit often stay in a big keg or a barrel for a very long time, and then the juices turn into wine. One thing to remember is that alcohol itself is not bad; it's when people drink too much alcohol that it becomes bad.

Teaching children to drink responsibly is a way of acquainting children with alcohol who otherwise, would not consider drinking it. The children learn that 70% of all adults drink alcohol at least occasionally each year. This means that 30% never drink and would teach their children never to drink. But the children of the 30% who think drinking is wrong are lulled by the schools into a feeling of security by thinking, "I have been taught how to drink responsibly."

This curriculum, K through 12, recommends:

> "If any of the children are confused, they can be recommended to a school counselor, a school nurse, a peer counseling advisor of the school, a local alcohol counselor, a mental health center and use hotlines."

This recommendation provides many references for agencies and keeps them in business. Many social workers have mixed-up lives and recommend different lifestyles from parents. Why not have the children counsel with their parents? Yet, the subject of alcohol is recommended to be integrated into many basic subjects and often is called a "citizenship" subject.

And you might like to know where I got this material. I got it from the curriculum that was written and put out by the Arizona Wholesale Beer and Liquor Association. Their letter to our Senators said,

"Attached is a copy of our new Preventing Alcohol Abuse Program introduced into your State schools. I thought you would be interested in the latest of our efforts to encourage responsible consumption of alcoholic beverages. This program is intended for students in high school, in junior high and grade school, providing them with important information on the relationship between alcoholic beverages and the body.

"And through the years, it used to be known as the Enjoy in Moderation program. Our members realize more than anyone that alcoholic beverages are not for everyone but also we know that responsible consumption among adults can add to the enjoyment of life."

We already have this program in 80 of our schools.

TESTIMONY OF————————————————
Angela Hebert

In the school year of 1980-81, our elementary public school became a desegregation receiver school, and was, therefore, eligible for a new federally-funded program. At a special meeting for parents, it was presented well and sounded very good. In the area of school counseling, it was decided that a counselor would be available when needed, and services would be used only with the consent or presence of the parents.

This was near the close of school in the spring of 1980. That would be our third year there. In September, 1980, this practice continued for a short while. In a regular communiqué to the parents, it was stated that the present counselor had been replaced; the name was given, and that was all the information that was given. We assumed that the same thing would continue and that counseling services would only be used if necessary, and with the parent's consent.

The next thing I learned, weeks later and quite accidentally, was that the counselor was coming into each classroom once a week for one hour, and the teacher had to leave the room. We found this out because my 2nd grade son came home from school one day and asked me what a contract was. He said the counselor had asked the class to sign contracts and hand them in. My 2nd grade son wouldn't do that because he didn't know what a contract was. I saved the contract and have it in my possession today.

Obviously this created a situation where my children's classrooms were being interrupted, and learning time was being taken away without our knowledge or consent, let alone the fact that no one was present to monitor what this new and unknown counselor was doing with my child's mind.

I then asked our three children who attended school at that time several questions and became very upset with what was going on. My 6th grade son stated that he would become demented if he continued in that counseling class. The counselor had evidently presented the class with life threatening "survival" problems and usually one had to decide upon the lesser of two evils.

We requested that our children be dismissed to the library each week when these sessions took place, and our request was granted. Prior to this, I had discussed the matter with my children's three teachers, separately. Not one of them seemed to favor what was happening in the school, and I learned more upsetting things.

That same year, Planned Parenthood attempted to come into the 4th, 5th, and 6th grade classrooms with films that I consider were nothing more than child pornography. Under the guise of Health education, it was really sex and very pornographic.

After a meeting was held and the parents, who didn't necessarily hold the views that I do, rejected them for the 4th and 5th grades, they were not shown to those grades. Then, they viewed three films for the 6th grade, of which two were rejected. They ended up showing one film to the 6th grade class which I would not let my son see.

The year prior to this, the district nurse gave an excellent presentation to the 6th grade class boys and girls separately, which I viewed with the girls.

Another area that concerned me that year was the choice of films being shown to our little ones in the library, films that either had no meaning at all, or ones that presented a wrong attitude according to the way generations in this country have been brought up. One film showed how a little boy could get away with disobeying his mommy. Another taught children to "do unto others as they do unto you." This is very contrary to the Golden Rule, which was still being taught in the public school in Iowa when I left: "Do unto others as you would have them do unto you."

At the half year, my 6th grade son chose to go to a Christian school in our neighborhood. The following school year, all six of our children were enrolled in our neighborhood Christian school and we have been there ever since. We could no longer tolerate what was going on in our neighborhood public school. This is not an isolated situation; these things are occurring all across our land.

As a result of these happenings, it costs my very hard working husband over $4,000 per year for our children's education, and we receive nothing regarding education from our taxes. We feel our children are worth it, but many families cannot afford private education.

TESTIMONY OF_____

Patricia Broyles

I'm an elected member of a local school district governing board, but I'm speaking to you as a parent and representing only my own views and those of my husband, Phillip.

I'll be speaking to you about one particular program, TIPS. TIPS is a kindergarten through high school program with two specific goals. One is to promote and maintain positive student attitudes and behavior; what that means specifically is not written into the curriculum. The second goal is to assist students in meeting their responsibilities; to help ensure the safety and welfare of self and others.

Program development was initiated when the Virginia State Department of Education invited the Charlottesville and Albermarle County School Systems to translate the FBI concept of crime resistance into an educational program. The project was federally-funded and administered through the Virginia Department of Education.

TIPS stands for Teaching Individuals Protective Strategies and Teaching Individuals Positive Solutions. The teaching strategies for this experimentation include Values Clarification, decision making, psychological role-playing games, and other unproven teaching methods or techniques.

Some of the unproven teaching methods included in this program could be construed as psychological treatment since the role-playing technique is widely used by psychiatrists in a clinical setting.

In one 6th grade program, the children are to imagine themselves in the same situation as the school children who were involved in the Chowchilla kidnapping incident. This is a psychological game which surely merits the parents' informed consent.

The children are to decide what are their values based on the choices they make for survival. The values are to be determined by the peer pressure of the group.

In one 3rd grade program, children are to decide if lying is worse than stealing, or if stealing is worse than lying. Parents may not want their children to make psychological choices and moral choices on the basis of peer pressure at the 3rd grade level. Certainly, there is a need to inform parents of procedures for handling inquiries and complaints.

Some of the unproven teaching methods in this program at the 2nd grade level include involving the children in moral dilemmas. They are to decide if the parental rules described in the dilemma are either fair or unfair to the children in the families depicted. This is a heavy load for a seven-year-old. This aspect of the program certainly causes one to see the need for Hatch Amendment regulations.

The program overview of TIPS crime resistance strategies includes the following:

For kindergarten, examining personal feelings and those of others.

1st grade, comparing feelings with those of others.

2nd grade, comparing feelings and emotions, investigating causes of feelings and emotions.

3rd grade, examining attitudes and values, expressing and comparing values.

4th grade, relating values and attitudes, exploring how people and things influence attitudes and values.

5th grade, comparing attitudes and values,

ranking values.

6th grade, learning that rules and laws are based on values and needs, identifying attitudes toward authority.

7th grade, introducing, "victimless crimes."

8th grade, considering the concept of "unwritten rights."

This list is taken verbatim from the cover of the workbooks provided for this program.

The entire program deals with the formation and promotion of certain attitudes. To promote and maintain certain undefined positive student attitudes and behavior is goal number one in the TIPS Handbook. This is a program whose very foundation rests on the necessity for pre- and post-testing for attitudinal changes.

When children are subjected to such teaching, it must be only with their parents' informed consent.

TESTIMONY OF————————————————

Sherri Pitman

I am the mother of 10 children, seven of whom have attended the public schools here in Phoenix, Arizona. Three of my children were involved in a program in our school district identified as a Decision-Making Skills Program.

The methods used in this program were objectionable to my husband and me and we expressed these objections to our local school board members. As a result, we became involved in an extremely controversial battle with the teachers, the administration, and other parents in our school district.

The director of this program denied that any questions dealing with the personal values or attitudes of our children were being used. However, according to the testimony of the children, parents and other teachers, it became evident that such was not the case.

We also traced the strategies being used in this program back to the original source of a values education program written by Dr. Sidney Simon. This program was being implemented without prior written parental consent.

We found this Decision-Making Program to be very discriminatory against our Christian religion. I believe this type of values program is currently being used throughout the public schools of this nation. Therefore, it is the responsibility of any school administration to notify parents prior to the use of these programs with their children.

Currently, to my knowledge this is not being done in most school districts. Because so few parents are aware of these programs and their rights to protect their children from these programs, there has not been too much success in removing those courses from the school curricula.

One of the most difficult parts of being involved in this controversy was being unable to obtain the necessary information concerning the sources of this program. It took many hours of persistent pursuit in order to find out what rights I, as a parent, had concerning my children's curriculum in the public schools.

I would like to share with you what happened to me as a parent when I tried to implement usage of this right. First of all, I gathered documentation of this program going on in our school district for over one year, because it had been my experience that, when a parent opposed a program such as this, you became public enemy number one. They claimed it was your "hallucinations" and your "children's mental disorders" that were causing the problems, and that there was no such program in existence.

Therefore, I knew that if I were going to be effective in expressing my rights, I needed to have documentation. So for one year, I had children who were currently taking these courses tell their experiences to their parents if they were too young to write what it was they were doing. I had the parents take down the testimony and date it and have it notarized.

I had parents write down their response to listening to their children's testimony. I also talked to teachers who were using the program, who were extremely reluctant to give any information. I had one teacher express to me that she would lose her job if she showed any support at all for the parents who were questioning the program.

When I questioned her on this, that I thought this was America, the land of the free, she said, "they have ways." So there was a real reluctance on the part of the teachers involved in this program to give the parents any information on the program.

The director of the program was more than happy to give me the information, but what I received from her was only partially correct. Also, she maintained throughout the controversy that there were no personal questions. It was merely a decision-making technique to help children learn how to make decisions.

The funding for the program was coming through an organization called CODAMA, which receives, in part I believe, through my research, some funding from the National Institute of Mental Health. We were not ever able to get our hands on the direct line of funding.

We were told that it was a drug education program, and so the School Board adopted this program under the guise that it would help children learn how to make decisions so they would not be influenced by peer pressure, and therefore, they would be able to withstand drug pressure. Most parents supported the program because they believed this was the intent.

The actual strategies and things being used in this program, in fact, were Values Clarification strategies, and this is what I documented through the research.

I took the exact programs being used in our school district, went back to the source of Dr. Sidney Simon previously mentioned, and found they were verbatim out of his book. Even after six months of this controversy, they were still denying that they had ever taken the programs from any other source, claiming that it had all been originally written by this director.

So it was my word against the director of this program that there was any questionable content in it. However, because I did have documentation, I was able to produce testimony from the children, plus copies of their original sources.

We tried to stop the funding at the state level when it became available. We exposed where its source of funding was coming from. Because we had this kind of irrefutable testimony, we were able to get the program stopped in our school district.

Actually, they did not vote to stop it; they just did not renew the funding for it the next year. I have been called upon to work with parents in over seven school districts in this valley. I've had parents contact me from California and Colorado, asking how we were able to get this program stopped in our district.

My advice to them has always been that, if you are going to bring up this issue, you had better have your documentation. Those parents who have followed this advice have been able to stop such programs because, in our testimony to the School Board, we threatened to bring suit under the Hatch Amendment and to challenge their right to have these programs implemented without prior parental consent. Our district backed down just on the threat of this suit.

In studying all the Supreme Court cases which I could research dealing with parents' rights in education, generally what is the consistent thread of decision is that you, as the parent, have the right to demand certain things for your own children, but you cannot go in and demand things that will affect other people's children. So I have the right to protect my children and their value systems and those things which I am teaching them.

We took one program that was being used in our district to a child psychologist, did not explain to him any of our prejudices about it, and asked him to evaluate it as a psychologist. He would not give us his name, but we have a written report from him stating that most of the strategies being used were the same strategies used by psychiatrists in dealing with mentally ill people and that he would find them extremely dangerous when used by untrained professionals.

My only alternative after three years of effort was to remove my children. Because of the large size of our family, I had to go to home schooling; I could not afford private school tuition. I home-schooled my children for two years, and took on the responsibility of educating my children myself because I had no recourse through the public schools which I should have as much right to as any other parent in this country. Then this last year, a traditional school was started in our area, which is a school that allows parent involvement in the selection of the curriculum.

I happen to be serving as chairman of the Textbook Selection Committee, so I have the opportunity to review all materials being implemented into this school. My children are attending this school because, at the present time, there is direct parent involvement in the curriculum being used and a satisfactory process available.

This school was not easy to obtain. It was fought by numerous interest groups as establishing a private school at the taxpayers' expense, which I find ironic. We are the taxpayers and we parents have the right to have our children receive an education, the same as any other parent in this country.

Ann McClellan

I'm from Tucson. I served with the Citizens for Basic Education in Tucson.

I respectfully submit the attached testimony and documents as evidence that educators have used psychiatric testing and material on my children not only without my consent, but in all cases without my prior knowledge of their intentions.

The few examples that I've chosen to use are some of the many I have collected over the past four years from elementary, junior high, and high school classes my children have been enrolled in. I have become alarmed at the trend of educators to believe they are responsible for the psychological well-being of the students over and above their academic needs.

My first example was an exercise used in a high school Health class in which the teacher taught the normalcy of hating your parents. At the beginning of the unit, she asked "How many of you hate your parents?", and about three students indicated that they did. At the end of her very effective presentation, she asked the question again, and all but three students then raised their hands.

In my son's 3rd grade class, he was introduced to the virtue of therapy dolls. The class members created their own dolls and then were assigned to discuss their problems with their dolls before the class members.

In junior high, my daughter was subjected to an auction in which she was required to defend her religion and values under extreme ridicule from the group leader and from her peers.

In a discussion group with a list of 19 subjects to choose from, her group leader chose to talk for a few minutes about how to solve the problem of forgetting her locker combination, and the rest of a half-hour on how to deal with parents who embarrass the you-know-what out of you by discussing in detail the kinds of things parents do to create such situations.

In the 4th grade, and again in the 7th grade, my daughter was assigned to keep a personal diary that would be kept in the classroom. She was specifically informed she could write about her personal problems and family relationships even if they were bad because the teacher is her friend and would not tell.

In junior high again, one son and one daughter were given personal survey questionnaires in their English classes so the counselor could become better acquainted with them. Those surveys contained questions that are in direct violation of the Hatch Amendment.

It was interesting that, on this exercise, my daughter answered her questions according to peer pressure and how her friends thought that they should answer them. They even discussed how they were going to answer them collectively. My son answered his questions in a way that demonstrated his rebellion toward the exercise which he knew was being used unlawfully.

One exercise I consider to be the most offensive is called a Values Appraisal Scale. In this, many personal questions are asked about many areas of living. The students are then required to discuss their scores in small groups and compare them with a national average to help them see how normal or abnormal their views are. I would like to share with you some of the questions from that exercise.

I have a regular physical checkup by my doctor every year.

I will regularly take my children to church services.

I would rather spend an evening at home with my family than out with friends.

I have a close relationship with either my father or mother.

I have taught Sunday school.

I have regular dental checkups.

I believe in a God who answers prayers.

I enjoy giving presents to members of my family.

When I feel ill, I usually call to see a doctor.

I believe that tithing, giving one tenth of one's earnings to the church, is one's duty to God.

I enjoy taking part in the discussion at the family dinner table.

I pray to God about my problems.

I like to spend holidays with my family.

It is important to me that grace is said before meals.

They had to evaluate these questions on a scale of one to ten, then add them up and compare them with how normal they are with the rest of the community, in fact, with the rest of the United States.

I have heard every possible excuse for using these exercises. Some of these excuses include: (1) the educator needs to get to know the student better; (2) to stimulate or relax the class members; (3) to make the students feel better about themselves; (4) to open discussions; and (5) to help solve the student's personal problems. Not one educator has told me that any of these exercises were to help them better to teach math, English, reading, etc.

When I have confronted the teachers with the law, they have said: "I didn't know." I can testify that every teacher and administrator that I have talked to has denied knowledge of the Hatch Amendment.

If they know about it today, it's because I gave it to them and told them about it. I have heard the excuse, "I would have to get a legal decision on that." When I presented the Hatch Amendment to them, they have come back and said, "Well, this doesn't really mean anything," or "I thought it was okay because the exercise is not to be graded," or "It's not academic and it's not to receive a grade, and the primary purpose really wasn't to reveal information."

They have also told me that the law does not apply because the students were told prior to the administration of the exercise that they did not have to answer the question.

One teacher verbally attacked one of my daughters in the hallway of the school in front of her friends and degraded her for telling her mother what was being discussed in her classroom.

A principal in support of this teacher said to me, "I personally don't like counselors. I wouldn't want my child to go to a counselor if I wasn't absolutely sure of his credentials. I don't go along with some of the information that is withheld from parents, but I won't do anything about it." This man was totally supportive of the psychological manipulation going on in his classrooms by teachers less trained and qualified than professional counselors.

Sources for materials used in our district have been developed and dispersed through the federally-funded FOCUS program, the state STEREO program, and the Tucson Unified School District New Frontiers program. Some exercises have been used by the federally-funded La Frontera Mental Health Clinic located in Tucson. Many of the psychological surveys are found in career guidance programs and manuals. The use of psychological materials has become so widespread that educators are writing their own, and valuable academic teaching time is being used to facilitate them.

One of the newest programs in our district is called TIPS and is sponsored by the National Diffusion Network. This was overwhelmingly adopted by our School Board as a Crime Resistance program because it was offered free to our district.

TESTIMONY OF_____
Joyce Jensen

I'm representing the California LITE Committee — Let's Improve Today's Education — of which I am an area chairman. I'm the mother of six with another on the way. I'm a member of the pro-family coalition and the advisory board. I'm a certified secondary education teacher and I have worked in various positions in the elementary, junior high and high school level on the boards and committees.

In the beginning of our educational system, parents determined what would be taught in the classroom and the teachers followed the parents' direction. Today, parents are left to feel they have no say in education of the children, but must bow to the the whims of the teacher and the administrators.

We are greatly concerned with what is being done to our children in the name of education. Often, through the use of discussions, surveys, questionnaires, role-playing and other methods, teachers delve into the privacy of the students and parents.

This is done by encouraging the divulging of information of the most intimate and personal nature. These so-called teaching methods can be psychologically traumatic to a child. In most cases, the teacher is neither qualified nor authorized to help the child resolve the trauma; nor is that the intent of the exercise.

These methods can result in the same damaging effect as picking at small scabs, re-opening old wounds and enlarging them, leaving lasting scars.

When these methods are used in the classroom, the student's standards, religion, family and friends may be subjected to brutal and prolonged attacks by the group. When it is all over, if one has confessed all and has had his values and ideals smashed, he may doubt if there is very much in this life worth believing or defending.

His loyalties may now have been realigned away from his family and church and toward the group upon whom he has become dependent for his approval. His values of right and wrong become less important to him than his peers' approval.

As parents, we are greatly concerned with what is being done. As a protest to these types of teaching methods being used on my children, I went to the teacher, who was appalled when I accused him of the type of psychiatric treatment that was going on. I went to the principal, who was appalled that I would bother him. I finally met with the superintendent, who called a second meeting with other members of the district, including the psychologist from the district.

I presented to them the objectionable material, and cited the Hatch Amendment as a basis for my objections. As I would give examples, I was told: "Oh, we don't allow this. The teachers can't be doing this." They basically agreed that these types of materials could be detrimental to the psyche of our youth and could be in violation of the Hatch Amendment.

*TESTIMONY OF*_____
Helen Tapp
_____

I am an ex-Dominican nun, former school board trustee in Phoenix, Arizona, an educator since 1956 and have taught all elementary age children. Since my six years in the public school system, where federal programs flow freely, I have become increasingly alarmed at the lack of learning for learning's sake and the spontaneous joy of excelling.

I will attempt to identify specific programs, which, in my opinion, under the guise of getting back to the basics, have blatantly infringed upon the individual freedoms of not only the innocent young but have served to whitewash the cries of our confused and trusting parent population, not to mention the frustration it has caused the teaching profession.

Teaching another human being has always been considered an art form. Teachers today are being asked to use standard forms of presentation where uniformity once belonged only to subject matter. These appear to be subtle forms of differentiating the readily regimented teacher from the independent thinker. Unfortunately, when programs dealing with uniform presentation are mandated, the independent thinker is slowly jeopardizing his or her entire career.

Allow me to touch upon what I consider to be the most dangerous technique; ultimately, if it is used nationwide, it may shackle and imprison more minds than slavery could ever think of doing. What I am referring to is the concept called Mastery Learning.

I challenge each of you to carefully consider the following premise: Are we, average human beings, capable of mastering, that is, of becoming proficient in one given subject area while attempting to master six or seven others simultaneously?

That, in essence, is what mastery learning promulgates. Children are asked to strap themselves into a tunnel-like vision, mastering one concept at a time, unlike the tradition which introduces, meshes and integrates ideas, recalling and gradually reintroducing matter while maturation and saturation form an integral whole. This program (and many others like it) does not allow the child to advance forward until any one concept is thoroughly engraved. Is this reality?

I see the mastery learning concept as slowly stripping our youth of that uniquely American spirit of diversity and broadness of thinking which has helped save this nation during crises such as World War I, World War II and the Great Depression.

We have in our American elementary schools always been trained to know a little about enough areas that allowed us to freely change, study and develop in any area of our own choosing. Now, from the tender age of six or seven, we are asked to become experts on any one given idea, and not allowed to move forward until that idea is thoroughly grasped.

Of my 25 years in education, I find not only personally, but from observation, that few of us are physically or emotionally attuned toward grasping every fine detail of a principle, notwithstanding the fact that we may be very interested or motivated at the time. Most essential, however, do we all mature simultaneously?

Education through mastery learning strips one of the kaleidoscopic effect of learning. Students are tested, taught, retested, computerized, tested again, all on one concept until beaten or bored to death, while other major concepts are left to wait their turn or die for lack of time in which to study them.

It becomes quite clear that, if this idea of education is allowed to develop, then we will not only grow a crop of frustrated, ill-tempered, dull-witted members of society, but a totally illiterate one, since we strip the students of the very ideals of learning, that is, to touch upon all that is known in order to reach out and explore, to come back again to the tried and true, and eventually move on to new discoveries. Through mastery learning techniques, all subject matter becomes an end unto itself.

Surely, as in centuries gone by, we ideally work toward mastery. But should we, in the tender elementary years, ask for this kind of regimentation when and where there is so much to learn, so much to touch upon? Let us no longer under the guise of minimal requirements, deprive our citizens of their inalienable right to pursue life, liberty and happiness, and more important, the freedom to learn in a free atmosphere.

With federally-funded dollars and through the grand scheme of inaugurating minimal standard requirements, rather than the mass of students rising to meet the achievement of the accelerated, today's bored bright child tends toward complacency, thus, lowering the total standard. This, of course, as we already know, is a reality.

Teachers have been so caught up with government-required record-keeping that precious time is taken away from spontaneous high-standard growth. The most dangerous problem of all is mind-control programs which are now in operation and federally paid for. Is the plan of mastery learning a form of teacher control? Are we also funding this program of master formation?

No greater act of treason, in my estimation, can be performed than to establish a national uniform teaching program which may inevitably control the minds of this nation's youth. As the youth are formed, so does a nation grow. Hitler proved this by carefully training and mind-controlling his nation's young. Are we allowing the same stage to be set?

I have seen the signs of destruction vis-à-vis unrest and timidity among teachers and administrators who, at one time, were the inspirational leaders and educational guides but are now becoming federal and state paper-pushing puppets. The list goes on and on. Parents blame teachers; teachers blame parents.

As is true throughout history, where factions tear at each other, how easy it is for a controlling, supposedly all-knowing, third party to intervene and control. The Federal Government must stay out of the most sacred and fundamental element of a free society, education.

While students today in the 5th grade cannot tell you what geography or history are, one wonders if the reshaping effect has already been accomplished.

Government money spells federally-mandated reading material. Read your modern textbooks today about Russia invading Poland and find what amazingly distorted facts are presented and how many are deleted. Check with any neighborhood youth of 13 or 14 and determine whether he or she knows much, if anything, about Robert Louis Stevenson, Joyce Kilmer, Henry Wadsworth Longfellow, or about traditions such as "Old Folks At Home," "Swanee River," or "Home On the Range."

I am truly proud to call myself an American. I love my country and its Constitution and will continue to fight for academic freedom for our future leaders, our children.

TESTIMONY OF
Sherri Katz

I was exposed to the ECRI (Exemplary Center for Reading Instruction) Mastery Learning program by a seminar conducted by Miss Winterton while teaching reading for the Title I program in the Madison School District in the winter of 1978.

Teachers were asked to attend a five day presentation on what was called The New Reading Program, a mastery learning program funded by federal grants. Large binders containing scripts were provided for us. The scripts were to be memorized by the teacher. The scripts instructed the children to repeat, chant and point with their fingers. The scripts provided instruction for entire groups of children with a lock-step approach to learning for both fast, slow and remedial learners.

The scripts required 100% mastery of the stimulus words for the children to move on to the next task. Children were required to work for very long periods of time with few breaks.

If this program were to be used, there would be very little time for any other type of instruction. Stop watches were to be used, and children were to be pressured into responding within a very few seconds. The program provided for extrinsic reward for performance, and disapproval and isolation for nonperformance.

As a professionally and academically-trained reading specialist, and having worked in clinical settings with various types of children with various types of reading disabilities, I've always been aware of the need to correlate instruction with the child's learning style, and to provide a supportive, motivating environment to encourage children to enjoy learning and reading.

The mastery learning program is based on operant conditioning and Behavior Modification. This program is designed to hamper intellectual growth. This is not a reading program.

Furthermore, teachers who questioned aspects of the program during the seminar period were subjected to similar reward/punishment methods of harassment.

*TESTIMONY OF*_____
Jayne Schindler

I'm from Denver, Colorado. I'd like to share with you my concerns about public education and why I felt it necessary to appear here in person to present information on materials being used in Colorado.

Our son started to attend school about 1965 when the "open classroom" was a new experiment. Many parents thought this was just a phase. After all, it was new and modern, so why not go along, trust the professionals who knew best. But did they—and who are the professionals?

The experimentation programs had only begun. Old methods that had produced outstanding students of world acclaim were pushed aside to be replaced with new math, and occult courses for English classes. Here is a list of some of the types of classes: Family living classes, sex ed classes, the bionomics classes to promote alternate lifestyles so that our children would become more tolerant, abortion rights for minors, role-playing, lifeboat games, and more Values Clarification.

Educational test scores were declining. The educators wondered why. The Parent Teachers Association, the PTA, had campaigns against violence on television, and to promote more tax funding for teachers and school programs. More and more money has been poured into the system.

Still, the test scores declined. Parents were putting their children in private schools. The horrors of children involved in drugs, violence, suicide and sex are all at almost epidemic proportions.

Will someone listen? What are the parents objecting to? If a car manufacturer produced a faulty automobile, time after time, the public would cease to buy his car.

The PTA complains about violence on television. They should look at the school movies. Have you seen the movie, "The Lottery," where the mother is stoned to death in full living color? That's just one; there are many more.

Parents are told that the schools should teach sex education because some parents didn't explain it or talk to their children. We were told that sex education, kindergarten through 12th grade, would prevent venereal disease, unwanted pregnancies, and abortions. The reverse has been true.

Look at the bionomics course that I have brought with me. This test is so dirty that I cannot repeat it out loud; but our children are subjected to it in the public schools. I would like to know how a teacher would grade a course such as this.

Many of the teaching materials are close to being pornographic, if not actually pornographic. I don't know if you are familiar with the book, *Show Me,* which is in many school libraries. This book cannot be sold in a porno shop in Colorado because it would violate the child pornography laws, but it can be put in our public schools and libraries.

Does that mean that our schools are open game? Dirty words, disrespect for parents and authorities, are presented in many schoolbooks. The kids learn the words to write on the walls from their school books. How can we say we object to it in public but condone it in the schools?

When I asked one principal why he allowed books with such bad language, he replied, "Some kids talk that way at home and we need to make them feel accepted." Does that mean that our public schools are to reduce their standards to the lowest norm?

Our Governor of Colorado has established a Colorado Commission on Children and Their Families in order to establish the state's philosophy and policies on children. This Commission decries the statistics on drug abuse and child abuse. It developed an experimental program for three target schools, one of them being in the little town of Craig, Colorado, where population is approximately 8,000.

In this little town of 8,000, 400 people showed up at a school board meeting, complaining about this drug abuse program that had been put into their schools without their wanting it. They were overruled. They were told they were not professionals, that they must trust the teachers, and that the teachers knew best. One teacher even wrote a letter to a student encouraging the student to sneak around behind the parent's back and promote this program.

The teacher's manuals that were recommended, Tribes, Quest, and Ombudsman, focused on tribes. It's another Values Clarification manual. In the student manual, in the first few pages, the English is terrible and there are misspelled words. This was to be a program on drug abuse for the children of Craig, Colorado.

One of the programs in the schools is called Magic Circle. One parent, who is also a teacher, went in to see what Magic Circle was all about, and what her little girl was participating in. When she walked into the classroom, a little girl was crying. The facilitator told the little girl to quit crying and cut if off because "mommies are here" and "mommies don't want to talk about the things" they were talking about. But the mother said, "I'm an accredited teacher, and I would like to know what you're talking about."

The question of the day was, "Who died last in your family?" The little girl's grandfather had died, and she was extremely upset. Tell me, how is that child going to get through the rest of the day after being forced to play Magic Circle?

Another case involved a little girl who was adopted. A newspaper article was read to the class, and here is the question the class discussed. The little girl in the article is 12 years old and she's pregnant. The class was then compelled to decide what to do. By a class vote, it was decided that abortion was much better than adoption. The little girl who was adopted was almost destroyed to have her friends feel that she was better off dead than adopted.

Another class was given a little story about Georgey which asked the question, "In situations where a fib would do no harm, which loyalty, which value, is better?" The answer given was, "Georgey never told a lie, but in this story, if he tells on his friend, his father will beat him, so maybe the better value is loyalty and maybe he should lie." How are we going to teach our children to be truthful to police officers when schoolchildren are given materials such as this? Another class was asked, "What is the one thing your mom and dad do to you that is unfair?"

My husband is a Denver fireman, and he was most upset when he read the page that asked, "Your house is on fire, what would you go back in to save?" That is not what you should be teaching the children. They should be taught, don't go back into the house.

Other questions asked of schoolchildren include, "If the atomic bomb is going to fall in ten minutes, what would you do in the last ten minutes?" and "What would you like put on your gravestone?"

Remember, these questions were asked in what was called a "drug education" course. One of our mothers went and took the teacher in-service training, a two-and-a-half-day course. In the course, the facilitator, the teacher, drew an imaginary line on the floor. The teacher then walked to one end and she said, "On this end, we want to legalize drugs and on the other, you do not want drugs legalized."

The whole room moved to the end to legalize drugs. The mother was the only one on the other end. Can you imagine the peer pressure that it would put on a child in school to experience this demonstration in class? We are talking about illegal drugs. What kind of citizens are we going to raise for tomorrow?

These courses openly admit that they are "change agents." Change agents for what? Professionals for what? In this manual, designed for grades 4 through 8, there is a list of 15 experts, each capable of bringing about some kind of permanent change in one's life situation, who have agreed to offer their services to the members of this class. You must decide who can best provide the change *you* want. For example, you can pick Dr. Karen Horney; she will teach you to be an excellent sexual partner, to enjoy sexual relations, and to bring pleasure and fulfillment to others. This is for the 4th through 8th grades.

A child can't get through these courses without playing the "lifeboat game." There is room in the boat for only five, but there are seven people. The child is asked to decide who is more important, who are we going to save?

In other classes, the materials tell the pupils that "teenagers and youth have the right to make their own informed decisions concerning whether to drink or not to drink." With such materials that invade our privacy and undermine parental authority, my greatest concern is the suicide rate with our kids, and the drug and alcohol abuse that is going on.

We had an English course in the 7th grade junior high school whose title was Death Education. In the manual, 73 out of 80 stories had to do with death, dying, killing, murder, suicide, and what you want written on your tombstone. One of the girls, a 9th grader, blew her brains out after having written a note on her front door that said what she wanted on her tombstone. Her young boyfriend, also in the 9th grade, found her in that condition.

Our children are our most precious resource. I'm really concerned about the public schools. I would like to see them saved, to see them revived, and I think that can be done if all of these kinds of materials are removed and the parents could, once again, trust the public schools.

TESTIMONY OF_____
Shirley Mapes

I'm finding that many of the schools no longer feel that it's necessary to test children ahead of time for psychological health or behavioral health. They more or less *assume* that, upon entering into kindergarten, each child has a problem with his behavior and moral values. We need to have more open education so the parents can take a better look and see where these programs are coming from.

Many of the programs are labeled Enrichment, Multi-Exceptional Children, Decision Making, or Critical Thinking. These courses are labeled that way so as not to raise the suspicions of parents, but I've noticed, when going in and looking through the curricula, that it's always something different from what it's been labeled.

To further complicate matters, I've also found, particularly in the Tewksbury school system of Massachusetts, that the entire curriculum was being more or less rewritten. I have a sample here. This course was Social and Health Science curriculum for grade one. It's been totally retyped over, so really when you have a question about this type of program, all you're handed is a nice little brochure that they've typed up. All the individual items are elsewhere, so you have to continually go back to see if you can get your questions answered.

When I was first back east and introduced to the school system in Tewksbury, Massachusetts, my daughter was just entering kindergarten. I noticed that, being a four-year old, the first couple of weeks, she was under an awful lot of strain and seemed to be emotionally upset. At first, I thought it was probably just because she was undergoing a new change, a new environment, a longer day and quite a busy day at that.

But after a couple of weeks, it didn't clear up. She was constantly whining after school to the point where I was really quite concerned for her. I asked her if everything was going all right with the school children, if she was getting along with everyone, if the school teacher was all right. "Well, Mommy," she said, "you know, there are three people inside of me and one of them's a mad person." And she broke down and started crying.

After speaking with her for a lengthy time and questioning her long enough, I realized that she was being taught Transactional Analysis, which is better known as "TA." I realize that TA is psychological manipulation, mainly because they're teaching three role models that, they say, are an individual's three different people. They are trying to get you to stay in one role, which would be the adult role, the happy person. The other individuals in this are the adult who is the mad person and the child who is the sad person.

Anyway, I was quite upset about this and I mentioned to my child's speech therapist that I knew about the Hatch Amendment, and knew that it was against the law to psychologically test a child without parental permission, and therefore I realized that it would also be against the law to psychologically manipulate the child without parental permission.

A couple of days later, my child did come home from school delighted and said, "They aren't going to teach the three people anymore."

I also want to mention that when my child entered kindergarten, I, as the parent, had to fill out a bunch of quite lengthy forms on different developmental stages from her birth. They asked me if I had a complicated delivery with this child. They also asked me when this child went off the bottle. They told us that we would be doing the government a favor in filling out these forms. I'm just quite curious as to what those forms might have been for. Nobody ever explained it to us.

Another program that I've been quite upset with in the Tewksbury school district was what was called Anti-Parent Pressure. This is one course which I have to admit is very, very true to its title. It was definitely anti-parent.

The material in this book looked very much like it had been taken out of context, as though the author had written one book, and then everything was taken out of context and lifted from it and put into the book from which these kids were taught. The author of this book allowed you to come only to certain conclusions.

For example, if a child worries, the only conclusion that the reader was allowed to come to was that, if a child worried, his world was one of gnawing hunger when he was a child, that he had built the habit of worry because his mother didn't feed him on time. There was no other conclusion offered for these children to come to.

Here is another example. According to this material, if a child had a learning problem, it was from a possible two-year diaper rash, because his diapers weren't changed on time. According to the author, that diaper rash caused the tension that reduced your learning abilities.

The thing that bothered me about this material is that the author admitted that it was sensitive material, and that it should be gone over with the child along with his parent. But in our school district, for some reason, the teacher took it upon herself to be the acting parent for the 25-plus students. My son brought this book home by mistake. That's the only reason I knew that the Parent Pressure Program was even in the school district. He was told he was not to bring it home but, for some reason, he got it mixed up with his books and assignments and it came home.

I would like to state, too, that Tewksbury, Massachusetts, has an extremely high suicide rate for 14 through 20-year-old kids. This course, Anti-Parent

Pressure, was for the 4th through 6th grades. This is a time when children really need to know that their parents have their best concerns at heart. This book certainly didn't help that parent-child relationship at all; I would say it definitely hindered it.

The Fallout Shelter game is something that seems to be getting into our school curriculum in different states. It was given to students in December of 1980 at North Street School in Tewksbury, Massachusetts.

Another course my son was involved in was, strangely enough, for multi-exceptional children. It is called Guided Nurturance of Multi-Exceptional Students or GNOMES for short.

To obtain acceptance for this program, the facilitators presented it to the elected school board members. I asked one of the school board members if anyone had looked at or read the materials being used in this course to which this one member replied, "No," and just commented on how good the presentation had been.

In this month, the exceptional children's course was administered with parental consent. I've included in the master copy, various information from the course explaining it. It was given to the entire 5th grade class, not just the individual children who had been tagged.

The reason for giving it to the full class was that the facilitators felt that the whole classroom would benefit from the program, and the facilitators would be also training the classroom teacher to carry out the program's philosophy throughout the various classroom subjects.

Naturally, the majority of all parents, when told that their child would be in with 50 exceptional children receiving the same type of training, were filled with a parent's sense of pride. It certainly did that to us; we thought that some of the material, entitled "Decision Making" and "Critical Thinking," sounded very necessary and that our child could really benefit from it.

But I did think that maybe I had better look at the materials, and so I called and asked one of the facilitators if I could look at the materials because I didn't want it to be a course in values education or humanism. She assured me that it had nothing to do with that and that she'd be more than happy to give me the materials. She was very cooperative.

When I got hold of the materials, I was amazed in the introductory parts of the various books how many times it referred to Values Clarification and humanism. I can't understand how that woman figured I was going to be too lazy to read the material; or perhaps she thought I was just stupid; I'm not sure. In any event, it was very, very upsetting.

One of the books was called *Learning To Think and Choose.* The other one was called *Critical Thinking Book 1.* These were extremely depressing books. I went through them and basically took the courses as the children would. They had multiple-choice questions and, as the instructions explained in the introduction, there would be no easy answers. There were no easy answers, and it was terribly depressing to go through and try to answer those questions.

One of them, for example, is "Would it be better to have your arms cut off or your legs cut off?" I don't see anything educational about that at all.

I think it was an extremely depressing course that had nothing to do with responsible education. Repeatedly, the child was forced to choose values foreign to him. This course was designed to change the children's home-taught values, and particularly, their Judeo-Christian traditional values.

TESTIMONY OF
Sylvia Allen

I take very seriously my responsibility toward my children, ages 18 to 4, and feel that their education is very important. However, I am alarmed at the trend in education to not only educate but to indoctrinate.

My biggest complaint with some of these programs is the time taken away from the basic subjects that our children need so desperately to learn. When my son was in the 7th grade at Poston Junior High, I was very concerned about his grades. He was having trouble in English and Social Studies. Every other Friday they would have circle discussions. They would tell their feelings about different subjects. Also, he spent a lot of time filling out questionnaires.

My son did not like participating in these discussions and felt ill at ease. Besides prying into his personal and family beliefs, they were wasting precious time needed to help my son understand the subjects he was failing. I have included a page from his journal so you can see why I was so upset with his English; the spelling and grammar errors are terrible. They never corrected anything in his journal concerning grammar.

This same year, I was a leader in my church for the young women, ages 13 to 14. At a slumber party, one of the girls told us about her math class and how she really liked it because, every Friday, they talked about different things, instead of doing math.

I asked her what they talked about and she said, "Oh, everything. Last Friday, we talked about abortion." I asked her what was said and she replied, "Why abortion is a woman's right. She should have the say over her body, and besides, a 12-year-old girl has no business having a baby." I was shocked because the religious standard in this young girl's home is that life is sacred and that taking the life of a baby is wrong.

When I questioned her further, it was clear the other side of abortion was never given. My question is this: What does abortion have to do with math? How can this much time be wasted and be justified? What right did this teacher have to indoctrinate this class with his one-sided view?

When I went to the assistant principal, Mr. Budge, to talk about my concerns for my son and this girl, he explained that the math teacher was taking some counseling courses at ASU and was practicing on his class. I told him about the Hatch

Amendment and he said he had never heard of it and couldn't be bothered. Obviously, we need to attach regulations and penalties so that schools will be bothered.

Shannon Stearns

"In a barrio called the 'Devil's Corner' lived a very poor woman. She and her three children lived in a miserable shack that seemed to hang on a cliff by the riverside. Her husband spent his time and money across the river in Laredo.

"She ironed and washed for the other people. She even begged sometimes in order to provide her children with one meal a day. She herself ate practically nothing. It was a wretched life and every day brought new miseries. She did not ask anything for herself, but it broke her heart to see her little ones suffer. There was always a ray of hope. Her husband would come back and everything would be all right again.

"But one day, he came back to tell her he was leaving her and the children for a new woman. That was too much for her to bear. There was no exit to her long agony. She looked at the peaceful river below. Her children couldn't possibly face a whole life of misery. Poor little angels; they would be so much better in Heaven. God would clothe them, feed them, surround them with love. They would be so happy up there forever.

"On an impulse, she pushed all three of them over the cliff. They tumbled down into the water. They floated for a while and finally disappeared.

"She smiled for the first time in many months, satisfied that she had fulfilled her maternal duty. She could see all three of them with a shiny halo already up there eating a big plate of strawberry ice cream. She went to bed happy and fell asleep.

"The next morning, she looked around for her little children. Where were their caresses, their smiles, their tears? She suddenly realized what she had done. Wanting to join them, she threw herself into the river and drowned.

"Now, many people attest to the fact that, when the moon is full, one hears the moaning and the sobbing of a woman along the river. Could it be the mother who is still looking for her children?"

What did this story do for my daughter as well as the other 7th graders at Poston Junior High? Did it tell them perhaps, that death is the answer, or suicide, or murder?

My daughter felt this was a very sad story, and so did I. There was no grade given for this story. She could have stayed home from school and not missed anything that day.

What are the schools teaching my children? I believe schools are in the business to teach reading, writing, arithmetic and other academics, and not to make social changes.

Values Clarification and humanism have much in common. They're being taught in almost every grade and school across the country. Their beliefs and objectives consist of these: faith in man; God is non-existent; there is no right and wrong; all morals are situational and there are no absolutes.

These beliefs taught in the classroom cause children to re-think values taught at home. Then they must decide whether they should keep the old ones or go along with the norm of the group.

Here's an example. My daughter needed a schedule change at school, so I decided to talk with all the core teachers to see which teacher would be most suitable for my daughter. She had just come from Franklin School, the basic school in Mesa, and I was concerned about junior high.

This was my conversation with Mr. Judd. I asked, "When do you do Values Clarification? I would like my daughter dismissed during those times." He said he couldn't say because he does them at any time. He said, "For instance, last week during our literature class, we did a story about a man who owned a florist shop. He was selling three-day old flowers for fresh ones and getting the fresh flower price. An employee disagreed with this and he lost his job." Mr. Judd asked his class, "Can you always be honest in a business?" More than half the class said, "No, you cannot always be honest in a business." This is all he told me about the story.

I asked him, "How does this make you feel, Mr. Judd? You have now conditioned more than half the class that honesty isn't really what it's cracked up to be, that you don't have to be honest all of the time." He just sat back and smiled.

I talked with another core teacher, Mr. Valencia, and we began talking about honesty again. I told him that, in a business, it's a dishonest act when some people take home company pens from work. He said that, even though I believed that, other parents don't believe the same way that I do.

So I said, "Wouldn't it be better to leave these things out of school altogether? Most of these children will never attend college. This is their only time to get a firm foundation in the basic academics that will be with them all of their lives."

One last story I would like to relate is about the teacher I finally chose for my daughter, Mrs. Farren. I made clear my position that I did not want my daughter involved in valuing, questioning, etc., without my permission.

Mrs. Farren had passed out a paper on prejudice in which the students were to fill it out and pass it in. Lisa told her teacher that she could not fill it out and that her mother did not want her to. The teacher said, "Do it anyway."

The next day I was able to get this paper and I would like to share just a few of the questions that were on it:

What prejudices do you have against others? (religion, language, ethnic background, clothes they wear, freaks, punks, other)

Where did your prejudices come from?

(parents, friends, TV, movies, radio, newspaper, bad experience)

What are the biggest prejudices at this school? (religion, language, ethnic groups, clothes people wear)

Do you associate with certain groups on campus? (freaks, preppies, punks, jocks, other)

For that question, my daughter wrote, "just friends."

The last question was: "Comment?" My daughter, wrote, "Why do you have to know this?" And that's my same question, too.

My husband and I decided to go to the principal and tell him what had been happening, and just let him know our concerns. As we began to talk to him, he explained that we were "over-reacting" and this couldn't possibly be happening.

I handed him a letter that said I would like my daughter dismissed during these times, and that I didn't care if she went into the teacher's office, just as long as she wasn't there during those times.

He read it over and said, "This would be impossible to do. I couldn't do this. You know what I'd have to do to do this?" He gave us a long story of how inconvenient this would be, and he said, "You know, I have over a hundred students who come to this school who have not been able to get in because it's already filled up. Perhaps, Mrs. Stearns, you would like to take your daughter to some other school."

I said, "Well, we have been considering one other one." And he said, "What is that?" And I said, "A home school." He replied, "Well, Mrs. Stearns, I really suggest you home teach your daughter. Do you know what? This is the first time I've said this to any parent in 25 years."

My husband and I were flabbergasted because Lisa had done no wrong, and we hadn't either. In fact, I said all of about three or four sentences in our 15-minute conversation. We found that the principal was not cooperative enough even to be understanding.

Before I close, I would like you to know that I have seven very beautiful and intelligent children. This year, we have taken our children out of the public schools and are home teaching them. This has proven to be a great thing for our family. We have even discovered that we can read the books and answer the questions just like teachers do.

I've discovered too, that I have much to offer them. I believe my children can withstand the temptation of drugs, alcohol, smoking, and even bad language, but I fear that they cannot always recognize the lies that are found in the classroom at school.

Perhaps, my children will some day return to a public school, but it won't be until our legislators and educators allow our children to be moral, patriotic, honest, and God-fearing.

TESTIMONY OF
Linda Mace

In 1978, I received a Bachelor of Science degree in nursing. I made A's in psychology. I know that the very same methodology I learned for dealing with the mentally ill is being used for normal, healthy children in public schools at all grade levels, in just about any subject matter.

In fact, the most popular methodology today deals with mental and emotional processes, Behavior Modification, attitudes, mental states, and philosophical concepts. This modern psychologism, in spite of its apparent good intentions, is positively harmful to students and their families.

The rise in popularity of psycho-therapeutic techniques in the classroom has been accompanied by a skyrocketing incidence of suicide, drug abuse, alcoholism, and crime among the youths.

Before psycho-therapy became the norm in the classrooms, the most pressing problems included tardies and spitwads. Nothing is sacred in today's classrooms. The invasion of privacy of families has eroded the parent-child relationship by inserting a wedge of doubt, distrust and disrespect.

There is a class at Canyon Del Oro High School in Tucson whose motto is, "Question Authority." If not the authority of the teacher who's teaching, what other authority would it be? I believe they are teaching them to question the authority of their parents and their own religious leaders.

Students are being indoctrinated against the traditional beliefs of their parents. Teachers and counselors at every grade level are specifically using transactional analysis, Values Clarification, group think, and other psycho-therapeutic modes to manipulate the students away from their parents and their own religious beliefs.

These programs do not deal in reality; they use only perception. The student is taught to make his own reality in a false world without absolute rights or wrongs. This is faith in psychology. It offers no solutions, only more questions. These classes renounce the traditional concepts of family, community and authority, and replace them with a very vague, gray world of situation ethics.

The students are taught that, somehow, it is more interesting to be an isolated individual than to be a loving, obedient, respectful child. In fact, the term "childhood" hardly applies to students who have been robbed of their own innocence and plunged into psychiatric reality therapy.

I am Chairman of the Parent Citizen Grievance Committee to Marana School District. I was a member of the Citizen Task Force that surveyed the entire curriculum, K through 12. I work at knowing what is going on in the public schools, and I do know what is being taught.

One method for dealing with the mentally ill is called group therapy. The patients sit in a circle with the psychologist or psychiatrist and discuss their feelings about personal matters. The psychiatrist listens and is able to use the information he gathers from this non-threatening group situation to guide the patients toward a more healthy attitude.

The same technique is popular among classroom teachers today, though they are dealing with normal, healthy children and not the mentally ill. However, the teacher is not a psychiatrist. The manipulation of attitudes and behavior is not what the parents intend for their children to be exposed to when they send them to school.

One of the ways I learned that psycho-therapeutic techniques are popular in the public classroom was personally to survey the entire high school curriculum. I sat through whole class periods and attended the school for the full day every Monday for six weeks until I had surveyed the entire curriculum.

I studied teachers' lesson plans, supplemental materials, textbooks and student work. I have two spiral notebooks full of documentation. I found psycho-therapeutic methodology used in three out of five classrooms.

One history teacher showed me journals that he had his students write in every day. These journals are for recording feelings and personal information, which the student feels is important. The journal has nothing to do with history. There is no requirement for correct grammar. There is no stated objective regarding academic achievement. The teacher stated that he has some students who are not interested in history, so he uses this discussion of a more personal nature to get their attention.

These attention-getting devices also happen to reveal students' attitudes, values and emotional feelings, not to mention the fact that they take away valuable time from the study of legitimate curriculum. The President's Commission Report, *A Nation At Risk*, shows that our academic standards are suffering, and I do believe that violations of the Hatch Amendment contribute to this suffering of academics.

The parents do not know that their privacy has been invaded until after it is too late. It is usually after private information has already been shared in these personal journals that the parents find out about it, if ever.

In English classes, I find that political and religious subjects are very popular. They use surveys to gather sensitive information from the student population. Is it legitimate to gain private information just so the students can learn how to survey? How would you like it if your private life was discussed by a high school class?

This is what psycho-therapy is all about. The teacher does not have to intend to change the student in order to accomplish that end. The psycho-therapeutic technique works to change human behavior. If a teacher does not know the outcome of these techniques, he may innocently cause harm. Psychiatry is not a toy for amateurs, nor does it have a place in the normal classroom for teaching academics, but it is there just the same.

Tucson Unified School District is one of five regions for pilot-testing several federally-funded programs. These include Woman's Educational Equity Projects, Desegregation Projects, Title I Reading Programs, etc. The parents of that school district are

experiencing increasing amounts of psycho-therapeutic techniques, counseling, Behavior Modification, and invasion-of-privacy gimmicks.

Parents' response is to remove their children
from the public school and to seek alternatives. That
district is in one of the fastest growing cities in America today. And yet, the public school population is
decreasing rapidly. Schools are being closed in Tucson Unified School District. The population of com-
peting schools, at the same time, is growing rapidly.

As Research Chairman of the Citizens For Basic
Education in Tucson Unified School District, I can
testify that thousands of parents in that one school
district alone have signed petitions for a basic education school because they want their children to learn
academics, and not to be used as guinea pigs for
more psycho-therapeutic educational programs.
These parents camped overnight in order to enroll
their children in the only basic school in the whole
district.

I have seen psycho-therapy used in Home Economics classes where students discuss personal family matters without the parents' knowledge, much
less prior written consent. Most parents I know have
not taken a psychology course recently. They do not
necessarily recognize the Behavior Modification
techniques. They only found out after the fact, after
their private lives have been exposed in the classroom,
and after their children have been manipulated
against their own religious, political and social
beliefs.

Every public school and every teacher is affected

by federal dollars. Federal grants are used to a large extent to develop experimental programs that are tested in the public schools. They are too numerous to list and such programs are continually being developed.

The trend of using psycho-therapeutic techniques is so popular among educators today that a teacher may learn a new technique at a federally-funded seminar and then apply it in a classroom that is not specifically a federally-funded project.

Religious beliefs are constantly being assaulted in the classroom. My son was taught an occult game by his biology teacher without my prior knowledge or consent. In language textbooks in my own school district for grades K through 8, I found entire spelling lessons dealing with the terminology of the occult. The *Scope* magazine series used in Title I Reading in my son's school has an entire issue dealing with para-psychology.

School libraries are full of witchcraft, demonic and occult literature. That may be a minor thing to some people, but it is a serious matter according to my belief. Stories and situations dealing with the occult are prominent in the normal curricula today. This is a violation of religious beliefs. Occultism is a pagan religion. It has no place in public education.

Guidance counselors are becoming more numerous in public schools today. In fact, whole classrooms are spending time with a counselor who uses psychological therapy on students without prior knowledge or consent of the parents.

These parents become concerned by the changes

in the behavior of their own children and only find out later about the class sensitivity training session; and they're not pleased. Parents I know who have experienced this have taken their children out of public schools because they felt there was no alternative.

A specific example of a federally-funded program being used in Tucson and across the nation today is TIPS. Former FBI Director Clarence Kelley's idea for crime prevention became a federally-funded pilot program administered through the Virginia Department of Education.

TIPS stands for Teaching Individuals Protective Strategies and Teaching Individuals Positive Solutions. That sounds good. I have no quarrel with crime prevention or the protection of children. However, the methodology suggested in this program includes the use of fear, transactional analysis, and other behavior modification techniques.

In the 6th grade, this program uses the Chowchilla kidnapping and burial of a bus load of children supposedly to teach the importance of law. I asked the teacher about her experience in teaching this specific lesson. She said that, personally, it gave her cold chills, and that some of the children were confused and in tears; other seemed lost and upset; but others, she thought, handled it rather "adult-like," whatever that means. She didn't know if it caused nightmares, or whether there will be recurring negative effects on the children. Certainly, it was scary and the long term emotional effect is not known. It's experimental.

We do know that children can learn about law in a more positive way. The TIPS program also uses transactional analysis in teaching kindergarten and first graders how to deal with feelings and emotions. The stated goal for kindergarten has to do with examining personal feelings and those of others, introducing situations that could cause conflict.

Do you think a first grader needs to be introduced to a situation that causes conflict? In fact, feelings and attitudes are emphasized more than facts throughout the K-through-8 TIPS curriculum.

Of course, the teacher does not have to use all of the strategy suggested. The 6th grade teacher whom I interviewed said that she invited a psychologist into the classroom to discuss death. Do you see why many parents have difficulty with their children if they are constantly being exposed to psychotherapeutic techniques, from both federally-funded programs and their spin-offs throughout the K-through-12 curriculum?

Private, personal information is being solicited from children. These violations are not only prevalent, but psychologism classes have become mandatory for graduation in Ampitheater School District in Tucson and are under consideration by at least three other school districts in Tucson alone.

*TESTIMONY OF*_____
Judith Brown

I'm a teacher at Isaac Junior High School. I will relate my experiences with the ECRI (Exemplary Center for Reading Instruction) at the junior high school.

When this mastery learning program was first introduced at our school, only a few teachers were interested in piloting programs using it. The rest of the teachers were encouraged to observe and learn about the program.

The following semester, through the use of a variety of incentives and inducements, several of the reading teachers signed up for a workshop using the program. I did not attend the workshop because to do so meant to commit myself to using the program exclusively for a period of at least one year.

Those teachers using the program were rewarded in a variety of ways, which included free time, extra supplies, new desks, and rolling desk chairs. These were ostensibly needed to implement the program. However, the remaining teachers who were later coerced into using the program were not provided with these materials.

The administration let us know that all teachers were expected to use the mastery learning program. I was not impressed with it and, along with two other teachers at the junior high school, did not choose to use it. The three of us were subjected to a bombardment of subtle coercion tactics. These included being ostracized to some extent by our fellow teachers and administrators, given the most difficult and least-liked duties and assignments, and given a daily barrage of verbal praise of the program and questions asking *why* we chose not to become a member of the team, thus supporting our school and its policies.

Before the introduction of the ECRI program, my principal and I had interacted on a friendly basis, exhibiting mutual respect. However, after I declined to adopt the program into my teaching regimen, I was treated in a brusque, terse manner except when he was extolling the virtues of the program.

When it became apparent that I would not change my mind, the principal began seeking me out on a daily basis, questioning me about ECRI and encouraging me to adopt the program. Outwardly, this appeared to be a very friendly interchange, but it soon began to create a great deal of tension between us to the point that I tried to avoid meeting him whenever possible. As his subtle harassment continued, I began to suppress a great deal of anger toward him, creating more and more tension within me.

On October 30, 1979, as I was preparing a cup of coffee for lunch, the frustration and anger I had been suppressing erupted. I began shaking uncontrollably and was taken to Good Samaritan Hospital by ambulance. After a four-day hospital stay involving numerous testing procedures, I was released to outpatient therapy through Arizona Health Plan. I joined classes dealing with controlling headaches and tension and therapy sessions involving counseling and biofeedback.

By this time, the spasms were localized in my right arm which continued to shake uncontrollably most of the time. The biofeedback sessions were not helping me, so my counselor decided to try hypnosis, choosing a psychologist trained in hypnosis as my therapist. It was through my session with the hypnotist that I discovered that my problems stemmed from suppressed anger, the major portion of which was directed at my school principal.

My job is very important to me for several reasons. I love teaching and helping young people. It is the career of my choice and I wish to remain in it. I'm the sole breadwinner in my family. My daughter depends on my support and, if I lost my position, I would be unable to care for my daughter and myself. My health is also very important to me.

So I realized I had two choices. I could resign my position and seek employment elsewhere or I could give up fighting against the system and go along with the majority. After careful consideration, I decided to stay at my school and go along with the ECRI program. By this time, I was the only reading teacher who had not capitulated.

When I agreed to use the mastery learning program, I promised my principal that I would give it a fair trial. I learned as much about the program as was possible. I discovered that none of us was properly trained in the program and each teacher had adapted it to her own methods of teaching. All of my research into the program warned against doing this, that the program must be used exactly as it is designed without adaptation.

I used the program for two years and, as a classroom teacher, these are my objections to it. School districts adopt the program and then require their personnel to use it without sufficient training and without the necessary supplies and equipment. After the initial expenditure, the district did not wish to continue purchasing the supplies, but instead, expected the teachers to make do with what we had. For example, my district used teachers, who themselves were poorly trained in ECRI, to train the rest of us. When a representative from the Exemplary Center for Reading Instruction observed our program, she told our principal that it barely resembled their program. She tried to help us get back on the right track, but thought it was an impossible job.

When we adopted new reading texts, a summer workshop was held to set up the tremendous amount of material necessary to implement the program. Unfortunately, only two of the people attending the workshop had any idea of how to go about doing this and, as they directed us, we made a tremendous amount of mistakes. However, these are the materials that we are expected to use until our next textbook adoption.

Another objection is that the ECRI program uses a set pattern of phrases that the teacher must memorize and parrot, requiring exact responses from the students. This is highly objectionable to me for these reasons:

First, the teaching moment is lost. The teachable moment is that digression from the planned lesson (which is so important in any learning environment) involving answering the questions or discussing the problems which are uppermost in the student's mind at that particular moment. It involves questions brought to mind through the lesson, but are not necessarily a part of it.

I enjoy teaching, mainly because of the spontaneous interchange between teacher and student. Most of this is lost under the ECRI program. The parroting and response of set phrases leaves little room for spontaneity.

The students and the teacher are soon bored with the program. After the initial newness of the program wears off, we are left with a memorized pattern of question response which takes no thought process to complete. Students are soon able to parrot answers without the teacher's questions to prompt them. If students can respond without consciously thinking through their responses, why is so much class time being expended? Learning by rote has its purposes in education, but I believe valuable class time and certified personnel can be put to better use.

In addition to objecting to the coercion, the poor training, and the set question response patterns, I found that the time required in the teaching and the preparation of the program was far greater than the amount of time that I had available.

In the two years I spent teaching ECRI, I could never fit all of the various aspects of ECRI into the amount of available classroom time. Although the program requires much less paper grading than most programs, the amount of preparation necessary to implement it is formidable. Each grading period, I would have one or more students still on the first mastery test, so far behind the work being presented that there would be no chance of catching up. Therefore, both the teacher and the less motivated students quickly reached the point of frustration.

My experience with mastery learning has not been pleasant. I believe I gave the program a fair chance. I made every effort to do my very best but I found that poor training, lack of necessary materials, and inadequate time for the preparation and delivery of the various aspects of the program quite defeated me, as it did the majority of the teachers at my school.

At this time, six years after the program was first implemented at the junior high, I do not know of a single teacher at my own school still using it.

V.

Excerpts from

Official Transcript of Proceedings

BEFORE THE

U.S. DEPARTMENT OF EDUCATION

In the Matter of:

PROPOSED REGULATIONS TO IMPLEMENT
THE PROTECTION OF PUPIL RIGHTS AMENDMENT
SECTION 439 OF THE GEPA
ALSO KNOWN AS THE HATCH AMENDMENT

DATE: MARCH 21, 1984

PLACE: CONCORD, NEW HAMPSHIRE

Elizabeth Soper

The NEA Journal, *Today's Education,* January 1969, stated:

> "For one thing, the basic role of the teacher will change noticeably. Ten years hence, it will be more accurate to term him a learning clinician. This title is intended to convey the idea that schools are becoming clinics, whose purpose is to provide individualized psychosocial treatment for the student, thus increasing his value both to him and to society."

The question should be asked, by whose standards will his value be increased, and who gave permission for amateur psychologist teachers to use the students as guinea pigs? The term "treatment" presupposes that all the students are mentally ill. That federally-funded programs experiment with children in an all-out massive campaign of Values Clarification can be amply demonstrated. The National Diffusion Network facilitator centers in all 50 states were set up for just such a purpose.

For example, Facing History And Ourselves clearly violates the Hatch Amendment provisions. It requires students to keep journals of the most private and compromising nature.

Another example is Positive Attitude Toward Learning. A teacher training program states on page 29:

> "Worthy of a special category is role-playing or sociodrama or dramatic impersonization, as it is variously called. The delight most students take in play acting makes this an important value-eliciting strategy, and any kind of potential or real conflict situation is useful in role-playing, or any situation in which real feelings are often concealed. Consider situations in school, in the family, and the playground, at work or in politics or government."

This is clearly an attempt at Values Clarification. Professor Alan L. Lockwood, Assistant Professor of Education, University of Wisconsin, says: "Values Clarification embodies ethical relativism as its moral point of view and Values Clarification is a form of client centered therapy."

Dr. Richard A. Gardner, M.D., Associate Clinical Professor of Child Psychology, Columbia University, College of Physicians and Surgeons, states in an article in *Parents* Magazine in 1978:

> "In my opinion there is no question that therapy is a form of brainwashing. The therapist, whether covertly or overtly, imposes his values on his patients."

Leslie Chamberlain is quoted in the November

1973 issue of *Intellect*: "The concept of learning a particular amount of content as a preparation for life is obsolete and must be abandoned." That is planned illiteracy. No wonder Johnny can't read! His rights must be protected!

Consider the awful Fallout Shelter program in some Grade 8 Health classes. Children are given the task of deciding which six out of ten people shall live; they must eliminate those too old or sick or unproductive. This is disgusting and clearly must be regulated in the public schools.

Lester Kirkendall, a major force in sex education and a member of the editorial board of *Humanist* magazine, tells sex education teachers this: "Just sneak it in as an experimental course and see how people react." How can parents react when such hideous material is hidden in perfectly innocent sounding social studies and health curricula?

Kenneth Killworthy gives teachers, in a book called *Social Studies for the Seventies,* one last word of warning: "All records which teachers have of children should be kept confidential and placed in a safe place where no one can find them." Clearly parents and students need all the protection they can get from such people.

Hiding behind slogans such as "separation of church and state," "academic freedom," or "professionalism," a single-minded group is bent on changing national values and policy tomorrow by indoctrination of pupils of today.

In the *Congressional Record* of August 23, 1978 Senator Orrin Hatch stated:

"Much of the money authorized in particular titles of the ESEA goes for very worthwhile and necessary forms of tests, medical surveys or other scholastic or aptitude examinations which are above reproach, but there has been raised a tremendous outcry by parents, PTA officials and others who have serious reservations about some of the nonscholastic or aptitude tests, the psychological probing and other nongermane, often mind-bending, surveys being conducted in elementary and secondary schools without the knowledge, and much less the consent, of the parents or guardians involved."

TESTIMONY OF————————————————
Eileen Bowie

I am a wife, widow, mother of five children and grandmother of eight. "Gap" seems to be a very popular word today, so let's talk about the literacy gap. It is a shocking figure, now widely admitted, that one out of every five adults is functionally illiterate. That means that those people can't read the help wanted sections of the newspapers, can't fill out a job application, can't read the directions on the medicine bottle, and can't take a written driving test. These people are not dumb; it's just that they haven't been taught. So our corporations and our armed services have to put in their own courses to teach their employees how to read and write, add and subtract.

Many of us saw this coming long before it received so much press in the country. Years ago, the main problems that teachers seemed to have in the class-room were passing notes, whispering, and chewing gum. Today the problems include teenage suicide, vandalism, rape, drugs, drinking, premarital sex, unwanted teenage pregnancies, and beating up teachers—in addition to not being able to read and write, add and subtract.

We like to think that we have progressed from year to year, but that doesn't seem to be the case in education, does it? Instead of teaching our children to learn the basics and to learn something about the principles and values that made our country great, it appears that many students are spending a great deal of time on anything *but* the basics.

There has been much discussion about the new curricula on nuclear war. These curricula are not de-signed to inform or educate. Rather they are de-signed to instill fear, guilt, and despair. They are de-signed to sell pacifism and to divert our country's spending away from national defense and to every type of domestic handout. The courses are designed for our children to spend many depressing hours listening to dramatic descriptions of the horrors of nuclear war and radiation.

No wonder there is a movement in our country today by dissatisfied parents to remove their children to alternate schools, private schools and into home teaching. I agree with President Reagan that educa-tion is the issue that people care about, and I also agree with him that money is *not* the solution. It is restoring the basics, the values and the standards that alone can provide a good education.

Instead of ABC's recent seven-million-dollar production, "The Day After" (which was a dismal failure), the network could do a great service to our country if it would do segments on the classroom courses referred to in the Hatch Amendment so that many parents may be aware of what is going on in education today.

Surely the media can accurately discover the new illiterates in their twenties and thirties, and let each one tell his own horror story about the way he was promoted through grade and high school but somehow was never taught to read. A rebirth of trust and credibility would reward the major networks and their local affiliates for this great service.

If General Motors is forced to recall millions of automobiles at General Motors' expense and have to make good on its mistakes, then the schools should be required to recall illiterate graduates and give them skills for which they, their parents, and the taxpayers have already paid.

TESTIMONY OF————————————————

Alan C. Thomaier

I am a member of the Board of Education in Nashua, New Hampshire. All my life I have been involved with young people. I have been a profes-

sional baseball player, a coach, have served on the
scout committee, been a religious instructor for high
school students, fathered five children, served as a
police officer for six years and as an elected school
board member for over eight years.

For too long I have been concerned over the
manner in which the secular humanists have been
undermining morality, patriotism, and a sense of
values in our youth. For example, in six years on the
police force, I ran into only one problem of drug
abuse with an adult. Now, according to an article in
our local *Nashua Telegragh,* students in the towns of
Hudson and Nashua can obtain drugs any time they
want in our high schools.

In 1979 an article was in the *Union Leader* stating
that a survey taken in our New Hampshire schools
showed that 5th and 6th graders were now using
drugs and alcohol.

In 1976 another newspaper article revealed that
there was an epidemic of teenage pregnancies. Also,
on the same page was an article revealing that teachers and librarians in the state of New Hampshire
wanted immunity from the obscenity laws. Why?
Pretty obvious.

All over the country there has been an uproar by
parents, school board members, teachers, etc., over
the one-sided materials being forced on our children
by the humanists who now almost totally control our
public schools. The amazing part is that roughly
20% of those refusing to use the materials in the
schools have been teachers and administrators themselves, and that in most instances federal funds are

used to finance the materials or organizations promoting this anti-God and anti-family material.

When Terrel Bell was U.S. Commissioner of Education, he stated that parents have a right to expect that the schools would support the values of the parents in the home. But, when some of us object to these materials, we are branded as "book burners" and "censors." Studies have revealed that these tremendous problems of youth started when prayer, good school books, discipline, moral values, dress codes, etc., were taken out. They replaced social studies with new innovative programs, sex education, etc. Few parents were aware of what was happening in the schools because most of the materials were audio visual cassettes, educational TV, mimeographed sheets, and paperback books (with the usual four letter words). These materials do not go home.

Some years ago we had a workshop on Title IX for teachers, and they showed a film put out by the National Organization for Women (which has received federal grants). This organization has probably done more to undermine our morals and family values than any other group. In 1978 as a school board member, I led the fight to remove *Ms.* Magazine from our school library. I called it a piece of trash. A former principal of our school also fought to have it removed. The magazine had the usual four-letter words and five pages of ads where young girls could send away for cordless vibrators, gasmotrons, erotic toys with which to have fun with their friends, and various lesbian ads. One book used with this was the *Gay Mystique* written by a homosexual who told the reader that sex with men was better than sex with women. That book was paid for with federal funds. This was removed after I complained. The student in court said she was using *Ms.* Magazine to do research on lesbianism, homosexuality, abortion and witchcraft. Our library had many books promoting these views. Books donated by myself to give opposing views were not put on the same library shelves.

The question I always ask is, why don't we teach children how to read and write, about our heritage, and how to go out and earn a living? The local papers would not print the material out of *Ms.* Magazine.

All over the country, schools are putting in literature guidelines that are stacked against the parents. In the *Ms.* Magazine case, I had to go to a committee composed of the librarian, the teacher using the magazine, the department head, the principal, and the assistant superintendent of schools. They were judge and jury. Between the federal funding in the schools, and the threat of a lawsuit from the American Civil Liberties Union and the humanists, parents, teachers and school board members are scared to death to challenge the materials.

Another federally-funded program was used in an elementary school in our city. The children were given articles out of newspapers such as those promoting disarmament, gun control, and the horrors of nuclear war. They were all too young for these subjects and were given only one side. They were encouraged to use diaries and told that what was in the diaries would not be revealed without their own full permission. Can you imagine that a very young child might write true or untrue things about his parents, etc., and then reveal this to other children who live in the same neighborhood who could bring tales home to *their* parents? This could create some dangerous problems.

In May 1975 the *American School Board Journal* revealed the results of a survey of school board members and administrators: 86% of them were concerned with the prospect of graduating dummies from our public schools. We have watched a very serious erosion of basic education during the last 15 years, and most of them stated they are in favor of returning to fundamental schools. One stated that most of these innovations of the past decade have been dismal failures. The bubbleheads have had their fling and, in the process, have done irrevocable harm to millions of children.

It is time to go back to what education is all about. Our children need learning, not the fun and games of permissive classrooms. Programs like new math, open classrooms, sex education, sensitivity training, and role-playing have been total failures. All over the country there has been an uproar because our students, who graduate from high schools, can hardly read, write, add, or make a living. Instead, they are taught how "the Communists are persecuted in our country," about family planning, acid rain, the horrors of nuclear war, that businessmen are evil, and everything that is negative about America. No wonder so many of them are depressed and get in trouble! They were taught nothing positive.

The school board members voted overwhelmingly to go back to having fundamental schools which teach the phonetic system of reading, the Palmer method of writing, and basic arithmetic skills, to reenforce parental values, morality, prayer in school, citizenship and personal responsibility. Where these fundamental schools have been set up, parents are standing in line to get their children in. Teachers also favor them. Our children are our most precious possessions and we have a right to protect them against the humanist change agents.

TESTIMONY OF_____

Carol Eremita

I am a parent and mother of four children, and I will tell you what happened to me as briefly as I can. I dealt with the Hatch Amendment three weeks after it became law.

Two of my four children, one in the 2nd grade and one in the 5th grade, were subjected to psychological testing in 1978 as part of an experimental Behavior Modification program called Schools Without Failure. This is a canned program developed in a reformatory for delinquent adolescent girls, and is the brain child of William Glasser.

The program is very well dealt with in his two books *Reality Therapy* and *Schools Without Failure,* so I will not take time to fully explain the programs in my testimony. I will, however, bring to your attention two points that worry me greatly. I come to this hearing and speak with the background of a nurse. I've dealt with informed consent on a professional level in nursing.

Glasser's program was brought to my school and unanimously approved by my School Board with very little prior knowledge of the program. Only brief and superficial information was given by our superintendent of schools, and we had only minimal discussion at a single meeting. From the time I first brought a complaint to the School Board in 1978 until 1982 when the board finally revoked the program, not one original voting member had read either of the books. Very few parents took the time to read the book or even research the program.

I'm afraid that almost any program could be passed through a school board in this manner if information is only selectively offered as it was at my school. It becomes a particularly serious problem when the possible results are considered. Informed consent simply becomes an ambiguous term unless we define first the needs, the alternatives, and the possible side effects, good and bad. The possibility for liability for damaging results from psychological manipulation should be considered. I think that this should be mandatory, in order to have a liability clause to see who is going to take the blame for this stuff.

Since most of the programs are promoted as bold new thrusts, and are at best only questionably effective, true informed consent requires that the parent fully understand that these methods are experimental. The parent ought to know that it might not work and that it is probably going to cost a lot.

My second concern is the availability of the materials to parents. I had an interesting experience when I went to the school and asked for a copy of the tests that both my children took. I was told that the school had a responsibility to protect my children's privacy! Interestingly enough, the data had already been put into the University of Maine computer, so protection of privacy really wasn't the big issue.

When I insisted that I be shown a copy of the test, the superintendent (after legal consultation) allowed me to inspect a blank copy, that is, one that had not been touched by a child, in his presence, in his office. He defined the terms. This, in itself, would put many parents off and discourage them from pursuing the matter.

How accessible is accessible? I felt duress was present there at the office. I've talked with a friend of mine who is a physician and a lawyer. We've talked a lot about informed consent. He told me that he could probably obtain a surgical consent from any patient simply by giving selective information along with his expert opinion.

Chairperson Monika Harrison (the Department of Education Hearing Officer): Unfortunately, I have heard the same story in each of the other hearings. Parents who have become aware that certain materials were being used, thought that, as citizens of that school district and as parents of children in that school district, they could just go down and say, I would like to see Johnny or Mary's paper, and they were surprised to find that somehow that wasn't something they were supposed to see. Every one of these parents talked about the element of duress. Many of them have had far worse situations. Some of them, for example, are allowed to talk to their children's teachers only when accompanied by an associate superintendent or the superintendent. They waged battles for any number of years; clearly the primary aim was to wear them down and to get them out of the classroom.

So I'm not insensitive to your story. I guess I've just heard so many over the last week that there isn't any element of question in my mind.

TESTIMONY OF———————————

Anne Pfizenmaier

American youngsters graduated from high school 25 or 30 years ago and entered college without needing remedial courses in math and English. Teenagers who went into the work force 25 or 30 years ago were able to offer math and verbal skills to an employer. The Armed Forces, 25 or 30 years ago, did not accept functional illiterates. So what has happened?

During these last 25 or 30 years, the philosophy of John Dewey has taken a giant step into the classrooms of America. While the foot in the door may have then been only a size 4, the heavy boots of progressive educators have since managed to stomp out nearly all of the traditional teaching methods and philosophy that made our country great.

In 1974, regulations were passed to ensure that parents could investigate the content of educational materials in the classrooms. Some of the materials became an issue in many communities, but it was next to impossible for parents to question the educators. Parents were confronted by a solid block of intimidating professionals who claimed to have the so-called expertise to direct young minds—and expertise supposedly beyond the mental grasp of the untrained mother or father. Children themselves feared repercussions from school authorities if their parents began to show interest in the content presented in the classroom.

The usual cry that parents were attempting to "censor" and "ban" certain instructional materials was raised by the entrenched and tenured teachers who battled for intellectual freedom—*theirs*.

In my town, Hingham, Massachusetts, a public high school English class was asked to name any of the Ten Commandments with which the student disagreed. This questioning of authority thus reached the level of man's highest behavior guidelines upon which the laws of our land are based.

The John Dewey education system is finally bearing fruit. The National Education Association (NEA), of which he was a member, grew by leaps and bounds. The NEA soon reached a membership of more than 1½ million, having learned to disregard authority and set its own codes of behavior on the basis of "if it feels good, do it." Students' lack of discipline and basic skills have created social problems that undermine the nation's economic, judicial, political, intellectual and ethical stability.

Economically, because of their inability to perform in the marketplace, youngsters are incapable of supporting themselves and wind up on welfare. Politically, more and more taxpayers' money is demanded by single-issue, self-interest groups. Congress has voted to fund programs to do what our educational process failed to do.

In my town the importance of "relevance" in today's education was exemplified by this passage in an 8th grade English textbook:

"Write a suicide note." [The following is the example given in the text.] "I am finally going to do it. Unemployment drives me crazy. Inflation makes me angry. The cost of living turns my stomach. Big business raises the cost of candy and gum. Teachers expect too much. School takes away my freedom. I can't communicate with my parents. My parents don't understand me. I have said my goodbyes. I fought a good fight, but I have met defeat."

That depressing advice was supposed to be "relevant." It was taken from an "activity" approach to Basic English, Part 2, published by the New England School Development Council in Newton, Massachusetts.

Ethically, our young people no longer have the traditional guidelines that made our nation, under God, great in world influence. They have adopted for themselves an Eleventh Commandment: Thou shalt not get caught.

In order to evaluate the effectiveness of the socialist-oriented progressive education of the NEA, a system of tests had to be devised. It was necessary not only to determine whether or not the process had been effective in the schools, but also to what extent it had invaded family life.

Students and parents alike had become so accustomed to testing that the far reaching ramifications of the procedure, and the ultimate use to which it would be applied, was of no particular interest to them. It was significant, though, that schools began to include classes in sex education, child care, parenting, and so forth, in their curriculum, subjects which have never before been considered within the purview of a public education system. These subjects, which have such great moral connotations, should not be entrusted to a faceless group which is never held accountable for the consequences. Since families can and do live with the consequences of such instruction, that instruction should be left entirely up to them.

The NEA has publicly asserted that its goal is

power. Over ten years ago, a spokesman for the NEA said that teachers would no longer be teachers — they would be change agents. They would be clinicians. Have our schools then become clinics, experimental laboratories, under the second largest union in the country?

Over a hundred years ago Alexis de Toqueville toured the United States. His wonderful appraisal of our country was summed up in his comment that America is great because it is good, and that if it ceases to be good, it will no longer be great. We cannot keep our nation good if we sacrifice our young people to satisfy the curiosity of the scientists and psychologists under the guise of education.

*TESTIMONY OF*_____

Ron Figuly

I operate a small business in Conway, New Hampshire. I am the father of two children, one of whom has completed high school and the other is in her freshman year.

The purpose of my testimony is to give evidence of the bias of a few but apparently very influential psychologists in education who are promoting curricula which are oriented towards pacifism and unilateral disarmament. Using the National Diffusion Network as an access facilitator to the minds of American students, they virtually ignore the need to defend the United States. They fail to focus attention on the reality of the unprecedented build-up of offensive weapons by the Soviet Union.

In his remarks to the Senate on August 23, 1978, Senator Orrin Hatch stated:

"In Wisconsin, there is a program, publicly funded in part by ESEA money, entitled Future Directions of Family Planning in Wisconsin. It is a program providing so-called 'peer evaluation training' in sex education from kindergarten through the 12th grade. The program provides all forms of contraception information, pregnancy and abortion referral education, and even services to persons as young as ten years old without parental consent. Though originally set up as a condition for Title X funding of the state family planning programs under the auspices of the Department of HEW with the endorsement of Planned Parenthood, the program certainly has not won the endorsement of many parents and other citizens who protested the program. This is one dramatic example of many which I will be prepared to present before my colleagues during the impending debate on ESEA. It is a betrayal of education's basic purpose. It is a kind of thing which our Parental Consent Amendment would correct."

At Kennet High School in Conway, New Hampshire, the Family Planning Program is a very busy factor in the life of the students, as evidenced by a series of articles in the school newspaper on sex subjects such as teenage pregnancy, birth control, and methods of how Family Planning can help. The articles in the newspaper were covered by three students under the supervision of an English teacher and printed under the direction of the graphic arts department. Using Family Planning resource materials, these youthful writers launched into the details of Family Planning programs being implemented in Kennet High School. The article states that the High School "works in close connection with the Family Planning Clinic and Calcenny Mental Health Clinic," both under a common leadership. The "school nurse" acts as the liaison.

When my wife spoke to the school nurse about the health education program at school, the nurse told her that she delivers female students' urine samples to Family Planning clinics for pregnancy testing. I never thought that schools work to educate therapeutically and test young girls for pregnancy. I always thought that schools had to do with developing learning skills and knowledge.

Next came glowing accounts of the advantages of Family Planning. For example, teenagers are encouraged to use contraceptives. Family Planning services "require no more than an individual signature on a minor consent form and it no way involves parental permission and knowledge."

Family Planning makes it known that "birth control is available to them should they find themselves becoming more sexually active. Family Planning is a clinic that may aid in the handling of this responsibility."

That's responsibility? There is no indication in the article that sexual activity outside of marriage is called fornication, or that fornication contributes to family dissolution. No mention is made about the dangers of herpes, AIDS, syphilis, and gonorrhea. Nothing is said about the uncertainty of contraceptives in preventing pregnancy, or their potential and/or possible health hazard, or that abortion is the taking of an innocent human life.

Students are informed that "Family Planning is easily accessible and free of complications." Just a front door away from the school nurse's office will do the trick, and the matter remains strictly confidential. No parental consent is required. "For teenagers in this area, the Family Planning Clinic is a hassle-free and easily accessible aid in dealing with the many problems that may arise in a sexually active teenage relationship."

I never thought that schools were to be a clearinghouse for free-wheeling teenage sexual activity.

Senator Hatch in making reference to this kind of activity, said:

"This whole problem came about when schools started becoming more concerned with children's attitudes, beliefs and emotions rather than providing them with basic education. What we have today is a situation where dramatically fewer young children can read, write or count, but who have become worldly wise in stories about sex, drugs and violence. This does not speak well for the long-term emotional stability of the child. Such implicit value changes, which tend to teach the very young about drugs and sex, challenge their faith in their parents and constitute the most vile threat to the American family unit. The techniques used to change young children's attitudes and values are an invasion of privacy in the first degree."

One example of this is the National Diffusion Network Program entitled Ethical Issues in Decision Making. This program uses Professor Kohlberg's moral reasoning situation ethics.

The second part of my testimony has to do with the indoctrination of students with a certain bias through federally-funded nuclear education. One such program available through the National Diffusion Network is called Facing History and Ourselves. This is a federally-funded program by the Department of Education for 8th and 9th grade students. It is another effort by the anti-defense establishment in close collaboration with such psychological organizations as the Educators for Social Responsibility and the U.S. section of the International Physicians for the Prevention of Nuclear War.

Any curriculum which (borrowing the words of those who professionally evaluate it) is "controversial and experimental" is clearly designed to change students' attitudes on political and social issues. Any program which uses pre- and post-testing to evaluate students' attitudinal outcomes presents problems for a free society.

To substantiate these contentions, let us look at

the following quotation from Facing History and Ourselves, a Project Evaluation by Dr. Marcus Lieberman, Harvard Graduate School of Education, published in *Moral Education Forum*, 1981:

> "During the first year of the FHAO program, we wanted to 'cast the widest possible net' to capture changes in the students' moral, ego and social development. Not surprisingly the junior high school students who took all these tests complained bitterly about the difficulty in answering the questions posed in the protocols. (It became particularly difficult to persuade those students who had experienced a unit on resistance to continue with the tests!)

> "While the advantages of 'casting a wide net' to capture any changes had seemed like a reasonable approach, the emotional response to what students had perceived as a high level of abuse had been unanticipated."

The intent of this program, to my mind, is manipulative and has no legitimate place in a school curriculum. I can imagine a very probable and realistic scenario in which a teacher, burdened by his or her deep commitments to pacifism, unilateral disarmament and the inevitable direction of history, could recycle the students through this program until the students' responses correctly match the view of the teacher as evaluated in the post-test protocol. Also, I can imagine the probability that this information could be used by deeply sincere and dedicated individuals in the Department of Education to achieve similar objectives on a national scale.

TESTIMONY OF———————————————————
Jim Hopkins
————————————————————————————

I am from Wolfeboro, New Hampshire. I think it imperative that the people assembled here today be made aware of the fact that public school classrooms are being rapidly politicized, particularly over the issue of peace and disarmament. This disturbing trend is popping up in all parts of the country. One such program, called Crossroads, Quality of Life in the Nuclear World, is now in use in public school systems in at least 30 states. Developed in 1982 it is a "peace education" curriculum available in three units, for social studies, English and science.

Another program called Choices — A Unit on Conflict and Nuclear War, was put into practice in the 1982-83 school year by the National Education Association on a field test basis in classrooms in 34 states. It should be noted that this testing was done not only with the assent, but with the active collaboration, of the departments of education in most or all of these states.

In other words, taxpayers' money went into the implementation of Choices for the National Education Association to introduce such a program into the classrooms of our public schools without a national consensus.

Where is the NEA's often articulated effort to emphasize scholastic excellence? The avowed purpose of these courses is to allay the fears and despairs of the young by showing that adults are trying to solve the difficult issue of the threat of nuclear war. The idea is ultimately to prepare the young to set us free from the threat that endangers the world by teaching them the effect of a nuclear bomb on the human body and the environment. What would it be like to be the survivor of a nuclear war? What are the issues behind the arms race, the effects of an increased military budget, and of social cutbacks on the quality of life?

With the world's greatest statesmen having difficulty solving international relations and the threat of nuclear destruction, how in the world can we expect children to make constructive contributions to these grave issues?

The basic premise of Choices is that junior high students are being increasingly faced with the international debate on the threat of nuclear war. In order to help these youngsters overcome their fears and despair over this issue, say the authors of these programs, they are supplying them with "age-appropriate materials," designed to show the choices necessary "to insure a peaceful, secure future for the United States and the world."

These programs from the National Education Association fail to mention that they themselves and their cohorts in the nuclear freeze movement were the ones that selected and defined the so-called "choices" presented to the unsuspecting students.

I see nothing wrong with the idea of helping teachers with lesson plans who are devoting classroom time to discussions of the nuclear threat. What is wrong is that the powerful teachers' union has its own views on these issues and is asking its members to fill their kids' heads with slanted propaganda, rather than helping the students to understand the number of different points of this very complex area.

Schools and individual teachers receive advocacy materials from many sources. However, they must exercise objective professional judgment in deciding whether or how to use them. The important factor whenever such materials are used in the classroom is that they be identified as such and that a balanced presentation be made to include an opposing viewpoint.

The 1.8 million member National Education Association claims that the 144-page lesson plan for Choices is unbiased and contains opposing views, but the material includes only 20 lines of copy from the office of the President and just 3-½ pages from the pro-defense Committee on the Present Danger. All the rest is devoted to a one-sided presentation favoring nuclear disarmament without adequate explanation of the need for a strong defense. It is not a question of being for or against nuclear war; everybody in his right mind wants to avert the horror and the devastation of nuclear conflict. The issue is how do we manage to do that.

In this National Education Association curriculum, the United States is portrayed as far superior to the Soviet Union in nuclear arms, a view not supported by national intelligence estimates. At the same time, completely ignored in the text, is any mention of the massive Soviet arms buildup, the greatest in the history of mankind. Ignored also are the lessons of Munich and the need to determine strength to prevent the very nuclear holocaust which the NEA warns about. Not being taught is the fact that the surest way to war and senseless destruction and the misery of tyranny is unilateral one-sided disarmament.

These programs are not only conducted at the junior high school level. At Public School No. 3 in New York's Greenwich Village, a group called "Kids Outreach" conducted a classroom discussion of nuclear weapons, war and atomic holocaust for 2nd, 3rd and 4th grade students. The discussion included the showing of a film entitled "Arms Will Make the Rainbow Break." One of the nine-year-olds said it was so scary that she felt "like I should just cut my head off."

Should we really be surprised that the suicide rate among the young has increased 41% in only four years? This is a national tragedy.

In order to develop self confidence, courage and a sense of responsibility needed in the adult world, children must grow up in an atmosphere of optimism and hope. The schools can do much to help with this development, but not by teaching courses which frighten children with a grim future and push them further into despair. This may not be the aim of these courses, but it is what they accomplish. These children don't develop fright on their own. They are responding to the paranoid fears of anti-nuclear adults and organizations which knowingly, I repeat, knowingly spread false and distorted scare stories. When the nuclear debate is forced into the classrooms to influence innocent children, we can no longer remain silent. Exploiting children too young to reason for themselves is a tragedy of the education process. We must stop this dangerous manipulation of young minds.

TESTIMONY OF

Mary Blaisdell

I'm from Concord, New Hampshire, the mother of four children ages 10 to 19. I am a registered nurse and presently I'm on the Concord School District's Health Committee as well as other educational committees and parents' groups including the Lamplighters of Concord, which has as members over 500 parents.

I would like to point out a few examples of our curriculum here in Concord. Students are asked who they'd vote for for President, but the teacher will not reveal who he's voting for. The implications may be (1) voting is not a personal, private privilege (2) a child's vote usually reveals his parents' choice, and (3) when a teacher won't say how he is voting, it creates a double set of values. It's difficult for parents to get the needed information as to what's being taught, and when and by whom, because it's time consuming and because it's an integral part of a child's whole curriculum.

I am referring, for instance, to Health, although

there are other parts of the curriculum that deal with what we are talking about, too.

For instance, in the Health curriculum if there is a part that you object to your child taking part in, if it's integrated into his social studies course, it would mean he would have to miss part of his academic training. If it is taught as a separate entity by itself, and Health is mandated in the school system, it could jeopardize his going forward in his classes.

Another part that is difficult for parents is that sometimes the program titles are deceiving. For example, the Me Me program is presented as a drug prevention program. Most parents would be very pleased to have a drug prevention program in their school, but if they had time to really look into this program, they would find that one part of the program is informational and the other three-quarters deal with values, attitudes, etc.

I brought in a very small portion of the Health curriculum here in Concord. If a parent were to go to school and say he would like to know what's being taught in the Health curriculum, chances are he would be given this outline of scope and sequences. I'm just referring now to the 3rd, 4th and 5th grades.

Under "individual" you would find "behavior choices, consequences, interpersonal relationships, communicating, making decisions, clarifying values, helping and asserting." Under "family" you would find "understand rights and responsibilities of family membership, roles of family members, communications, family, interreaction, family decision making, values in family." Some parents might say "that's fine," and yet it doesn't tell you a whole bunch.

If the parents want to go further to know what's in the curriculum, they may be given the "activity packet" which is given to the teacher in order to implement these particular goals and objectives. Here are some of the questions and activities in these packets, to name a very few.

Class discussion: How do you feel when someone who sits next to you does not look or smell clean? What do you do?

On a daily basis, encourage students to focus on feeling good. Ask them to share their ideas on how they feel as they go about.

Have students in class talk about a problem they recently faced, and how they solved it, using the decision-making process.

Complete at least a five day daily dietary intake chart, and keep a health and "feelings" journal.

Discuss feelings which family members may have upon the arrival of a new baby.

Discuss what issues are considered when parents make a decision to increase family membership, and introduce the concept of family planning as a method of controlling the decision. Role-play issues which are related to reproduction and its purpose.

Classroom discussion of why boys and girls don't go out with each other when they are younger, but choose to do so as they get older.

Make them talk about older brothers and sisters and uncles, etc., who are dating, and comment with observations.

Students should write an essay entitled "The Person I Marry." Discuss the function of boy/girl relationships. These include learning what one wants in a marriage partner.

Discuss the impact of family activities and personal feelings of self-worth. Identify influences that affect the family health habits and lifestyles, such as knowledge, education of parents, parents as role models, and religious beliefs.

From the following list of personal behavior, students can discuss who they know who encourages them to do this, discourages them to do this, or forces them or prevents them from doing something.

Focus on fighting between brothers and sisters. First, how do students feel at the end of an argument. What was the argument about? If appropriate, talk about how parents feel, and about how students feel when parents fight. How do they deal with this anger, fear or whatever. Complete the worksheet entitled "Stress In Your Family."

Play a game of "Simon Says." How do you feel about following the game. How well do you follow along with everyone else?

How would you feel if everyone could go to a dance, but your mother wouldn't let you? At the bottom of this list, it calls for values voting and values interpretation.

How many of you would raise your children more strictly than you were raised? How many of you think there are times when cheating is justified?

How many of you regularly attend religious services and enjoy it? A note to the teacher says that voting is an excellent way to introduce specific values issues into the classroom.

Write an essay with a picture of your parents. What do your parents do? Write a description of whether students like or do not like to be similar to their parents.

Complete the worksheet entitled "The Talents of Their Parents." This worksheet has on it a list of skills and talents. Put an X beside those which apply to your mother or father: good cook, friendly person, good listener or helper, hard worker, good mechanic, makes decisions well, good parent.

Discuss misuse of some substances by parents, for example alcohol, valium, etc.

All through this curriculum, as well as other curricula, the pupils are given this decision-making process. It's not just in Health. This is a probing of a child's values, attitudes and beliefs. It is based on Values Clarification, which is also referred to as mind control, conditioning, sensitivity training, and psychological stripping.

The results of Values Clarification prove that it does not reinforce existing home values. Instead it is producing a generation of confused, emotionally disturbed children with no set of values or morals.

A plaque hanging on the door of a doctor's office here in Concord reads: "*No* decision *is* a decision." You have to think about that for awhile, but it is true that *no* decision *is* a decision. Educators would have us believe that they do not teach values or Values Clarification, but teaching *no* values is indeed *teaching* a value. They fail to see that they are dealing with children, not with adults who have maturity and experience to draw from.

The tragedy of all the experimentation of educational theories and teaching methods beginning in the 1960s was that the experiments were not carried out on mice or hamsters in a laboratory, but on real live children who, in their journey through the classroom, would never pass that way again. The second tragedy is that the same students are some of the teachers of today.

I realize there are problems, but the classroom setting is not the place to deal with them. I remember, when training to be a nurse, we were cautioned about psychological questioning of our patients, as we were not qualified to help an emotionally disturbed individual. Yet this goes on every day in the classrooms by teachers who are unqualified in this area. There is a big difference in education between the teaching of responsible information versus teaching through analysis and disrespect of others. We as parents are responsible for our children. We can't be in school with them every day. We have to have the right to choose what's best for them.

TESTIMONY OF————————————————
Valerie Walsh

I was involved with our school system very much. I was a volunteer at the local elementary school where my son was enrolled, and I was the publicity director for that school covering most of the events for one and a half years.

I was surprised when a letter came out stating that the children would be participating in a program called Me Me. I was vaguely aware of this drug prevention program. I remember a school board meeting in the spring when a gentleman professed his displeasure regarding the program's activities. However, I also remembered feeling very secure in the thought that parental permission would be sought and an orientation program put in place for the parents, prior to the use of the program.

The administration assured everyone at that school board meeting that this would be so. Shortly thereafter, I asked the school principal about the date of orientation night and how the school went about securing parental permission. I also asked if he could secure any material regarding the effectiveness of the program. He assured me that he would give me all that information as soon as he could. Because I wanted to be informed on the program, I read as much material as I could, including the two manuals containing the entire curriculum as well as any material referenced therein.

I interviewed the author on the telephone, the guidance counselor who reviewed the program at the local school, the assistant superintendent in charge of curriculum development, a project coordinator at Concord, and other school administrators who had used or were about to use the program. The list of interviews really seemed endless. However, I felt I needed background information for articles to put the school in a very positive light; I also had a self-serving interest because my son would be participating.

After four weeks of research and intensive interviewing, I felt that many people had sincere concerns regarding the program. I sat at the meeting with the principal and the guidance counselor at my son's school. I asked a school board member to be present, so he would be privy to what we discussed.

It is now November 4, 1982. This is four weeks after the letter came home. I asked several questions at that meeting. I had many, many more. However, I had no doubt that my concerns would be listened to. During the meeting I was invited to serve on a committee whose goals would be to address my concerns and modify the program where necessary, if they felt they were valid.

After more in-depth discussion on several points, the principal started getting argumentative. I really couldn't believe this. I also felt he had an unbending attitude in regard to the more personal aspects of the program. I started to point out the Hatch Amendment and other laws and their relation to the program. During this part of the discussion the principal said: "So what if those laws are in place! What do they mean to me?" I reacted by saying that I felt the laws were in place for a good cause and reason, and that they protected children from disclosure of personal, private matters.

The principal then suggested that, if I didn't like what was being used in the school, I did have the option of leaving the system. I explained that I had no plans to leave the system and that the only reason I wanted the meeting was to obtain answers to my questions and have my concerns at least addressed.

However, with his attitude permeating the room, I felt I was being placed in an adversarial position and was not comfortable with that position, as I felt very positive about my school and all the people in it. We did close the meeting on a more friendly note, and the principal felt that every concern that I had would be addressed by serving on the committee.

As I stand before you today, I am still waiting. The committee was never formed. The parent orientation night never came to pass. I never saw the supporting data on the effectiveness of the program. Parental consent was never asked for. I will remind you that the meeting took place November 4, 1982.

To the best of my knowledge, none of the above has yet come to pass today. The School Board at subsequent meetings let the program stand as is, with no review. Late in February, I met with various people within the Department of Education in Concord. After several hours of explanation, and much give and take during the discussions about my concerns, I asked the commissioner what he would do if it was his child. He suggested that I remove my child from the system.

In August the school contacted me and explained that a room had been set up to accommodate 16 other children whose parents disagreed with the program's activities. It sounded like everything was coming together.

However, prior to this I had specifically asked the grade placement coordinator that I wished to have my son placed first and foremost according to his academic standing regardless of Me Me. After contacting the school on this late development, I could not get any assurance that he would be placed academically. We had to decide whether to sacrifice his academics or his mental health. I stated to the administration that my main concern involving my son would be to maintain a continuum relative to academics and, further, that in no way should that development be impinged upon by the use of a social program I had concerns about.

After much consternation, my husband and I in late August decided to do what was best for our own child in all respects. We opted for the suggestions of both the principal and the commissioner of education. My child is now in private school.

The story seems to end well for my child. Yet, I have a second one coming. I truly feel that my child's right to a public education was thwarted and that the federal law relating to students' rights was disregarded.

From extensive research and interviewing the appropriate key people, I found that there are sincere differences of opinion among most educators themselves. Some experts in educational matters and medical professionals question whether the techniques will enhance or injure mainstream students or should be used at all on reasonably well-adjusted children. It is like applying chemotherapy when the patient doesn't have cancer.

I had followed local procedure to have my concerns addressed to no avail. I have discussed my concerns with teachers, with the guidance counselors, with the principals (and I do use the plural because it was more than just one), my school board members including chairman of the School Board, the New Hampshire Department of Education, and the federal Department of Education at the regional office in Boston. Some of the people were sympathetic to what appeared to be this injustice; yet others said, so what if the law is in place. Other said, that's a local issue.

I stand before you and ask, as I have countless times before, what do I do when our local and state educational officials refuse to comply with or even refuse to acknowledge the existence of the laws? I do not believe that this is just a local issue. Through my intense reading and interviewing, I did find that similar problems exist in other states on the very same issues.

*TESTIMONY OF*_____
Robert Duarte
_____

To continue funding of the Me Me drug program is not in the best interest of the Federal Government. Therefore, it was one of 13 National Diffusion Network programs from which federal funding has been removed. Out of the program's 600 pages, only one alone is drug information. The rest are nothing but Values Clarification.

This is advertised as a drug prevention program, and yet nowhere is there any expectation that drug abuse will be reduced by using this program.

We have heard a lot today about the Values Clarification process. No one here could state what the moral basis of that process is, not even the Commissioner of Education. That process is applied to moral questions extensively in the school system with little children; no moral code is permitted to enter into the discussion.

The problem we have is that Federal Government money got this program into 38 states. When I talked with Mr. Cartwright of the National Diffusion Network last week, I asked him if they informed the facilitator centers in each state that this program is no longer funded and why, and he said, "Oh, they are well aware of it." Then I asked, "Have you directed them to inform the school districts that this program is no longer funded and why," and he said, "That's not our prerogative to do. We can't do that." So the problem we have as parents is that here is a program now in use for all children, grades one through six, and nobody is telling the schools that this is not a good program.

Let's look at what they claim they are going to teach in this program and then look at the exercises that they make the children practice. Now in this one here, it is claimed that the purpose is to help children understand the concept of honesty. They immediately ask the children,

> "How many of you have ever lied? How many of you seem to be lying more than you used to? How many of you think that lying is also bad? How many of you think it is okay to lie if it makes someone feel good?"

Then they go on to say, "If Grammy sends you a dress you don't like, what do you tell her?" And they go on to say why it is okay to lie if it makes somebody feel good.

The last statement in this exercise is: "Finish the following statement: I would lie if _____." The child is then told to get up and share his answers in front of the class. Look at what is being practiced! The children are practicing imagining situations when they would lie, but they are never asked to imagine times when it's wrong. They never do that. So the exercise does not do what they claim they are going to teach.

VI.

Excerpts from

Official Transcript of Proceedings

BEFORE THE

U.S. DEPARTMENT OF EDUCATION

In the Matter of:

PROPOSED REGULATIONS TO IMPLEMENT
THE PROTECTION OF PUPIL RIGHTS AMENDMENT
SECTION 439 OF THE GEPA
ALSO KNOWN AS THE HATCH AMENDMENT

DATE: MARCH 23, 1984

PLACE: ORLANDO, FLORIDA

Shirley Correll

I am currently a doctorate candidate in education. Someone is tampering with the soul of America. This tampering has operated on intellectual deceit, clothing itself in phrases which have been designed to give the appearance of progress, while dismantling religion, culture, beauty, truth and order.

It goes by many names. It calls itself sensitivity training, change agents, learning clinics, psycho-educational clinics, psychosocial treatment, psychotherapy, sociometry, role-playing, attitudinal surveys, diaries, journals, psychodrama, encounter groups, simulation or survival games, group dynamics, open classrooms, inquiry learning, Values Clarification (more honestly called values mutilation), moral education, awareness training, consciousness raising or awareness, transcendental meditation, ungraded education, middle schools, magnet schools, character education, contemporary literature, death education, abortion and contraception education, sex education, population control, evolution, new age education, psychology, parapsychology, astrology, mythology, classes about religion, in-service training, family living, character citizenship, alternative schools (such as the Scarsdale School which sends children to Red China), globalism, interdependence, health education, drug education, mastery learning, super learning, new math, ecology and environmental education, parenting, child development, Behavior Modification, Kohlberg's moral reasoning, esperanto, metrics, operant conditioning, MACOS, Magic Circle, DUSO, QUEST, TRIBES, TAD, SELF, look-say methods, PPBS, management by objective, accountability, minimum competencies, taxonomy, multicultural education, multidisciplinary and interdisciplinary approaches, gifted education, foundations, and on and on and on.

These programs have born fruit. They have systematically diminished any real acquisition of knowledge as understood in the traditional sense of the word. Swarms of mind manipulators have been exploiting our little ones and laying waste our educational system for their own purposes and benefits. They are not shy in publishing their direction but, in keeping with their covert methods, they publish but do not publicize. Their writings are meant for each other and not for the public.

So when informed and alert citizens attempt to get materials which should be available to the public, they get the run around, such as we have gotten from the National Diffusion Network.

I have personally watched some of the sensitivity training which has given so much status and financial gain to those who openly call their methods "brainwashing." In Polk County, we rewarded these opportunists with one-third of a million dollars in one program alone, paying children $10 and teachers $20 to attend. A revolution is not difficult to bring about when you have limitless resources and can pay people to be brainwashed.

These programs are designed for the total management of society. Anyone who is honest can admit no less.

Should we tolerate the spiritual and political deception which exists? A resounding no. The law is clear and directs itself toward solution. First, the regulations must be clear and they must be enforceable, which they are. Second, there must be the intent to enforce, which there is not.

Who should be entrusted with such an undertaking? The PTA fully supports the exploitative programs and will defend them. When I was president of the Polk County Council of PTAs, I was well trained in their techniques. They taught us how to whip the parents into shape by mini-courses and workshops and so forth. We soon learned how to use the brochures on "extremism" to define any objecting parent as an "extremist." I felt that the values they were labeling "extremist" would most likely fit most of society, if they wanted to be honest about it. When I didn't support the sensitivity training which the NEA manual defined as brainwashing, I was given to understand that social acceptance, both at the school districts and higher levels of PTA, would be withheld. This form of intimidation works very effectively on many people who are not strong enough to deal with such methods.

*TESTIMONY OF*_____
Raymond O. Lewis

One program introduced into our schools was and is perhaps the most controversial subject of the day: sex education. Children now can expect to get 13 years — 13 years — of this particular subject, ranging from kindergarten through their senior year in high school. Thirteen long years.

William V. Shannon, our Ambassador to Ireland, made the following observation about our children when he was a member of the editorial staff of the *New York Times*:

> "As America's children return to school, many conscientious parents are genuinely uncertain whether they may be delivering their children into enemy territory. Much of America's popular culture adds up to a con-spiracy to destroy the innocence of youth and to force upon children premature knowledge of ways of acting that they can understand intellec-tually but not cope with emotionally. The new sophistication is more than a passing phenome-non of the 60's. Its evil effects can be seen today in the grim statistics in suicide, now the second leading cause of death among persons aged from 12 to 24 years and occurring at a rate twice what it was a decade ago."

Mr. Shannon goes on to urge teachers to "halt their headlong flight from intellectual and moral standards and make schools once again places of challenge and decorum."

Everyone here no doubt knows the results of compulsory sex education in the schools in Sweden, and of the abhorrently drastic rise in unwanted pregnancies, abortions, and venereal diseases. A petition signed in Sweden by 200,000 people in support of an appeal to the Minister of Education, sent by no less than 140 physicians, declared that children misunderstood instructions in sexual matters. In retrospect, it would seem that the children did not misunderstand; the message they got was loud and clear.

A few months ago my wife and I attended a seminar right here in this city where we had the opportunity to see a Planned Parenthood movie on sex education. The scenario was between two high school students who were dating. This was about their affair, her consequent pregnancy, and ultimately their hasty marriage. To be sure, one scene after another, close up and in living color, showed nakedness, their lovemaking complete with sound effects, gyrations, music, "the works," all too real. After the marriage, they were stuck miserably with each other and stuck with a baby they didn't want. This movie began and ended with the most foul, disgusting street language one can imagine. The only relief from the rotten language was the violent, passionate love-making scenes.

I wondered as we watched just how many beautifully innocent young people, even how many Christian teenagers, were exposed to this filth in the name of education.

The new sex education movement accepts homosexuality, masturbation, bisexuality, group sex, and other practices as merely varying aspects of human differences in lifestyles. So after the introduction of sex education in Sweden, illegitimacy (which had been declining) subsequently rose.

The emphasis is no longer on having the ability to read, write or solve mathematical problems. The emphasis is now on making Jimmy and Jane socially enlightened. Instead of exercising competitiveness in the classroom, which has always been a lively factor in the American free enterprise system, we instruct them through situation ethics, Values Clarification, and strategies to put down the barrier of prejudice toward homosexuals, lesbians, and radicals, and instead, accept them with community brotherhood.

We have stripped from our teachers their sacred responsibility to teach morals and have replaced these duties with programs for change agents. Our children are forced into assuming adult attitudes. For example, instructions on abortion, contraceptives, their uses and availability, are given young people who are still in the adolescent state, often not even mature enough to put them into use.

I call attention to the human rights attitudes now being advocated for children's rights, which is placing a great strain on discipline. A Child's Bill of Rights, written during the International Year of the Child at the White House Conference on Families, promoted radical social changes, outlined special reforms considered essential to the true liberation of all children, including the right to sexual freedom, to conduct their sexual lives with no more restrictions than adults, the right to "nonsexist" education, and the right to all sexual activities that are legal among consenting adults.

Across the United States, the moral survival of approximately 53 million children is at stake. They are all helpless captive victims within their classrooms. They are going to be compelled to accept any kind of education that we decide to give them, whether it is honorable, upright, pure and high-minded, or is indifferent, corrupt, depraved, shameful and destructive.

Any program or textbook that uses filthy, rotten pornography in films and group discussion, sensitivity training, brainwashing, and turns the kids on to sex in the name of education, should be outlawed — not federally funded.

In Lake County, Florida, where I live, sex education was started in — would you believe! — kindergarten, this past September. I could hardly believe it, and we did everything we could to stop it. By the fall of this year, the rest of the grades, six through twelve, will have courses in sex education. Someone has decided that it takes 13 whole years to teach children something that could be accomplished through a regular biology or health class in a half hour.

TESTIMONY OF——————————————
Marilyn Lewis

I'm a grandmother and mother. I have with me one book which I find particularly offensive. It contains material covering every aspect of invasion of privacy of students. This book is a classic example of experimental attitudinal change in the raw. *Values Clarification* has it all: pre-testing, post-testing, exploitation, invasion of privacy, sensitivity training, brainwashing, situation ethics—you name it, this book has it.

Values Clarification is a handbook for teachers and students. It was written by Sidney Simon, Leland Howe and Howard Kirschenbaum. This book is based on 79 strategies and includes a seven-step procedure which allows the child to first thaw out previous values which have been instilled in him through his family, his home and the church. The student is instructed to set these values aside for the time being. During the second phase, the student may consider and select a new set of values which he feels is important to him. Phase three of this procedure simply instructs the child to refreeze his newly chosen values; he is committed to making them a part of his lifestyle, to act on them.

Now here are some of the questions that are discussed, male and female. There are no separations of boys and girls.

"How many of you think there are times

when cheating is justified?"

"How many of you approve of premarital sex for boys?"

"How many of you approve of premarital sex for girls?"

How many of you would approve of a marriage between homosexuals being sanctioned by a priest, minister or rabbi?"

"How many of you would approve of a young couple trying out marriage by living together for six months before actually getting married?"

"How many of you would approve of contract marriages in which the marriage would come up for renewal every few years?"

"Share your opinions on the illegal use of drugs or premarital sex."

"Tell where you stand on the topic of masturbation."

"Tell how you feel and what you actually do about alcohol or pot."

"Reveal who in your family brings you the greatest sadness and why. Then share who brings you the greatest joy."

"To whom would you tell that you have had premarital sexual relations?"

"To whom would you tell your doubts about religion?"

"To whom would you tell your method of birth control?"

This last question assumes that every girl discussing this in the class is on the pill.

Incidently, Values Clarification can be taught as an elective course, or it can be inculcated into various standard subject matter such as English or social studies.

Situation ethics and sensitivity training reek from this book. I would like to read strategy #77 found on pages 388 to 391 on the subject of diaries. (When I was a little girl I kept a diary and there was nothing there to be ashamed of, but it held my secret innermost thoughts.) But here is a direct quotation from the book.

"Diaries is a strategy that enables the students to bring an enormous amount of information about themselves into class to be examined and discussed."

For a whole week or longer, students and the teacher keep their own individual diaries, accurately recording all basic facts about any specific activities they find themselves in. If it is a disagreement diary, they record disagreements they were in, or they may record disagreements between other people which they witnessed. Students then bring their diaries into class and share entries with the group. Some of the suggestions for diaries are:

Budget diary.
Politics diary.
Religion diary.
Disagreement diary.
Male-female roles diary.
The affectionate and tender feelings diary.
The hostility and anger diary.

Is this type of so-called education anything short of experimental psychological maneuvering on the part of the educational system? Is this anything less than a rudely offensive invasion of privacy upon unsuspecting children and their parents?

In a time such as this when our young people are faced with enormous pressures, sometimes seemingly insurmountable, and oftentimes faced with compulsory reading material authored by intransigent, indifferent persons in the name of education, I am deeply dismayed.

TESTIMONY OF
Shirley Riesz

I'm from Osprey, Florida. I have a degree in elementary and early childhood education. I am a mother of three children.

In September 1981 I enrolled in a course of curriculum instruction and discovered that the emphasis of education had changed from the basic academics of reading, writing, arithmetic and reasoning to humanism, socialism, social relevance or social reconstruction, and technology, with academics at the bottom of this list. The professor and student teachers laughed about the fact that the parents and community in general still insisted on teaching children basic academics.

During this course I had to pre-intern in a local

elementary school, and I had the opportunity to see some questionable programs being conducted in a classroom.

The Sarasota County Drug Program sponsored by ESEA funds, would be more appropriately entitled something else, namely, Values Clarification. Instead of approaching the problem of drug abuse directly with indisputable facts, this program seemed more determined to find out a child's personal thoughts than to prevent drug abuse. The lesson I observed had the students discuss their feelings about a pig. The students thought of a pig as a dirty, sloppy animal, while the teacher wanted them to think of the pig as a happy animal who always looks like he has a smile on his face.

Now, what does this lesson have to do with drug education? Absolutely nothing. What does this lesson have to do with monitoring and manipulating students' values? Absolutely everything.

In most of the curriculum, the spirit of experimentation pervades drug abuse education. The concern is with personality structures, decision-making skills, and choices. It encourages students to make their own decisions and to understand their own values in order to develop their own personal code.

Although the original emphasis of this program is for the teacher to remain neutral through the Values Clarification process, the curriculum developers now consider it progress when the teachers encourage guided choices. When I asked how these guided choices would be controlled to be the appropriate choices, the reply was that it would be controlled through the student.

If you know anything about peer pressure and faculty pressure at school, you will understand my concern about a student monitoring teachers for guided choices. The students are afraid of other students and the teachers. If there is suspected wrongdoing (even in minor detail) on the parents' side, you can be sure that the children are being trained how to openly discuss and identify abusive parents.

Another school curriculum, called Health-Life Management Skills, includes not only personal hygiene, first aid and safety, but also an in-depth study of personal, social and family relationships. The purpose of this course is to train students to assess dysfunctional and self-defeating behavior in peers, recognize situations beyond the peers' control which cause dysfunction such as skirmishes among family members, abuse, integral dependency of a family member, and status defenses. The methods used in the peer counseling project, such as group dynamics, can set the stage for monitoring and invading the privacy of our homes.

Verbal permission is obtained from the parents of potential counselors who, in 12 sessions, learn interviewing techniques, solicitation techniques, how to elicit responses and when to remain silent.

These trained facilitators are then equipped to identify lonely, unwanted, isolated younger students who can be counseled by these trainees on a voluntary basis without their parents' knowledge. Sometimes facilitators are assigned to these younger children as a result of a psychological recommendation or parent conference.

At a town hall meeting during the fall semester of my course, Mr. Trulington addressed the meeting about educational excellence. I asked him about the global studies program being partially underwritten by the Institute of World Order and the Aspen Institute of Humanistic Studies. He stated he was unaware that we were accepting the ideas of these organizations. He emphasized that it would not be a separate course, but would be implemented as an interdisciplinary approach.

Our county was chosen as one of 30 in the nation to implement the Global Studies Program. It is designed to prepare our children by the year 2000 to be good citizens in a global society. The Global Program, according to our local draft, is to "prepare young people to be humane, rational, participating citizens in a world that is becoming increasingly interdependent. The course states:

> "Americans need competence to make decisions based upon an understanding of our heritage and commitment to democratic values and a responsibility to self, society and the world."

The goal of Global Education is to prepare all youths to accept a world government for all systems and a global interdependence.

In our present Global Awareness Program, a typical guide is a variety of objectives which focus on this world, such as world cultures, world interests, world civilizations, world religions, international contemporary history and future studies.

The emphasis is placed *not* on facts about the world, but on the mastery and methods of sociology. When students totally lack factual information dealing with history, while emphasizing the development of social science skills through inquiry methods, the end result is that the program promotes changes in the attitudes of students regarding American and Western history.

The January 1982 issue of *Social Education* presents the following statement:

> "The purpose of Global Education is to develop in youth, the knowledge, skills and attitudes needed in a world of limited natural resources and increasing interdependence."

Social studies teachers are in a key position to play a leading role in bringing a global perspective to the school curriculum. Education is no longer defined as development of the intellect in order to help the student make independent decisions to determine his behavior as a free man. The current objective of education is to monitor the learner's desirable change of behavior. This desirable change in behavior has nothing to do with discipline in the academic kind of hickory stick variety. It simply means the educator now has to monitor the student's feelings, emotions, values, and loyalties in order to manipulate desirable changes in affective domains. These programs are designed and exist to bring about total change—change that will transform our constitutional republic into a humanist/socialist participatory democracy.

The local School Board in my county has admitted to me that, with all the federal and state mandated programs in the curriculum, they have approximately 2% control of the total program.

To preserve our children's academic freedom and excellence, I wish to insist that an effort for local control of the curriculum be instituted to preserve the individuality of each student, teacher and subject against a global school plan that would indoctrinate all children.

TESTIMONY OF_____

George L. Crossley, Jr.

I am the pastor of the First Baptist Church of Lake Monroe, located in central Florida, and I speak as one who has become deeply concerned as a result of interacting with local school systems during the past few years. The thrust of my statement will be directed at the controversy which has occurred when educators determined that they were the final authority regarding the types of instructional materials and library books being used to educate children.

My first real experience in this area was in Lake County when a group of parents brought some sex education materials to my attention which had been purchased. These materials, which numbered some 120 tapes, video tapes and slides, and 16- or 8-

millimeter films, had been purchased without even the knowledge of the School Board.

They had been purchased in preparation for a sex education program which hadn't even been voted on by the people of Lake County. I reviewed all of the materials and they absolutely shocked me. I had no idea there were materials like that available to be shown to children or to be used to educate children.

I reviewed the materials and I found that they attacked the morals and the religious values held by many parents in Lake County. From age 12 on up the materials promoted homosexuality as an alternate lifestyle. The library books in the elementary school levels gave specific instructions on masturbation. Books in the junior and senior high levels frankly, were, just downright pornographic.

The materials generally don't give two sides to an issue such as, for example, premarital sex. They promote the idea. They don't suggest it is not a good idea. They quite boldly advocate a position which is amoral and directly attacks religious values being taught to children at home by parents and by religious leaders.

This has caused children — and I have dealt with this personally — to wonder whom to believe, their parents or the educators. The Florida public health agencies have been dispensing birth control pills to girls as young as 12 years old without parental knowledge or consent. I have had the misfortune also of having dealt with some young girls who have taken advantage of that situation and ended up getting pregnant anyway.

Sex education is promoted in many programs from kindergarten through 12th grade. When followed through completely, this course changes the views of children regarding the absolutes of right or wrong and the relationship of parents to children. It attacks religious values directly as bringing children into some kind of bondage.

As a pastor I have had to counsel with young people who have been faced with the struggle of whether to believe and do what they are taught at school, or believe what their parents taught them at home.

The only views on the subject of abortion allowed in the Orange County schools are those brought by Planned Parenthood. Planned Parenthood, in my humble opinion, is the federally-supported answer to Murder Incorporated. They have paid for 70,000 abortions through that organization alone during this past year.

Judy Young, who represents a private organization, True Life Choice, a non-profit organization, went to the Orange County schools, and sought an opportunity to present alternatives to abortion. She was turned down without even a decent word of explanation other than that her views were "controversial." Her organization is willing to financially and emotionally support young girls and young women who become pregnant so that they might have good prenatal care and that homes may be found for their children if the mother feels unable to care for them.

Public educators in the state have even felt compelled to force their political views on the children in order to influence parents regarding some specific item as, for example, Amendment #1 which is going to be voted on in November in this state. My children, who are members of my church, have told me quite clearly that in the public schoolroom during classes, people who oppose the passage of Amendment #1 had been brought in to influence the children and their parents to vote that way on Amendment #1.

I have some real problems with the concept of public tax dollars being used in that particular manner. I am not saying that a teacher doesn't have a right to her own political views. I am just saying that I don't think the classroom is the place for those views to be shared.

What right have educators to try to influence children to pressure their parents to vote one way or another on any issue during school time — either by teachers or those brought in by educators? Isn't classroom time supposed to be spent devoted to basics in the areas of reading, writing and arithmetic? Are we to pay public educators with our tax dollars to force their radical views on morals, religion and politics upon our children, and just say nothing about it?

When a group goes to a public school board meeting, questioning school library books or instructional materials because they discriminate on the basis of race or creed or for religious reasons, they are defending their civil rights. But when somebody like me comes before a school board to question the choice of instructional materials and school library books because they attack the Biblical concepts being taught to children by myself and parents I represent, I am accused of being a "censor." I don't understand the difference between the two.

If I am a public-spirited citizen when I question how the County Commission spends my tax dollars on a specific project, then how am I a narrow-minded person and a "censor" if I question how the school board spends tax dollars on any given subject? The pressure and intimidation put on parents for standing up and speaking out against materials which manipulate and influence the minds of their children is reprehensible.

TESTIMONY OF_____

Beth West

The Sarasota Drug Education Program funded under ESEA is used in 40 counties across the State of Florida. Written in 1976, revised in 1982, it is composed of three parts: One part, called Something Else, contains 24 lessons for grades 4 through 6. Another part, called Right On, contains eight lessons for grades 7 through 9. A third section of this program is called The Red Sea Place in My Life for grade 11. Less than 50% of the material actually deals with drug education. The rest of the lessons are group therapy, self-analysis, psychotherapy, and Values Clarification.

Many activities are beyond the responsibility and expertise of a classroom teacher. Children are subjected to sophisticated psychotherapeutic techniques without the necessary safeguards, without parental knowledge or permission, and without their own consent. Role-playing, sensitivity training, peer pressure, handwriting analysis, and TM-type relaxation are included in this curriculum.

The following are some of the objections voiced by parents citing specific examples from the programs:

1. The privacy of student and parent is seriously invaded in the activities of the program Something Else. It asks the student to list his secret fears. He is then threatened with having them read to the class. The student must choose a positive position on a sensitive issue, such as abortion, anger, friendship, etc., and publicly affirm it, *or* complete open-ended sentences, such as "I am sad when _____," "I am good when _____," or "I am bad when _____." In the lesson called Right On, students are asked to write a plan for self improvement.

2. Many activities break down the natural bonding of the child to family, fostering mistrust and alienation. On page 5 of the Elementary Teacher's Guide to Something Else, the teacher is to "create feelings of love and belonging within the group." On page 17 the teacher is to build an "esprit de corps" within the group. In lesson 5 of Right On we read that "one of the top goals of this activity is to provide students with a no-drugs message that their peer group has approved."

3. Activities in Right On and the Red Sea Place

ask the child to disregard legal, moral or familial standards and choose for himself the values he will hold and publicly affirm. "Be nonjudgmental. There are no right or wrong answers since each person is expressing an opinion about the topic. The teacher must not indicate that he agrees or disagrees with what a student contributes." This quotation is from page 5 of the "Successful Class Meeting," a supplemental pamphlet.

On value strategy sheets, page 50 of Right On, students are to rank from bad to worse six negative incidents. This causes the child to rationalize that some things like cheating on a test are not so bad because other things, like deliberately running over a dog with a bike, are so much worse.

On page 66 in lesson 7 of Right On, good things are defined as "good according to the way you feel or the way they make you feel." None of these exercises upholds the community norm of morality or the authority of the law.

4. Particularly offensive is the activity called "voting on values" in which the 6th grade child questions the authority of home-taught and/or religious values. "Come back to some of the old statements, values, at a later time to give people, students, a chance to change their minds and indicate so publicly." These are the instructions for activity 16 of Something Else. Values up for discussion and voting include sexual behavior, cheating, lying, friendship, obeying school rules, and anger.

TESTIMONY OF CHARLOTTE COONEY 357

TESTIMONY OF_____
Charlotte Cooney
_____

I am a mother of six from Jacksonville with six and a half grandchildren. My subject today is parenting education as included in the federally-funded programs. What is parenting education and why should anyone object to such a nice sounding course of study? Well, I'll tell you.

Almost all parenting classes are structured after Dr. Thomas Gordon's program set out in his book *Parent Effectiveness Training*. All you need do is just read this book of instructions, as I have, to realize parenting courses are not all that they are cracked up to be and that the philosophy involved takes discipline completely out of the home, replacing discipline with permissiveness.

For instance, Dr. Gordon's method of teaching recommends a "no-lose problem solving" in which children and parents sit down and arrive at solutions acceptable to both—the old game of the parent giving his rules, the child giving his demands, and the parent compromising. This is called a "no fail" solution.

Dr. Gordon claims "it is paradoxical but true that parents lose influence by using power and will have more influence on their children by giving up their power or refusing to use it." In other words, you, the parent, have no rights. He continually uses the word "power" to describe the parent's desire to influence or guide the child. That is an ugly word and he knows it.

Here is another example of how bad this training

is. On page 9 of Dr. Gordon's book, the child says to his dad, "You're a dirty, smelly stinkbug." The father responds "You're really angry at me." This is really in the book!

· I could cite many examples that downgrade parents and teachers and encourage the parent to let the child do his thing, however and whenever he wishes.

Dr. Gordon's training is humanistic, revolutionary, detrimental to the child's best interest by telling parents they do not have to be consistent or pretend to feel loving toward a child, or feel love and acceptance toward all your children. He advises against setting limits or moralizing, he promotes role-playing, he disapproves of guidance by parents, he encourages disrespect for parents, he compares humans and animals repeatedly, he encourages lying, and downgrades parental authority, he promotes world government, he advises a family split-up in certain cases, he advocates modifying behavior of parents or else having the children fire you, he pushes children's rights (intimates you have no right to your children), and he promotes sensitivity training and downgrades schools.

Between Parent and Child is another parenting book. It tells you how to talk "childrenese." George Will in an article wondered, "Did Tom and Nancy Lincoln talk childrenese to little Abe? Did they read, *How to Raise a Brighter Child*?"

A project called Education for Parenthood has been launched by the Office of Education, Office of Child Development, and the National Institute of Mental Health. The project includes "development and curriculum for secondary school students called Exploring Childhood." In this program high school and junior high school students work with young children while learning about human development and their own identity. Does this sound as though this course would teach students to be good parents or how to find themselves?

Exploring Childhood also pushes for child development and kibbutzes, the day-care centers in Israel where the government used to raise your children for you on a 24-hour basis and allow you only occasional, brief visits.

A class in parenting skills was given in a community school in Duval County to help us teach our children about sex. Our children could probably teach us a thing or two, but we were curious. In class we were requested to fill in different words for sex-related terms such as masturbation, sexual relations, homosexuality, female and male sex parts. At the top of the list was 69.

Each participant was asked to read the lists and the related terms added on by the class members. The primary purpose of this deal was to desensitize parents into using four-letter words with their children.

We were privileged to view Sol Gordon's movie "About Sex," which included a glimpse of a couple having at it in bed, babies fondling themselves, homosexuals, and so forth. The verbal advice accompanying the viewing stressed that masturbation was normal, not harmful, and that parents should "butt out." Abortions were also encouraged and the film told how simple the operation is and how painless.

Sol Gordon's "Ten Heavy Facts About Sex" was recommended in literature distributed. This comic book was banned from the New York State Fair in 1972 after Judge Gabrelli pronounced, "This so-called comic book encourages children to engage in homosexual experiences, is pornographic, and shows that nothing is really wrong with oral and anal sex." Associate Justice Main agreed, adding, "It suggests sodomy is acceptable and it condones and encourages homosexuality and bisexuality."

We do not need any "parenting education" classes in our schools.

TESTIMONY OF _____
Frankie Anderson

Since Values Clarification is a part of a larger humanistic movement, let's examine what the humanist educators say about why we send our children to school. John J. Dunphy, writing in a 1983 issue of the *Humanist* magazine, proclaims:

"I am convinced that the battle for humankind's future must be waged and won in the public school classroom by teachers who correctly perceive their roles as the proselytizers of a new faith: a religion of humanity that recognizes and respects the spark of what theologians call divinity in every human being. These teachers must embody the same selfless dedication as the most rabid fundamentalist preachers, for they will be ministers of another sort, utilizing a classroom instead of a pulpit to convey humanist values in whatever subject they teach, regardless of the educational level — preschool, day care, or large state university.

"The classroom must and will become an arena of conflict between the old and the new — the rotting corpse of Christianity, together with all its adjacent evils and misery, and the new faith of Humanism, resplendent in its promise of a world in which the never-realized Christian ideal of love thy neighbor will finally be achieved."

Paul Blanchard in his article entitled "Three Cheers for Our Secular State," writes:

"I think the most important factor for moving us toward a secular society has been the educational factor. Our schools may not teach Johnny to read properly, but the fact that Johnny is in school until he is 16 tends to lead toward the elimination of religious superstition. The average high school child acquires a high school education, and this militates against Adam and Eve and all other myths of alleged history.

"When I was one of the editors of *The Nation* in the twenties, I wrote an editorial explaining that golf and intelligence were the two primary reasons that men did not attend church. Perhaps today I would say golf and a high school diploma."

G. Richard Bozarth says in *The American Atheist:*

"And how does a God die? Quite simply because all his religionists have been converted to another religion and there is no one left to make the children believe they need Him. We need only insure that our schools teach only secular knowledge. If we could achieve this, God would be dead and shortly due for a funeral service."

TESTIMONY OF

Sandra McDade

I am a resident of the state of Louisiana. I have four school-age children and one preschool child.

I began studying the problems addressed by the Hatch Amendment in 1972 before the Hatch Amendment was constructed and passed. I became very disturbed at the personal value exercises and just plain prying that goes on in the public school classroom. I was even more distressed when I learned that the reasons for the values exercises were to change the attitudes and values of my children. The manual for the Values Clarification approach to teaching in the classroom is, of course, *Values Clarification* by Sidney Simon. The purpose of the book is to change the values of students in certain areas such as politics, religion, work, school, love, sex, family and money—basically all those things that I once was told parents were supposed to handle. I find that the Values Clarification approach is "to help young people brought up by moralizing adults to be prepared to make their own responsible decisions."

These illegal teaching methods are brought into the classroom basically in three ways: (1) textbooks (incorporated in almost every grade level in every subject), (2) outside sources, and (3) counseling.

For several years now I have been reviewing textbooks and looking at them before they were adopted. I have found that, almost without exception, all of the books incorporate questions and activities that are in violation of the Hatch Amendment. Since my time is limited I will quote only from one book. This book was adopted for use in one of the high schools just this last week. The book is *Exploring Career Decision Making* by McKnight Publishing Company, copyright 1978.

I would like to read from the credit page of the book just to let you know who produced the book. "The development of this project was paid for by the Education and Work group of the National Institute of Education, Department of Health Education and Welfare." Therefore, this is a federally-developed book. Now I would like to quote just a few of the things the book does. Only about one chapter is on careers; the rest of the book is on changing values. For example, on page 8, "Do you want the same things that other members of your family want? Are you any different from the other members of your family? Do you want the same things you wanted a year ago?"

Or look at page 68: "Another way to look at

yourself is to examine your boundaries. What do you think is important? Read the following questions and show your answers in the following manner. If you agree, raise your hand. Disagree, thumbs down. Don't know, fold your arms.

"A. Do you think children should have to work for their allowance?

B. Do you think students are losing respect for their teachers?

C. Do you think familiarity breeds contempt?

D. Do you think money should be spent on aerospace projects?

E. Do you think men should stay home and be husbands and fathers?

F. Do you think women should stay home and be wives and mothers?

G. Do you think most students feel free to talk about anything with their parents?

H. Do you think young people should limit the size of their families to two?

I. Do you think there are times when cheating is alright?

J. Don't you think most people cheat sometimes?

K. Do you think most adults understand young people today?

L. Do you think most adults ever understood young people?

M. Do you think there should be a law assuring the minimum wage income?"

I could go on and on. These basically deal with controversial issues. They are stated in a one-sided manner.

Next, I would like to talk about outside sources. Two sources I personally encountered are a series of Values Clarification kits offered to the community by the J. C. Penney Company and one by the Gannett News Service. The J. C. Penney kit could not be taken out of the Shreveport area; therefore, I could not bring it. However, it is a series of open-ended questions, just like the ones I have just read to you. It calls for various exercises that violate the Hatch Amendment if it is used in the classroom. It is used in several schools in our area.

Now, the bad thing about this is that it bypasses both the School Board and any state authority. It is designed for the teacher to pick it up and carry it straight to the classroom. The Gannett News Service materials are basically the same. They are designed for the teacher to order. You will find them advertised in the paper. Some of their questions are interesting:

"Dead-end Exercise: Find and write an obituary that you think would fit you."

"All in the Family: Find the TV family that is most like yours."

"Games of Life: Pick out the team on the sports page that is most like your life and tell why."

"What's in the stars? Read your horoscope for the day. Tell what is true for you and why. Write your wish horoscope for tomorrow."

I highly resent this last question.

Now I have a personal experience to relate for you. It shows how, even though the school system requires a written permission slip to subject the child to counseling, this was bypassed in the interest of intimidation.

In 1976 I was a candidate for the Irving Independent School Board in Irving, Texas. I lost the race to the president of the School Board who had been president for 20 years. What followed was the final blow that caused my husband and me to begin looking for suitable education for our children.

Our oldest child, who was in the 3rd grade at the time, came home a few weeks after the election and told us that she had been sent to the counselor and asked questions like this:

"Do you like your parents? Would you rather live some place else? Do your parents spank you? Do you think that is child abuse?"

This child had been adopted by our family three years earlier, so you can imagine the traumatic feelings that she had. She got the impression that we had initiated these questions to her so that she might then be moved to another home.

Naturally we were puzzled. We thought that there must be some mistake. We went to the school, and her 3rd grade teacher told us that, indeed, our daughter had been taken out of the class, but only for the purpose of speech therapy, she thought.

We knew that, in order for her to be sent to speech therapy, a parent's consent was required. We went to the office and asked to see the form. It could not be produced.

Then we went to the speech therapist. We asked the speech therapist how our daughter was doing. She had never heard of our daughter. She said, "I don't know her. I have never had her in speech therapy."

To make a long story short, we were finally able to come up with the fact that she had, indeed, been sent to a counseling session. Nothing was on the books, and nothing was in the files about her counseling session. But I talked to two teachers who admitted that a very common use of the counseling sessions was to intimidate parents who asked questions.

TESTIMONY OF

Doris D'Antoni

For many years I have been active in PTA, having served on both the local and county council of PTA's. Polk County had a federally-funded curriculum in a school in our area which was experimental in nature. The newspapers were full of controversy with hundreds of parents complaining to the School Board. The federally-funded curriculum was vulgar, designed only for political and moral corruption. These programs were also brought to the attention of our county council of PTA's.

As a result of federal funding, we had sensitivity training which is a systematic assault on authority.

The teachers' manual, "Issues in Human Relations Training," page 47, refers to this method as coercive thought-reform or brainwashing. The president of our County Council of PTAs observed this technique and brought a committee of concerned citizens together with the superintendent of public schools in order to voice their concerns over the psychological manipulation of children. Children were taught to challenge the authority of the home.

My own children and grandchildren have been exposed to death education in the public schools, a clear violation of their religious rights. This depressing subject is not suitable to dump on a child. In one program in our county, little first graders made their own coffins out of shoeboxes.

Federally-funded sex education programs have introduced our children to sexually stimulating, perverse and promiscuous programs. Sol Gordon has trained both parents and teachers through use of our tax dollars. I resent the vulgarity of this man training our children to use four letter words. He was paid for the corruption of our children! I enclose a copy of a sex education comic book, used in our state, which promoted masturbation, homosexuality, oral and anal sex.

In another program in our county, the Federal Government funded an "engineered classroom" approach. The public school and the mental health clinic signed a contract to work together on children who did not perform in various areas to the school's satisfaction.

Our schools have been completely changed

through the influence of federal funding. The training received by college teachers is more manipulative psychology than educational and academic preparation. Much of this direction has come from the Federal Government in such programs as the Florida State University program which redirects the whole approach to education, including the use of a systems approach to teaching. Programs throughout our state have set up regional centers which restructure in-service training for teachers, curriculum and the methods used.

Graded concepts have been phased out through federal-funding and replaced with three-ring circuses called individualized education, complete with team teaching, middle schools, and a host of other strategies designed to destroy traditional education and replace it with useless experimentation which is expensive, but in the long run produces uneducated illiterates. It takes great skill to take so much money and eager people, and direct them in such a way as to spend money, time and energy in nonproductive and damaging programs. Russia could not have planned a better strategy for the bleeding and ultimate internal destruction of our nation than what has been accomplished in our public schools. That is basically what the Federal Government itself admitted, when it stated in the 1983 report, "A Nation At Risk" that, if a foreign power had done to our public schools what has been done, it would have been considered an act of war.

A thorough evaluation of federal funding, through the Pacesetters in Innovation Program,

ESEA funding catalogs, the Florida State University program, and others will show that the Federal Government systematically decided to restructure our education. Academic scores have dropped in direct relation to the increase in federal funds. This is no mistake. The program is a political one and the abuses are absolutely clear. The Department of Education has clearly shown not only that it does not desire to enforce the Hatch Amendment, but that it has been its biggest violator.

TESTIMONY OF_____
Gail T. Bjork

I am the mother of two girls, ages 11 and 14, who attend Palm Beach County Public schools. I am an art educator and, though not presently teaching, I have taught and substituted in public schools in New Jersey and Florida. I have been an active volunteer during the years my children have attended school. Presently, I am a freelance writer and photographer.

I was a spokeswoman for the Coalition of Religious Integrity which stopped the federally-funded teaching of Transcendental Meditation in public schools in the mid 1970s. In this $100,000 lawsuit, the courts upheld what parents and the courts had initially told school bureaucrats. This teaching was forbidden in Civil Action #76-341 because the courts determined that the schools "sought to effect a secular goal by the propagation of a religious concept." At present, I am spokeswoman for People for Academic and Responsible Education, a group representing hundreds of parents and teachers in the Palm Beach area who are opposed to the insidious use of controversial teaching methods on our minors who attend public school under compulsory law.

When my daughter was 12 years old, she was given a questionnaire by her 7th grade Health teacher without my knowledge or consent. She was asked many personal questions including being required to give her views about life after death. She was asked: "What reasons would motivate you to commit suicide?" Five reasons were listed from which she was expected to choose.

She was given a list of ten ways of dying, including violent death, and asked to list them in order of "most to least preferred." She was asked what should be done to her if she was terminally ill. Two of the five choices offered her by the framers of this questionnaire were mercy killing.

You cannot convince me of any positive benefits of this approach to controversial subjects thrust upon unsuspecting minors. The manner in which these questions were presented to my child was not only an invasion of privacy, but violated the deepest moral and ethical teachings of our home. The ways we would teach our children to deal with terminal illness were completely left out of the choices presented to my daughter. The authors built *their* values into the answers, but conveniently left *our* values out. School authorities have defended this type of questioning to us by saying that the method "teaches children how to think." A truly objective review of these types of material will show that the authors do not help children to think; what they in fact do is to tell children *what* to think. This is indoctrination and manipulation of young minds of the most hideous sort.

Hundreds of thousands of youngsters across this nation are being coerced into discussing matters of private morality and family life each day in the classroom through manipulative methods such as Values Clarification. No doubt the teachers' motives are sincere, but motives, or a teacher's good intentions, are irrelevant to this issue.

In Palm Beach County, Values Clarification and similar affective education techniques are continually being promoted in the classroom through textbooks and curricula in both required and elective courses, and through continual teacher training workshops held throughout the school year.

Our officials effectively beat around the bush when asked by parents if these programs are federally-funded. No doubt they have the Hatch Amendment in the backs of their minds when offering their incomplete response. What we have been able to find out in our county is that most of these programs began with the use of federal funds. Officials will not say if federal monies continue to subsidize affective education.

Values Clarification and similar techniques have been criticized by responsible educators in such professional journals as *The Phi Delta Kappa, Educational Forum, The Journal of Moral Education,* and *Principal* magazine. The Fall issue of the American Federation of Teachers magazine, *American Educator,* states:

> "Values education is a distorted version of Horace Mann's advice to keep controversy out of the school. Operating on the mistaken assumption that there are few shared values that can be taught without indoctrinating, such courses imply that all values are relative and subjective. It is not surprising that courses in Values Clarification and morals education have been criticized by reputable educators and philosophers."

Dr. Richard Baer, Jr., professor of ethics at Cornell University, is one of the nation's leading experts on the Values Clarification/Affective Education controversy, and he has painstakingly compiled the criticisms of scholars concerning these techniques. In the April 4, 1982 issue of *The Wall Street Journal* he writes, "Values clarification indoctrinates students in ethical relativism," in an ethical religious philosophy which teaches that there is no right or wrong regarding moral issues except what seems right to an individual in any given situation.

Continuing, Dr. Baer writes, "The use of Values Clarification in the public schools constitutes a direct violation of the First Amendment protection against the establishment of religion" and "a substantial proportion of content and methods of Values Clarification constitutes a threat to the privacy rights of students and their families."

My daughter's Gifted Program, which is partially federally-funded, contains much Values Clarification. One principal reviewing some of the contents responded by saying it was "sick." At the time I signed my daughter into this program when she was in the 7th grade, I had no idea whatsoever that these types of methods were part of the program. I wonder how many other parents have ignorantly done the same as I.

Let me close my testimony by quoting from an article which appeared in the October 1982 *American Bar Association Magazine* entitled "Update on Law Education." The article, "A Conspiracy Against the Inner Life," examines the affective education/morals education controversy. In it, a Rumford, Maine, junior high school principal named Robert Doiron said, "A student's attitudes and values are his. They should not be compromised or changed via a school setting."

Why should normal, emotionally sound young-sters be subjected to Values Clarification? What is wrong with his present values? Who says they need to be changed? To what? Why should these techniques, which were designed primarily for mental patients, be foisted on helpless, captive children in the classroom? Who are the experts decreeing that *all* children be exposed to such techniques? For what reason? Why should such intervention in the pupil's life be a legitimate interest of the school?

TESTIMONY OF_____

Jacquelyn Thaden

As a former home economics teacher in the public schools, I am deeply concerned about the changes taking place in today's classrooms. A few years ago I taught Values Clarification. I thought it was a great opportunity to teach children about values from a moral standpoint. I didn't stop to think that, if someone else taught my children from a humanist viewpoint, their values would be completely different from mine.

Humanism teaches that sometimes lying and stealing are acceptable. For example, many state-adopted textbooks in Florida promote Kohlberg's moral reasoning. This process presents situation ethics, telling the student that he or she has reached the highest stage of moral reasoning if he or she will break the law for a good reason.

A value system alien from traditional values is infiltrating many of the behavioral science textbooks. Children 12 to 14 have to make moral decisions regarding death, suicide, mercy killing, alternate lifestyles, sex, homosexuality, incest, rape, and other controversial and personal issues. Children at this age are very vulnerable and depend so much on what other people think. What right does anyone have to interfere with the establishment of these family values? Families are the heart of America and to interfere with these values is like setting off a time bomb that will destroy America.

Kohlberg's moral reasoning breaks down the value system (which parents have spent years developing) by getting children to question their own traditional values and telling them they are more mature if they develop their own value system.

One example of interfering with family values is a process called Magic Circle. Students are asked to sit in a circle and discuss their feelings. Its purpose is supposed to develop the "whole child." I thought doing things like this was such a good experience when I was teaching. But I didn't stop to realize that some of these programs are motivated by a godless philosophy which conflicts with that of many Americans and the purpose for which this country was founded.

The Magic Circle is often used as a dangerous tool designed to break down value systems. Students are encouraged to discuss their personal feelings. They are often provoked into sharing more about themselves, their problems and their families, and they are made to feel uncomfortable. If that happens to us, it makes us feel embarrassed. However, youngsters of this age are stripped of their defenses when this happens because they have not fully developed their value systems, and they depend so much on what other people think. To have the values that parents have spent years developing attacked, and then openly stripped away, is one of the greatest violations of our personal freedoms.

The supplementary idea guide for Magic Circle says, "The basic atmosphere of each circle should be one of acceptance. Moralizing has a judgmental quality." For a teacher to sit there and listen to a child tell about something he has done wrong, for example, stealing, and not place a value judgment on it (for the sake of "accepting" the child) is like saying that the teacher approves of the behavior. It is innate in a child to believe that, if the parent does *not* disapprove of certain behavior, then that form of behavior *is* acceptable to his parents.

It is one thing for a teacher to make a student feel acceptable, but accepting a non-moral form of behavior is a totally different ball game. Doing this in front of his peers reinforces the desensitizing of moral standards. Any teacher who participates in this program is messing with something very delicate called the child's conscience, and that is very wrong.

Magic Circle is a form of sensitivity training that is supported by our tax dollars. It does not belong in the public school system. I think we must ask ourselves, is the purpose of education to teach children about values? Absolutely not. We need to get back to the basics and remove from the public schools these dangerous extracurricular activities that destroy what America is all about.

*TESTIMONY OF*_____
Nelda S. Reis

I am from Mulberry, Florida and I am entitling my remarks "The Death of a Teacher." I taught school in Georgia and California for eight years from the early '60s to the early '70s. I witnessed at first hand the deterioration of our public school system which I now prefer to refer to as the state school system.

When I began my teaching career in 1962, I was an idealist, thinking that I could have a positive influence on the lives of young people and be in a situation mutually beneficial to both student and teacher. I felt that my reward would be the satisfaction of a job well done, and the students' reward would be the receiving of good instruction from a caring teacher.

In 1962 some of God's principles remained in the schools. One of them was that the teacher was the authority figure in his or her classroom and the parents were the authority figures in their homes.

I was most aware of the down-spiral trend as the years went by and the philosophies of John Dewey and B. F. Skinner and others were perpetrated upon the classroom and we became what was called "progressive." It was really regressive. Students were taught to make their own decisions based on their own value systems, disregarding the "old fashioned" ideas of their parents and their early training. They were taught, "if it feels good, do it," "a thing is wrong only if it hurts another person," and "everything is beautiful." These teachings set up confusion, doubt, and frustration in the students which festered into rebellion.

I became a casualty of the state school system in 1971 because of the gap between the idealistic state rhetoric being expounded by the educational leadership ("let the children decide what they want to learn" and "give the children a free environment") and the stark reality of abject chaos in the open-pod, individualized-instruction farce of a middle school.

My goals could not be realized. I could not impart knowledge because no one could hear. I was helpless to enforce discipline and build rapport because I had no control of the three pods literally on top of my own class.

At that time in my life, I was not a Christian and did not have the knowledge or the power to be an overcomer. So, I confess to you, I buckled under the pressure of chaos.

Why, you ask, would such a conscientious teacher, who is now a Christian with the power to overcome and withstand such pressures, *not* go back to the classroom? As a committed Christian I would have to violate my conscience to teach the prescribed curriculum in today's schools. My spirit and my conscience are incensed by the manipulative and occultic base of much of the content. I know there are thousands of bright, conscientious would-be teachers who are in the same position. The sad result of our dropping out is the opening we leave for liberal, new-thought, new-age teachers who identify and promote the tearing down of traditional values and their replacement with a utopian-tranformation value system.

In closing, may I relate a practical problem I encountered this week to crystalize the point of my remarks. I bought a new scale, digital and expensive, because I started at Weight Watchers and needed to know my true weight. It weighed three to four-and-one-half pounds heavier than the scale at Weight Watchers. My old cheap scale, on the other hand, weighed three to four pounds lighter than the Weight Watchers' scale. I had a dilemma—which scale was true, if any?

The behavorial-scientific, situation ethics approach might be to invite over three friends and ask each of them to represent one of the scales in question. Each one would give me the pros and cons of each scale, and then I could decide, based on the information and what I "felt," *which* scale told the truth. Am I likely to know how much I weigh? Even the most liberal of you would have to say no. What is my problem then? It is that I would have no standard by which to measure—no reference point. I would be left in confusion, doubt and frustration.

To have true weight or values, we must have a standard, a reference point, by which to measure.

TESTIMONY OF————————————
Diane Williams
————————————————

I am a wife, mother and homemaker. My husband and I have five children, two of whom attend public school in Sarasota, Charlotte County, Florida. I am not here to discuss issues so much as I am here to represent the young man whose picture is in front of you. He would have liked to come here today, but due to the Florida State Compulsory Attendance Law, he was unable to attend.

Our oldest son, Roy, is an honor student at Lem Bay Junior High School. He was chosen student of the month and citizen of the month, both for the school year 1983 and in the present school year. He is in the 8th grade. My husband and I have taken much love and care in teaching our children values based upon our convictions.

Roy enrolled in Home Ec class in the first semester of this school year because I thought it would be a good idea for him to know something about food nutrients, and knowing how to fry an egg couldn't hurt either.

Shortly after classes had begun, I was kidding with Roy one day in the kitchen about the way he was operating a can opener and other kitchen utensils. I asked him how he was doing in Home Ec class. He described something that was going on in the classroom that had absolutely nothing to do with cooking or nutrition.

He told me that the students in the class had

been asked to act out a family situation which resulted in teaching my son how to go about getting us to comply with his demands instead of continuing obedience and respect to us as his parents, as had been his practice.

I was very concerned and I asked to see the book which the teacher was using to teach these values which were in direct opposition to our and Roy's convictions. We requested verbally and in writing that Roy be removed from this class because his values were being threatened and other rights of privacy were being violated. The guidance counselor refused our request. He said that there was nowhere to put him because the classes were overcrowded. I insisted once again that he be removed from this class. I am sorry to have to report to you today that he did have to finish the semester in Home Ec class. Because we were unaware of any Pupil Rights Law, he was not allowed a change of class.

Soon after that, we began inquiring about Roy's other classroom activities. We found that our son was experiencing similar mind-changing techniques in most of his other classes. We found that his personal convictions and values were challenged over and over again.

I visited the school principal, but his only response was to assign Roy to a "media center." I had seen the media center and I knew that it was a nonconstructive place for my son, so I suggested that maybe he could use library time until we could resolve this problem.

While in science class, Roy's teacher was instructing students about the technological development of man. He was told that it took many, many years for man to develop skills such as the wheel, tools, and the use of fire.

Roy opposed this idea based on the Biblical account of Cain and Abel, who were second-generation efficient farmers and herdsmen and used fire for their altar sacrifice to God. His teacher cut him short and detained him after class; she told him she did not want him to remain ignorant.

We have raised our children to respect authority, so he did not respond any further to his teacher, but I know how damaging this was to Roy.

I know now that this was in violation of the Hatch Amendment. I believe Roy could have been spared some of the embarrassment, harassment and trauma brought on by Values Clarification and other mind-changing techniques, had we been aware of this law.

Excerpts from

Official Transcript of Proceedings

BEFORE THE

U.S. DEPARTMENT OF EDUCATION

In the Matter of:

PROPOSED REGULATIONS TO IMPLEMENT
THE PROTECTION OF PUPIL RIGHTS AMENDMENT
SECTION 439 OF THE GEPA
ALSO KNOWN AS THE HATCH AMENDMENT

DATE: MARCH 27, 1984

PLACE: WASHINGTON, D.C.

Malcolm Lawrence

I live in Chevy Chase, Maryland. I appear here today on behalf of the Maryland Coalition of Concerned Parents on Privacy Rights in Public Schools.

The Coalition has long been disturbed by the problems related to psychological probings, non-academic testing and invasions of privacy of students and their homes on the part of the school system in the State of Maryland.

Concern over the privacy issue in Maryland led to a joint resolution in the State Legislature in 1977, which stated:

> "In the public schools, personal information is often solicited from students in the presence of other students. Children, especially younger children, may be unaware of the negative consequences of extensive self-disclosure. Additionally, school personnel have significant power to affect the lives of students and their families.

> "Resolved, by the General Assembly of Maryland, that the State Board of Education is requested to study the various roles of the public schools in protecting the rights of students."

Yet, to this day, no action has been taken at the state level to properly address this problem in Maryland. Snooping into private matters is still business as usual in Montgomery County and elsewhere in the state. I cite two recent examples.

I attach a February 8, 1984, article from the *Damascus Courier-Gazette* describing parental displeasure over a high school questionnaire on religious practices given to 950 students. The survey was part of the Middle States Evaluation Program that plans to send a team to the school this coming October to dig deeply into the "total community picture."

A February 21, 1984, enclosure from the *Washington Post* tells of a pilot program in Montgomery County, employing the use of personal journals from kindergarten to junior high school. The principal of an elementary school is quoted as saying, "It's a wonderful way of bridging the gap between home and school because teachers really learn about the children's lives."

She also stated, "One of the problems is the parents who sabotage us. They are still doing what was done to them. They are still correcting the children's work, saying 'it's no good,' which means that the kids will never show them anything again." How is that as an example of anti-parent propaganda?

Our contacts in other states confirm that instructional materials and practices used in classrooms openly use psychological manipulation and invasion of student privacy. Permit me to name just a few of the techniques: non-academic personality tests, questionnaires on personal life and views, family, autobiography assignments pertaining to personalized moral and legal dilemmas, log books used as supplements in language arts and social studies, diaries, journals, compulsory K through 12 life science curricula, sociograms, group contact sessions and talk-ins, strategies specifically designed for self-disclosure such as the Zig-Zag technique, contrived incidents for self-revelation, blindfold walks, isolation techniques, role-playing, psychodrama, sociodrama, Values Clarification strategies, and life-death survival games.

These techniques draw information from the students and permit the manipulation of their attitudes and personality development. Many of the techniques are based on federally-funded programs, and it is of little consequence to the classroom teachers whether a particular curriculum is federally-financed or not. The point is they are being used and the children are at risk in the classroom.

The infusion of these curricula and techniques into the school system has occurred over the past two decades as a result of a major shift in emphasis on the part of curriculum developers and educators from cognitive academic learning to the psychological development and social adjustment of the child in the affective domain, that is, his feelings, attitudes and opinions.

The shift was a reflection of the national, lucrative wave of pop psychology. The objective of the educators became one of re-socialization, at the expense of scholarly academic achievement. This is why our nation has failed to do a proper job of educating our youth who are, after all, the real victims in this tragic development.

There are only so many hours in a school day and the educators have, in effect, squeezed essential basic learning skills and sciences out of the school door to make room for personality development and attitudinal adjustments on social issues.

TESTIMONY OF——————————————————

Charlotte Iserbyt

I am a free-lance writer on education and politics and most recently served as a special assistant in the Office of Educational Research and Improvement, U.S. Department of Education, which oversees the operations of the National Institute of Education, the National Diffusion Network and the National Center for Educational Statistics.

Citizen testimony has revealed the expenditure of billions of dollars to deliberately bring about the handicapping of a generation or more of future voters through federally-funded drug, sex, death and immoral values education courses (which, of course, encourage drugs, sex and suicide), treasonous global education courses (which alienate our children from their roots and prepare them to accept a planned, controlled global society), and programs in law-related education (which produce adolescent versions of the Legal Services Corporation's lawyer activists in our communities).

For anyone who questions the subversion of our schools, shocking evidence is found in Pacesetters in Innovation, Behavior Science Teacher Education Program, and Professor Havelock's Innovations in Education, all of which were federally-funded.

Pacesetters says, "Forces which block the adoption of new ideas will be identified and ways to overcome these forces will be explored." "Teachers who are seemingly impervious to change will be sought out and trained on an individual basis." "A program of professional reorientation was used where teachers and administrators have been hesitant to adopt education innovation." "Parents should understand that they are not free from this restructuring, and are also given psychotherapy, as well as the students."

I took Ronald Havelock's course, which instructed me how to sneak in all the mind-bending techniques and humanistic courses and methods, without getting caught, and how to identify the resisters in my community of Camden, Maine. Of course, I was a resister.

Last but not least, in the destruction of traditional education, one finds the National Diffusion Network, which is the federally-funded transmission belt for psycho-social-political programs, at least half of which use methods of pre- and post-testing for attitudinal change, methods which clearly are in violation of the Protection of Pupil Rights Amendment.

One National Diffusion Network program, Positive Attitude Toward Learning, instructs teachers in the use of Jacob Moreno's psychodrama and states,

> "Worthy of a special category is role-playing, or sociodrama, or dramatic improvisation, as it is variously called. The delight most students take in play acting makes this an important value-eliciting strategy. Any kind of potential or real conflict situation is useful for role-playing, or any situation in which real feelings are often concealed. Consider situations in school, in the family, on the playground, at work, or in politics or government."

Role-playing is used in most of the National Diffusion Network psycho-social-political programs.

The verdict is in. The U.S. Department of Education is guilty of destruction of academic learning, morality, love of country, and respect for and love of family.

An immediate investigation of the federal role in education is imperative, at which our representatives could be informed that the head of the Nebraska Board of Education told the principal of the Faith Christian Academy in Nebraska that "Fundamentalist parents have no right to indoctrinate their children in their beliefs," saying "We are preparing them for the year 2000 and life in a global, one-world society."

If our elected officials, who are sworn to uphold the United States Constitution, agree with that shocking statement, we Americans should be told this on the Today Show.

*TESTIMONY OF*_____
Cindi Weatherly

I'm from Watkinsville, Georgia.

In 1978 Senator Sam Hayakawa of California stated before the U.S. Senate that he felt that attitudinal testing and teaching was:

> "the result of a flourishing heresy, a heresy that rejects the idea of education as the acquisition of knowledge and skills. Instead, the heresy regards the fundamental task of education as therapy. . . . To inquire into the sexual attitudes and beliefs of eight-year-olds, to probe into their psychic and emotional problems, real or imagined, rather than into the level of their intellectual achievements—these are serious invasions of privacy, and messing around with the psyches of young people does not stop with testing and inquiries. There are exercises in psychodrama, role-playing, touch therapy, encounter groups and other psychological games that have no academic significance whatsoever."

Things haven't changed since 1978, except for one little thing. The heresy now classifies and condones these activities as the acquisition of life-role skills. With the advent of Competency Based Education (CBE), the student became fragmented into five life-role functions: (1) the learner, (2) the individual, (3) the producer, (4) the consumer, and (5) the citizen.

This meant that there would be teaching, evaluation, testing and assessment of the student's progress toward the goals set in each of these categories. Thus, the Protection of Pupil Rights Amendment has been circumvented and ignored because each state has adopted these CBE goals as graduation requirements, and how can it be determined if a child has achieved his or her performance objectives as an individual without attitudinal and psychological testing?

Programs recommended by the National Diffusion Network (under NIE originally) have facilitated most of the curriculum changes that have been required by Competency Based Education and other educational innovations.

The National Center for Educational Statistics maintains a series of handbooks entitled State Educational Records and Reports Series, which outlines and categorizes every minute detail of information that can be acquired about a child, teacher, administrator, bus driver, parent and neighborhood, and includes detailed categories for educational research information.

Each local school system in the country is being asked to adopt the prescribed accounting procedures, sometimes at great cost to the states and localities, all for the sake of a unified accounting system. This process is based on the Planning, Programming, Budgeting System, which involves mandated goals and constant readjustment of resources to ensure that the goals are met.

If our financial resource reporting is going to be

unified by such a system, then are we not but a step away from unified goals for our educational outcomes? This is a step toward a mandated national curriculum and interstate and interregional tax and financial management revisions.

In 1982 Dr. Benjamin Bloom published a book entitled *All Our Children Learning,* wherein he stated, "The purpose of education and the schools is to change the thoughts, feelings and actions of students." This focus certainly correlates with NCES's definition of affective objectives: "Those statements specifying the acquisition of particular attitudes, values or feelings."

This attitude toward what is important in today's educational process is borne out in an ESEA Title II program called Thinkabout. This is a National Diffusion Network recommended program consisting of a multi-media approach to teach life-role skills or life-process skills.

Page 34 of Georgia's grant proposal for Thinkabout funds graphically depicts the Bloom taxonomy approach. It shows that, for the 13-year school experience, there will be a constant emphasis on health and physical education which will consume approximately 15 percent of each school day. Emphasis on basic 3R skills training will decline from 85% at age five, to finally 20% of each school day by age 18. By age ten (4th grade), the time spent on the basic 3R's will be less than 45% of the school day. A growing emphasis on life-process skills, beginning at 7% at age five, will rise to approximately 95% of the school day by age 18.

Life-process skills are defined as critical thinking, problem solving and decision making. Thinkabout is a multi-media program that includes a video component designed to introduce social and moral dilemmas for open-ended visual presentations.

The dilemmas deal with subjects including peer pressure to lie, choosing friends, making moral decisions, and conflicts with parents and others in authority. There are pre- and post-tests available with these units. The psychological counseling technique of Values Clarification, and use of Lawrence Kohlberg's stages of moral reasoning (which is also a Values Clarification process), are two privacy-violating strategies fundamental to Thinkabout.

In 1982 the Department of Education's initiative, entitled "Basic Education Skills Through Technology," or Project BEST, was launched as one response to nationwide criticism that the basic skills were not being taught.

To my consternation, upon reading Georgia's narrative response to Project BEST, I found that Georgia's focus "includes improvement in study skills, problem-solving and decision making," and, under the program component "C," it reads, "implement the Thinkabout program." Project BEST represents an $855,000 effort that is being used in part to perpetuate programs that violate the Protection of Pupil Rights Act.

Another program funded under the National Diffusion Network sanction is entitled Educational Community Opportunity for Stewardship, or ECOS Training Institute. This program performs a vital function for the aforementioned integration of curriculum. ECOS is a process whereby local school system personnel are trained to take existing curriculum material and infuse "intruder concepts" into it.

Under the ECOS definition, curriculum infusion consists of "incorporating the concepts, knowledge, skills, values and activities of an innovation or intruder into the content of existing subject matter curricula."

The purpose for which the ECOS training was adopted in Georgia at over 30 school system sites was to infuse the "life-role" skills required by CBE into the existing curriculum. The ECOS training is also referred to as a state model for the Competency Based Education instructional program, with graduation requirements mandating that a child demonstrate "skills and understandings necessary to improve both physical and mental health, to use leisure time in a profitable and fulfilling manner and to establish a personal family world which is mutually beneficial to the individual and to members of the family."

There would be no way to assess these skills without violating the Pupil Rights Amendment because of the social and psychological nature of the skills. With the help of ECOS training, it is also difficult to isolate the time and program used to teach, test and evaluate performance in these areas. Thus, ECOS itself is the violator of the Pupil Rights Amendment.

Having had children in the public schools in the State of Georgia for six years, living in a neighborhood surrounded by families with children presently attending public schools, and knowing the number of programs and curricula in use, funded by a variety of sources which violate the Pupil Rights Amendment, I have yet to find any other parents who have been notified of the possibility of their children being exposed to such programs.

TESTIMONY OF
Phyllis Chaplin

My children are currently ten years old, eight and a half, and five years old, and they are all in elementary school at this time.

My first experience with the Magic Circle curriculum was when my son was in first grade. The Magic Circle was kept private from the families of the student. The counselor I spoke to, who was the facilitator, said that they should not exchange the information received there because the family's items were private but not private for each other, so that they could present whatever they wanted to, to each other — and that I should keep in mind these are first graders, and you realize they normally talk about how everything is in other people's families.

So, the school didn't want the information to be given to parents, but they did want it for themselves.

A child was put into Magic Circle, in just a normal setting and at an impressionable age. The facilitator said it does not work well with older 5th and 6th graders because they are already too unimpressionable by that time.

The child, as I mentioned, was told not to tell his family, but everyone can speak when they raise their hands and tell the group anything that they want to about their home or anything that bothered them. At the end of this, they all voted openly; they all raised their hands to show they agreed or disagreed with the values statement that was given. After this, they would rub each other's backs and give each other hugs, and then change partners and rub each other's backs and give each other hugs again, to promote group caring. This is what she said.

I attended one of these Magic Circles, not by invitation, but by finding out what time they were held and entering. This is what I saw. The facilitator was the school counselor; she took over the class from the teacher and arranged the chairs in one large circle.

She began to talk about dying and was asked questions concerning this. When I walked in, she said to the children, "Parents sometimes get the wrong impression when we talk about death and dying, so I'm going to change the subject." She then spoke about ideas of right and wrong behavior in various forms to each other. After picking out certain children and getting their opinions on this, she called for a non-private vote. To me, a non-private vote for first graders means that all the children raised their hands because peer pressure is so great.

I asked a child later if they voted on things that they didn't like, and he said that the facilitator told him things that were not correct to him. He said, "They told me to lie." I asked him what he meant.

He said, "Well, they told the story about the boy who cried 'wolf,' and when a boy cries 'wolf' he should not squeal on his friends, because *that* is crying 'wolf.' " But, he added, in Sunday School they told him that it was lying if you hid the truth.

Later I spoke with the counselor and asked if they voted on religious things, and she said, "Yes, we voted that religion was a way of celebrating holidays."

Magic Circle was kept a secret until the end of the year. Then a questionnaire was sent out; I wrote on the questionnaire the suggestion that the parents be involved and told about this so that they could be included. I thought this was a very practical matter, but they did not include this suggestion the next year.

*TESTIMONY OF*_____

Delores Brown

I'm from Asheville, North Carolina. As a former teacher and now a full-time mother and homemaker, I am deeply concerned about the shift of emphasis in education today.

In recent academic testing of the eight most industrialized countries of the world, American students never ranked first or second in comparison with students from the other industrialized countries. In fact, we ranked last seven times. We were among the worst in mathematics and not much better in science and geography.

One-fifth of the 6th grade students tested could not even locate the United States on a world map. Yet, why should this surprise us, when the NEA has said, "Schools will become clinics whose purpose is to provide individualized psycho-social treatment for the students, and teachers must become psycho-social therapists."

I want to show how this philosophy and these psychological techniques have been incorporated into the federally-funded Ombudsman Drug Education curriculum. This is an affective drug education program and is the only drug abuse prevention program approved for use with 5th through 9th graders by the U.S. Department of Education's National Diffusion Network.

The book states that it is designed to "reduce certain psychological and attitudinal states related to drug use."

It does not emphasize any information or facts about drugs, per se. How can a child be expected to make any kind of responsible intellectual decisions about the harmful effects of drugs without some cognitive knowledge of the subject, some facts, the harmful effects, the benefits, or the results of drug abuse.

Yet page 15 states that the leader must be free to "accept them, (the ideas or feelings of the students) without striving to correct behavior or values. Change is ultimately the responsibility of the individual student. A leader cannot assume the responsibility for that change."

This curriculum is 152 pages long, and yet only

four pages make any mention of drugs, either directly or indirectly. The program is divided into three phases. The first phase is self-awareness followed by a series of exercises that permit students to gain "a wider understanding and appreciation of their values as autonomous individuals."

The second phase is communication and group skills. This is a kind of sensitivity training that brings about group consensus. Page 91 states, "Students develop their own values statements for the group. The leader should make it clear that there are no right or wrong answers." The children then decide about such things as church attendance, if parents should have more than two children, if parents have the right to say what can and cannot go on in their own homes. How many ten to 14-year-olds do you know who always happily agree with parental authority?

On page 92 we come to the first drug-related issue. Remember, there are no right or wrong answers. The children discuss such statements as: an alcoholic is not a drug addict; it's okay to try anything once; a drug dealer is just a business person like anyone else; and, it's impossible to become an alcoholic just by drinking beer.

On page 102, again the teacher is instructed to stay neutral and then the children are asked, do you think it's all right to lie, cheat, steal, break laws once in a while, or only at certain times? Why is the choice of "never" never given?

On page 111, the children will use decision-making values clarification techniques to decide whether marijuana should be legal. How can a ten-year-old discuss this without some cognitive facts?

On page 117, the class plays a survival game and decides which three people to eliminate from the group. This frightening strategy desensitizes children to the worth and dignity of human life. Therefore, euthanasia and infanticide take on a whole new meaning for the child as he evaluates the lives of those listed in the survival game, according to their age and contribution to society. Where does that leave the sick, the elderly, the retarded, or the handicapped persons? This was the same strategy that was used in Nazi Germany.

Parental rights to instill in our children the sacred values that we hold dear must be respected by the school system and protected under the law.

Finally, in this drug curriculum, on pages 124 to 125, we find exercises in death education. The children write their own epitaph or obituaries. This also desensitizes children to any uncomfortable feelings that they may have about death and dying. I am convinced that this attitude is reflected in the rising increase in teenage suicide.

Pages 127 to 134 deal with sexuality exercises and page 135 is a sensory awareness exercise using touch therapy.

Again, I ask, what does this have to do with drug education? These are some of the reasons that I feel we urgently need the Hatch Amendment enforced through regulations.

TESTIMONY OF————————————————
Snookie Dellinger

I am from Charlotte, North Carolina, and I, too am going to speak on the Ombudsman curriculum.

We have just recently had a 5th grade class go to a museum in Charlotte where they observed a film on childbirth. The parents did not receive a letter. One of the children fainted, and the parents still did not know what that child had seen or what had caused this.

Secretary Terrel Bell has stated that the Federal Government should not establish curricula. Yet, in essence, that is what has happened with the federally-funded National Diffusion Network programs. One curriculum of which I speak is Ombudsman, an affective values program which violates the Protection of Pupil Rights Amendment.

It was designed for grades 5 through 8, to be taught a minimum of two hours per week for a full semester, and is structured to change a child's values by psychological and attitudinal examination and testing activities.

Although this curriculum states it is for grades 5 through 8, we have had it in the 4th grade in our schools in Charlotte-Mecklenburg.

Some of the activities are designed to force choice by eliminating a "no opinion" or "mixed feelings" category. Later the students must reverse roles as they do the activities.

Examples of some of the issues on which they

must take a stand and later reverse roles, after they are told there are no right and wrong statements, are:

Is it okay to do anything once? Is it important for a child to attend church or synagogue? Is a drug dealer a businessman? Is it impossible to become an alcoholic by drinking beer? Do parents have the right to tell you what you can and cannot do, when to come home? Is it okay to steal, cheat or lie?

They decide if marijuana should be legalized. They have to make a choice between marijuana and alcohol (which is no choice at all).

This curriculum is written under the guise of reducing drug use. Ombudsman does not even emphasize information on drugs. It simply creates problems for children by not giving them an answer and telling them there are no right or wrong answers. The problems created by the curriculum many times end up in suicide for these students.

Ombudsman makes the assumption that all the students are at high risk psychologically in their attitudes favoring drug use, rebelliousness, negative social attitudes, low valuing of school, poor teacher-student relationships, poor parent-child relationships, and low self-esteem.

The children go through a series of experiential values activities to help them become aware of themselves (as if they had never known who they were), to love themselves (which creates me-ism), and to communicate these affective ideas (even if they conflict with parents and religious teachings).

A survival game which my 7th grade son participated in required him to eliminate five out of ten whom they did not have room for on the spaceship. This is a subtle way to accept genocide, to become desensitized to euthanasia and infanticide, and to destroy religious beliefs (for the clergyman is always the oldest, or nearly the oldest, and he is certainly to be eliminated).

My fourth grader was involved in death education. He had to write an essay on our pet that had died two months prior to this. It took us an hour and a half to get him to sleep because of the problems this created in his 4th grade mind. Why did he have to write a report on his pet that had died? He had to draw a picture of the pet, and he had to read his report to his class. It is interesting that animal death education precedes the human death study in the Ombudsman curriculum. Is it any wonder that our children in this nation cannot read, write or count, when so much time is spent in our nation's classrooms on such activities!

TESTIMONY OF
Phyllis Schlafly

I am president of Eagle Forum. I am a member of the Illinois bar and, with six children, have a lifetime interest in education.

All across the country, classroom courses masquerading as sex education are in fact violating the letter and spirit of the Protection of Pupil Rights Amendment. Let's take a look at the most up-to-date example of classroom sex courses written for use in public schools K-12 (kindergarten through 12th grade).

The New York City Board of Education has just published a new Sex Education Program (SEP). It is 293 pages long. That's about 283 pages longer than is necessary to instruct pupils in the facts of life; the rest is classroom fun and games designed to subject pupils to psychological treatment, to require pupils to reveal information about sex behavior and attitudes, to require pupils to discuss psychological problems potentially embarrassing to the student or his family, to invade his and his family's privacy, and to elicit critical appraisals of other individuals with whom the pupils have close relationships.

One of SEP's major teaching tactics is roleplaying, that is, getting pupils of every age to act out roles in various psychological situations. It is a powerful form of psychotherapy. SEP requires pupils to act out these situations: (1) pretend your parents are getting a divorce (p. 74); (2) pretend you are having a conflict with your parents (p. 75); (3) pretend someone you know is pregnant; discuss the options she has to choose from "including teenage marriage, adoption, single parenthood, foster care, extended family, abortion" (p. 92); (4) pretend your boyfriend tells you he has syphilis or gonorrhea. (p. 128)

Another teaching technique is called the Grab Bag. The teacher tells the pupils to write "descriptions of different situations in which couples are having sexual relations but are not planning on a pregnancy." The papers are put in a grab bag and drawn out one by one. The pupils discuss and evaluate the various methods of contraception and select the best contraceptive "to fit each particular situation." (pp. 166-167)

SEP grievously invades the privacy of the pupil and his family. Big Brother may not be watching you in 1984 but, with SEP, Child Is Spying on Parent. Pupils in pre-kindergarten through grade 2 are told to tell the class what happened "in their home when mom was having a baby," (p. 34) and to "discuss what are some of the ways your parents show love for each other." (p. 37)

Pupils are told to discuss "what is your present relationship with your parents," (p. 75) and to tell about times you disagree with "decisions made by your parents." (p. 46) The child is instructed to "describe your family," (pp. 72 & 177) and to "interview a grandparent or older adult in your family" and ask all sorts of personal questions. (p. 72)

Of course, being a public school course, SEP does not tell pupils that premarital sex is wrong; the teacher would be forbidden to do that. Instead, the pupil is instructed "to identify and evaluate the choices involved in sexual expression." The choices then listed for the student are "abstinence, sexual fantasy, masturbation, hugging, kissing, petting, exploration, intercourse, nocturnal emission or wet dreams, sexual preference, homosexual preference, homosexual experience, gay, lesbian, bisexual, transvestite, transsexual." (p. 137)

SEP forces explicit discussions of sexuality and genitalia on little children at the kindergarten and primary grade levels. (p. 30)

A persistent undercurrent of SEP is its attempt to teach pupils to be tolerant of homosexuals. "Experimental sex play" with persons of the same sex is described as "not unusual" among 5th and 6th grade children. (p. 63) "Homosexual experimentation" is described as normal behavior of 14-16-year olds. (p. 19) SEP states that "most child molesters are heterosexual males and not homosexuals." (p. 139)

SEP requires the child to make critical appraisals of gender-identity values within his family at home. The pupil must reveal whether it is "an advantage or disadvantage to be a boy or a girl in your family." The pupil is required to "list various household jobs that are performed by males, females, or both in your family," and then the pupil is required to determine "sharing responsibilities in your own home." (p. 73)

In a patronizing way, SEP says that "school districts and high schools may excuse students from such instruction if requested by the student's parent or guardian." (p. 5) But that's not satisfactory; schools should be required to obey the Protection of Pupil Rights Amendment which forbids inflicting such psychological treatment on children and invasions of their privacy "without the prior written consent of the parent."

Furthermore, SEP states that SEP is "integrated into the entire curriculum and not just in specific courses such as biology and health," (p. 7) so it would be impossible for the parent to know that SEP was being given unless the school first notified the parent.

Another major violator of the Pupil Rights Amendment is the classroom courses in nuclear war. Incidentally, sex and nuclear war are the only two subjects which are taught K-12 (kindergarten through 12th grade). No other subject is taught for the entire 13 years of pre-college schooling—not English, math, science, or history.

It is clear from an evaluation of the five major curricula in nuclear war currently in use that they are not designed to teach pupils facts or history, but are psychological-treatment courses which produce fear, guilt and despair. The nuclear war courses invade the pupils' privacy about political affiliations and attitudes, and attempt to change the students' attitudes to conform to the authors' prejudices and politics.

One of the major teaching techniques used in the nuclear war courses is forcing the pupil to write a Student Journal in which he reveals to the teacher his private attitudes about the course, his innermost feelings, and private conversations with his parents, friends and neighbors about controversial issues. The following direct quotations from journals written by pupils who took a nuclear war course prove clearly that they had been subjected to psychological or psychiatric treatment in violation of the Protection of Pupil Rights Amendment.

"These days, I just try not to think about my

future, because I have a hard time seeing one. . . . I want to do something with my life, but who cares about me? Besides, we're all going to get blown up anyway." (Crossroads)

"Some of the discussions we had got 'pretty heavy,' and it was hard to handle! It's hard to spend 45 minutes a day talking about dying, and it's depressing!" (Decision Making in a Nuclear Age)

"I have learned that there is seldom a right or wrong but rather a right or left." "I'm conscious of having changed in the strength of my convictions on many of the ethical dilemmas we've confronted. . . . Where do I draw the line between right and wrong?" "We all, in our struggling humanity, have to clutch to our eyeballs to keep out the cold light of despair." "The most meaningful parts of the book [Elie Wiesel's *Night*] to me were when the boy stopped believing in God. . . . Maybe my faith is waning a little, just from reading about it. Unfortunately, this book will always be tucked in my memory." (Facing History and Ourselves, a federally-funded program).

These Student Journals prove that the courses constitute psychological treatment which produces despair, promotes pacifism, and shakes the pupils' sense of right and wrong. They are a sophisticated form of child abuse.

Another technique used in the nuclear war curricula is the Whip. This is the device of asking the pupil to complete a phrase by speaking the first words that come to mind. It is a means of probing the child's psyche to find out what is in his innermost thoughts. When the teacher says, "When I think of nuclear war . . ." the pupil is expected to answer "Death!" How gruesome!

Simulation Games are widely used in the nuclear war curricula to teach pacifist and anti-defense politics. The Token Game is one of several games featured in the NEA-sponsored nuclear war course called Choices. The pupils are given 20 tokens which represent all the money in the federal budget. The pupils are told that 9 out of 20 tokens are now spent on national defense and induced to make the "choice" that those tokens would be better spent on NEA-approved social programs. (Even the NEA arithmetic is false; only one-fourth of the federal budget is actually spent on defense.)

Another technique used in all the nuclear war courses is requiring the pupils to write letters to "Dear Soviet Citizen" and to "Dear Editor." The pupils are told to send their letters to "Facing History and Ourselves" in Brookline, Massachusetts. This clearly establishes the linkage between the federally-funded curriculum under that name and the other nuclear war curricula.

The sample letters provided to the students are part of the psychological treatment which produces fear and despair in the minds and hearts of the pupils. Here are some quotations from the sample letters presented in the curriculum called A Day of Dialogue.

"It's hard for me to seriously think of the future. . . . It is overwhelming to me, as it must be to you, that every human being on this planet must live each day to its fullest, because the next day may never come." (p. 177) "Fear and helplessness overwhelms me." (p. 175)

Putting aside the bad grammar of this last example, it is so sad that schoolchildren are deliberately taught to be afraid and are trained to feel helpless and overwhelmed. Children should be given hope, idealism, and faith in the future.

TESTIMONY OF_____
Mary Park Hilles

My first introduction to how schools have changed occurred five years ago. I saw a movie which was shown to 8th graders in the kindergarten through 12th grade Human Development curriculum in their Human Sexuality Unit. The movie was 20 minutes long and depicted nude masturbation in detail. It showed how men do it, women do it, why they do it, and where it feels best. Teenage actors were used.

I determined then to find out what was behind this K-12 curriculum. A teacher called me anonymously and said she had a copy of the 13-year curriculum guide and she would leave it in her top desk drawer. I could come in when she was out, take it, and use it any way I wanted. I xeroxed 200 copies, spread it around the school, and both the program and the principal were removed from the school.

For one year I read all I could unearth about new educational trends. I learned about Values Clarification, Kohlberg's moral dilemmas, psychological pre- and post-testing in behavioral modification programs. I learned that special interest groups were planning the curricula for the schools. I discovered that educators felt it their prerogative to change and mold the minds of our children. I realized it was "in" to be non-judgmental, that all opinions were to be treated as valid, that nobody these days knows what's normal and not normal, that parents are old-fashioned and usually wrong, and that situation ethics is more appropriate in today's pluralistic world since the secular school system has deemed we no longer have absolute values to depend on.

As a parent of four young children in the public school system, I learned that I did not agree with how the state, using federal monies, intended to take over the responsibility of educating my "whole" child. I had no intention of sitting back docilely and letting my children participate in open-ended discussions in sex ed, family living, citizenship ed, drug and alcohol ed, human development, etc., taught with the philosophy that there are no right and wrong answers and all opinions are valid. That just goes against everything I believe and stand for. I removed all four children from any class utilizing Values Clarification.

At that point I decided to write a pamphlet disclosing my observations. I wanted to show parents that the intent of education had changed dramatically since we were in school. I wanted to enable them to discuss with their children subject matter and teaching techniques prevalent in today's schools. Reading the actual books the children read, and discussing classroom procedures, opened a can of worms.

Another reason I wrote the pamphlet was that I felt it was vital to show my children that one person could take a stand and be heard. Three people participated in the pamphlet and we called it "PACT: Parents and Children Together." To date, I have had to republish it seven times. I have sold 40,000 copies to parents and organizations in 37 states and four English-speaking countries. I have corresponded with more than 1,000 parents whose discontents are numerous and specific.

They believe the point of schools is not to reform society but to teach children academic knowledge. They believe their children are now being considered more the property of the state than as individuals who belong to themselves and their families. They concur with Terrel Bell that "parents have the ultimate responsibility for the upbringing of their children." They are angry at federal intervention with their children's emotions, values and attitudes. They are tired of having the burden of proof rest with the parents. They are fed up with affective education.

I believe I'm fighting for my children's souls. I'm

fighting for them to have a conscience and to realize there are rights and wrongs and normal and abnormal behavior. A recent quote by Roger Rosenblatt of *Time* magazine caught my eye: "When the state starts imposing on the soul, democracy is in trouble."

TESTIMONY OF————————————————

Marcella Donovan

I am the director of the American Education Coalition, a national grass-roots organization of parents working to improve our public schools.

Federal money taints a number of programs at the local levels. For example, there is legal authority for sex education to be taught with Chapter One and Chapter Two monies. This is particularly interesting when one looks at the reaction of Planned Parenthood in Oklahoma when the state version of the Hatch Amendment was passed.

Planned Parenthood of Oklahoma City opposed the bill because of what they saw as the probable negative impact on sex education programs in the classrooms. Just after the Oklahoma victory, a Planned Parenthood Action Alert urged their supporters to express support for values teaching techniques in the public school curriculum because the impact of this issue can and probably will have a lasting effect on the teaching of family life, sexuality education, and most social sciences in Oklahoma public schools, current and future.

The Action Alert went on to say that the ability to use Values Clarification and other techniques aimed at teaching decision-making skills is important to the future effectiveness of current and future programs.

What this means is that Planned Parenthood knew exactly that the parents in Oklahoma would not like the programs now being taught. Therefore, Planned Parenthood had to make every possible effort to prevent the Parents' Rights Bill from passing, so that their programs could continue.

Another example of a federal program under the National Diffusion Network is Exemplary Center for Reading Instruction (ECRI). Last year in Kendallville, Indiana, this controversial program caused an outcry from parents and some teachers who objected to the teaching techniques to which children were submitted.

Under this program children were taught to read through Behavior Modification. Another aspect of the program is time-testing, which puts an inordinate amount of pressure on the children and leads to adverse side effects. Parents expressed concern about physical stress symptoms displayed by those children participating in the ECRI reading program.

Doctors have confirmed the parents' concerns that the symptoms are the result of the ECRI reading program. Symptoms included stomach aches, sleeplessness, vomiting, rashes, nightmares, twisting of hair, excessive blinking of eyes, and stuttering.

*TESTIMONY OF*_____
Lee Phillips

I am from Hatboro, Pennsylvania, and the mother of two sons, ages 22 and 13.

When my older son was in 8th grade, he participated in an affective education program which was conducted once a week, instead of social studies, for the entire 40 minute period. This program had no educational merit and was solely an attitude-changing process, using my child and his classmates as guinea pigs.

Bruce's class was taken to what is called a quiet reading room. There they played a game called Quaker Schoolhouse where all the children sat in a semi-circle with an empty chair in the middle of an open end, facing the pupils. All the students had to remain silent until one of them was willing to get up and sit in the empty chair and tell what was bothering him or her.

It could range anywhere from having a fellow student purposely push them in the hall to the fact that their parents were getting a divorce. The children were forced to remain in the room for the full period even if they didn't want to participate in this activity.

The counselor who guided this class made it very clear that they were not to discuss what type of class they were in or what they had talked about with anyone outside that room. As a result, I knew nothing about this class from September to December, when my son told me about it.

This playing with the psyche of my child by the school counselor who conducted the class was my first experience with Values Clarification. However, when I went before the local school board, I was told that game playing was not Values Clarification but a form of understanding themselves better.

I believe that disturbing side effects are created, such as frustration, when children relate personal problems to public school officials who do not have it within their power to solve these personal problems, whether it is a divorce in the child's household or drunkenness by one of the parents. The only thing this type of revelation succeeds in doing, is to open a wound which is beyond the child's province to control.

Nowhere on any school report was there mention of this program involving our children. Since 1975 there were numerous other instances where Values Clarification was used and had a negative result with my children.

Many articles have been written in recent years concerning "why Johnny can't read." Yet all over the country, schools are wasting precious classroom time on problem-solving topics, much to the detriment of our children. I always believed that attitude forming and changing was a realm of teaching which I, alone, had under my jurisdiction. I was under the impression that I, and I alone, had the right and responsibility for the psychological, political, philosophical and religious development of my children. Therefore, I would like the Hatch Amendment enforced because I and millions of other mothers in our country have not relinquished this right.

TESTIMONY OF _____
Beth Trotto

I have been an educational columnist for a local Maryland newspaper for over ten years. During this time many questionable programs, techniques, etc., have been brought to my attention.

The University of Maryland in 1980 admitted, in a proposal to the United States Army, to use Values Clarification psychology to try and change soldier attitudes and behaviors, that educators have been experimenting for 15 years with Values Clarification. Yet there is no evaluation yet on this highly questionable technique which continues to be used on unsuspecting children. Why not?

Even prisoners in jails have protection from such mind-bending techniques. They have to give informed consent. The burden of proof and enforcement has to be placed on the government.

The Federal Government's funding of these experimental programs is spelled out in Pacesetters in Innovation. This compilation of federally-funded programs, that were part of the original ESEA of 1965, shows parents the Federal Government's scheme to change the attitudes and behaviors of a whole generation of American children and their teachers through Behavior Modification, and sensitivity training. This book has now become a collector's item.

There never has been any protection of any kind for children who are forced, through state com-

pulsory attendance laws, into the experimental laboratory for social change that is called the American
classroom.

As if the 1965 programs weren't enough, the Federal Government then decided to create the National
Diffusion Network, which disseminates through a
very intricate state and local labyrinth, the so-called
"exemplary" federally-funded programs. A large per-
centage of these fall into the category of psycho-
therapeutic methods mentioned above, programs
that were approved by the Federal Government long
after the Protection of Pupil Rights Amendment was
passed in Congress.

To illustrate how other government agencies are
involved in the school curriculum, I refer you to a
grant from the National Endowment for the Hu-
manities. One of their many programs is entitled
Ethical Quest in a Democratic Society. It was produced in conjunction with the Tacoma, Washington
school system, and structured according to Lawrence Kohlberg's moral reasoning.

Kohlberg's theories—and they are theories—have
been disputed by many professionals; yet his seven
stages of moral development are included in a law-
related curriculum in Maryland. Kohlberg's sixth
level of development is universal ethical principles,
which he states can put the student in despair, and
his seventh stage is the cosmic or religious. This particular program is endorsed by the Maryland Bar
Association. What right do schools have to manipulate students into despair and then publicly ring
their hands and wonder why so many students are

committing suicide?

The National Centers for Disease Control have just announced they are going to conduct a study on the phenomenon of teenage suicides. I strongly suggest they start with the programs, instructions and methods used in the schools which give students a feeling of despair, that there are no tomorrows and the feeling of being cut off from their roots and families. I also suggest that the students be asked how many courses they have had on death education, writing their own epitaph, suicide notes, and lying down on graves.

Read the so-called courses on peace and see how they generate despair and a lack of faith in the United States of America and our Constitution. One has to question whether there is a move to shift our children's allegience from the United States Constitution to the United Nations' control. The NEA's bicentennial program was called A Declaration of Interdependence: Education for a Global Community. Where does the United States Constitution fit into a Global Community?

We should look at the close connection between the National Council of Social Studies and the education arm of the United Nations, called UNESCO. How about such organizations as Global Perspectives, Inc., whose national conference in May is entitled "Global Crossroads: Educating Americans for Responsible Choices" and is subtly designed to put international and global matters on the country's educational agenda?

Another agency that funds curriculum in Maryland is the federal Department of Transportation for Alcohol and Traffic Safety. It uses Sidney Simon's third force psychology Values Clarification techniques, wherein students are told to make up their own minds, not listen to moralizing adults.

Another interesting teaching technique that has crept into the schools to be used on trusting students is hypnotism. Federally-funded programs are allowed in Los Angeles and in other places. A Bulgarian technique has just been franchised in the United States, called Super Learning, which is a relaxed learning biofeedback technique.

Why is tax money being used for such techniques in greater and greater quantities? In one sex education workshop for teachers, given by a teacher whose school was judged exemplary by the Department of Education, she described a common technique of "guided fantasy," where students close their eyes and visualize themselves walking down a beach with a friend and imagine what can happen.

The World Future Society stated in its brochure about the announcement of John Marks Templeton's speech on global values, that "alienation is a necessary requirement for the creation of global values." You have to be cut off from your roots and family before a new beginning can come into fruition.

TESTIMONY OF_____

Naomi King

I am the president and founder of Parents Alliance to Protect our Children, a national, non-profit organization, based in Latrobe, Pennsylvania.

One federally-funded program on drug and alcohol abuse is entitled Here's Looking at You Two. It is steeped in Values Clarification. It covers the range from kindergarten through high school and contains self-concept, decision-making, and coping activities which certainly come under the Hatch Amendment.

Five-year-old kindergarten children draw "feely heads," which are silhouettes of their own heads, to which they add emotions. The "feely head" is put on the wall and a pointer used to pick out emotions which the child feels throughout the day. There is to be one "feely head" for school and one for home. Role-playing has become a part of language arts. Without seeing the "feely head" and the emotion the child secretly points to, the class is to guess which emotion it is, after the child acts it out. The purpose is to recognize feelings and how they are expressed.

At other points there are questions such as, "How do you feel when your mother or father doesn't have time to play with you?" Program activities include questionnaires and situations for discussion. Situations for older students which elicit feelings include, (1) your minister has been arrested several times for drunk driving, and (2) your father becomes the life of the party when he is drunk.

For senior high, there are "feel wheels" where groups of five or six students sit around the wheel and react to various statements by putting markers on a particular emotion on the wheel. There is the option to put one's marker on the area marked "sanctuary" if one chooses not to reveal his or her feelings.

Here's Looking at You Two activities can be incorporated in many subjects, including music, social studies, art, math, writing, reading, language arts, biology, psychology, and environmental education.

In all fairness, we point out that a letter to parents is recommended to advise that the program is being implemented, that it contains self-concept, decision-making and coping skills, and that parents are invited to attend segments upon giving one day's notice. But no prior written consent is required.

We do not know of any drug and alcohol education curriculum recommended by the education establishment that does not utilize objectionable techniques that we oppose.

The late Dr. Conrad Baars, well known psychiatrist, wrote a book in 1979 entitled *Feeling and Healing Your Emotions.* He stated,

> "With a 'feeling cult' gaining in popularity, we witness a growing movement to better the 'mental health' of our population. Led by the psychiatric profession, financed and directed by many government agencies, this movement launched a popular auxiliary front of non-, near-, and para-professionals rushing to the aid of their emotionally starved and disabled brothers and

sisters.

"An example of the effect of the corrupt notion that emotions and feelings are of greater importance than thinking and knowing is the rapid deterioration of moral values and behavior in youth.

"Responsible for this modern indoctrination, directly or indirectly, in my opinion, are the teachings, programs and philosophies offered by Joseph Fletcher's *Situation Ethics,* Sidney Simon's *Values Clarification,* Lawrence Kohlberg's *Cognitive Moral Development,* and SIECUS's Sex Education in schools."

TESTIMONY OF————————————————
Jacqueline Lawrence

I am a parent from Montgomery County, Maryland. We are a foreign service family. Our nine children have attended schools in England, Switzerland, France, Germany and the United States. The oldest three graduated from schools in Europe and the other six from Montgomery County public schools.

In spite of the fact that all of my children passed their college entrance examinations and, seemingly, received an adequate education, those who attended public school in Montgomery County were subjected to psycho-social courses of study that were manipulative and stressful. Their teachers used psycho-therapeutic strategies that were at times coercive and demeaning. My children and their friends frequently complained to me of gimmicky and even bizarre events in their classes.

In order better to understand what my children were experiencing, I began studying classroom curriculum materials and teacher-training manuals. I have worked with state and national education research groups, as well as parent and political education organizations, from 1968 to the present.

I understand now that my children and other students in American public schools were experiencing a new approach to learning, identified by educators themselves, as humanistic, psycho-social, psycho-medical, and affective education. The most commonly used techniques were, and still are, psycho-dramas, socio-dramas, role-playing, encounter groups, and the isolation strategy. How did these techniques evolve? They were originally applied in mental institutions for the mentally disturbed, and in penitentiaries for the criminally insane.

Among the leading developers were Jacob Moreno, a psychiatrist from Rumania, and Hilda Taba, an educator from Estonia. Both of them received federal monies from the Office of Education as early as the 1950s to apply their psychotherapies on American public school children for the purpose of improving personality development and social adjustment. Many teachers have attended, with federal funds, the Moreno Institute in Beacon, N.Y., for training in the use of psychotherapies in the classroom, as developed by Moreno.

Hilda Taba, with the use of federal funds, developed an eight-year social studies program designed to improve human relations in the classroom. Her areas of expertise are the sociogram, role-playing, and the use of personal diaries. She believed that it was important to know where the child stood in his beliefs, attitudes and feelings, so that the individual ethno-centrism would be reduced or eliminated and the group, or class, could then become more cohesive. Teachers attend special workshops before using the Taba program and the techniques she prescribed.

The most commonly used strategy is the sociogram. A sociogram is a diagram of students' social relationships. By studying social acceptance patterns, the teacher attempts to plan activities to enable isolated or rejected children to earn the respect of their classmates.

I would like to describe how this worked in a classroom in a Montgomery County public elementary school. The teacher asked the class to select one child who was usually left out and who seemed rejected. Denise was their choice. The 25 students were then asked to write three sentences explaining why they disliked Denise or what they disliked about Denise.

Their papers were read aloud in the class, with Denise present. The criticisms were presumably to help Denise improve her personality. However, at the end of the readings she sat weeping. As she walked home, her classmates beat her up and said that they would never like her.

In this situation, the class certainly became a more cohesive group, but what about the stress and emotional trauma and, indeed, the permanent change experienced by Denise? How can one measure the psychological impact on the victim of this group attack?

The Taba social studies program instructs children to write diaries. The strategy enables children to bring an enormous amount of information about themselves and their families and their peers into class, to be examined and discussed. The information is used to further determine personality traits and to provide a vivid and precise record of the attitudes, emotions, conflicts, anxieties and fears of the student.

Diaries are kept on file throughout the grades. There are as many as 15 kinds of diaries recommended for use in the classrooms including a budget diary to see if a child gets a fair share of the income, a religion diary, a hostility and anger diary, a low points diary, an affectionate and tender feelings diary, and a time diary.

Education today is inter-disciplinary. That is, teaching units or strategies are used interchangeably in various classes. Consequently, we see Taba diary-keeping in many subjects.

The use of diaries should be recognized as a psychological instrument that could provide information that is self-incriminating and potentially embarrassing to the student, his family members and his peers. This technique must, therefore, require the written consent of the parents.

Social studies have become a vehicle to promote a conceptual approach to learning. Students are manipulated to accept basic concepts or ideas through the use of the psychotherapies, usually psychodrama, socio-drama and role-playing.

Jacob Moreno describes an educational sociodrama as highly directed, purposely biased, pre-arranged and carefully calculated to arouse hostility or bias. He explains that the socio-drama can be used for the indoctrination of any set of values: religious, political or societal, to arouse the audience to a collective self-expression or action or social change.

How is this therapy applied to children in the classroom? I should like to cite the case of a public elementary school in Montgomery County which receives Title I funds to help its disadvantaged students resocialize.

There were problems in the school interaction between disadvantaged students and the rest of the school body. One barrier was language usage. Some disadvantaged children used harsh street language and were unacceptable to those who did not use such language.

A drama group, specifically trained with federal funds, was invited to the schools to perform a sociodrama for grades 2 through 6. The group put on a skit during which a stranger came to town to announce that God is dead. Immediately all the actors on the stage began using obscene gestures, doing obscene things, and saying obscene words. When the play was over the students went to recess and mimicked the actors' actions and words.

Language was no longer a social barrier and the group had become more cohesive. The children could now be obscene together.

Educators use an even more volatile psycho-drama for attitudinal change. I refer to the concept that we must prune away defective persons in order to improve the quality of life for the group. This drama involves murder.

One variation is as follows: eleven people are in a bomb shelter with provisions sufficient to last eleven people for two weeks or six persons for a month. The group is to decide which five are to be killed. Students are instructed to accept the situation as fact.

It can be readily seen that, once a student has acted out the murders, he has resolved the dilemma and, by his action, agreed to the concept of murder.

Such survival exercises have been written into federally-funded programs since 1971. Why have educators held on to this strategy with such tenacity for so many years?

A few years back I protested the use of this psycho-drama, but the Montgomery County school system persisted in using it. I appealed to the county child abuse task force, which prevailed upon the school system to discontinue its use.

However, the federally-funded National Diffusion Network continues to promote the life-death psycho-drama throughout the United States in a program entitled The New Model Me.

I recommend that psychological manipulation, through life-death decision making, be recognized as highly dangerous to the emotional welfare of children, unacceptable in federally-funded materials and, in fact, inappropriate for any classroom setting.

Further use of Taba's and Moreno's psychodramas, sociodramas, role-playing, situational-attitude scale tests, and all psychological instruments used to identify, observe and analyze children's beliefs, attitudes, emotions and feelings, is being called for in yet another federally-funded program, New Perspectives in Intergroup Education. This curriculum states that "the public school offers the greatest opportunity for changing attitudes and is a positive, intervening agent in the life of an individual child."

Taba's theory to diminish a child's ethno-centrism — what he believes and holds dear to him — is also espoused in the National Institute of Education program entitled Global Education: State of the Art. This program decries the ethno-centrism of American children who believe that America holds a superior culture and political system.

These programs and techniques dig deeply into and re-fashion the psychological and emotional areas of our children. Moreno wrote: "At last we sociometrists stepped into the breach and developed psychological and social shock methods which may well become scientific instruments of social action, preventives or antidotes against persuasion of purely political systems."

*TESTIMONY OF*_____
Rabbi Yeduda Levin

I'm the executive director of the Family Defense Coalition, which is a New York statewide inter-community, inter-religious coalition. I'm from Brooklyn. I am also representing the views of a multitude of Jewish organizations throughout the country, such as the National Committee for the Furtherance of Jewish Education, Torah Losoro, which is the national Jewish school movement of some 500 schools, the Union of Orthodox Rabbis of the United States and Canada, etc. There are no conflicts within the Orthodox and Traditional Jewish community on these issues.

We have been heavily involved in the City of New York. Very clearly, the sex education guidelines there deal extensively with asking questions of the children about what their parents do, with role-playing, etc. We think this is poison; and we would want the Hatch Amendment regulations to deal with that very specifically.

Another thing which concerns us very much — and we're talking now from personal experience — is the fact that alternative academic programs are not available many times. Therefore, for all practical purposes, the parent cannot and will not take the student out of the classroom when something offensive is being taught, simply because they have nowhere to go. It should state very clearly in the reg-ulations that there must be alternative academic programs for the parents who protest the teaching of the aforementioned methodologies.

Local schools should be informed that they will be legally and financially responsible to the parents, and even to the children in later years, for any psychological damage which may have evolved because of the teachings of Values Clarifications, mastery learning, etc.

I am shocked that something of such profound significance as the hearings that are being held today and in various parts of the country received almost zero publicity. After all, there have been six years of foot dragging on these regulations, and one has to wonder what kind of confidence this inspires in the parents of schoolchildren throughout America when we see that no mention is made of this in the press.

The New York Times has extensively covered problems in education and religion, such as those that are occurring across Europe and in Poland, with front-page stories. The report on excellence in education also was covered extensively. Yet, here, when we're talking about the concept of parents' rights, there is nary a whisper.

HOW PARENTS CAN
EVALUATE SCHOOL PROGRAMS

Here is a check list to help parents evaluate elementary and secondary school programs and materials. The "it" in these questions can be a curriculum, a textbook, a film, a teacher's manual, computer courseware, a workbook, mimeographed papers, or extra-curricular activities.

1. Is it anti-parent? Does it lead the child to believe that parents are ignorant, old-fashioned or out of touch with the modern world?

2. Does it suggest that the child not tell his parent what he is taught in class? Does it instruct the child not to take home the textbook or questionnaire or other school materials?

3. Does it encourage the child to seek advice from organizations or adults other than his parents (such as Planned Parenthood or a teen clinic)?

4. Does it present information which depresses the child, leads him to a negative view of himself, his family, his country, or his future? Does it produce fear, guilt, and despair in the child, instead of faith in his family and country, and hope in the future?

5. Is it preoccupied with death and tragedy? Does it encourage the child to dwell on unhappy or tragic events, or to foster and retain bad feelings such as hate, anger, and revenge? Does it require the child to write morbid exercises, such as his own epitaph or a description of the last death in the child's family?

6. Is it anti-parent and anti-religion by leading the child to reject the moral standards and values he has been taught in home and church? Does it lead the child to believe that there are no absolute moral standards, but

that the morality of an act depends on the situation?

7. Does it present courses about sex, suicide, alcohol, or illegal drugs in such a way as to encourage experimentation? Does it desensitize the child to the use of gutter language?

8. Does it use pre- and post-testing to measure attitudinal change?

9. Is it anti-religion? Does it lead the child to believe that religion is unimportant or out-of-date? Does it censor out all knowledge of the importance and influence of religion in American history?

10. Does it affirmatively teach the ideology of secular humanism or that all religions are equally valid? Does it have a constant questioning of values, standards and authority and teach that all moral decisions and lifestyles are equally to be respected?

11. Does it attack the child's religious faith by ridiculing the belief that God created the earth? Does it spend class time on such anti-religious elements as the occult, witchcraft, or astrology?

12. Does it force the child to make choices in hypothetical situations which require him to decide that it is all right to lie, cheat, steal, kill, have sex outside of marriage, have an abortion, or commit suicide? Does it pose hypothetical dilemmas which upset the child's moral values taught in the home, and induce him to seek the approval of his peers?

13. Does it spend class time on lessons, exercises and questions about feelings and attitudes, rather than teaching knowledge, facts, and traditional basic skills?

14. Does it force the child to play psychological games in class (such as Survival, Magic Circle or Dungeons and Dragons)?

15. Does it force the child to answer questionnaires or surveys that probe into the child's or his family's attitudes, feelings, behavior, customs, or political preferences, all of which invade the family's privacy and are none of the school's business?

16. Does it force the child to engage in role-playing of socio-political situations or unhappy personal problems caused by divorce, premarital sex, pregnancy, or VD?

17. Does it force the child to write journals, diaries or compositions which require the child to reveal private family information or to relive and remember unhappy events or feelings?

18. Does it require classroom discussion of personal and private matters which embarrass the child in front of his peers?

19. Does it force the child to confront adult problems which are too complex and unsuitable for his tender years, such as nuclear war?

20. Does it blur traditional concepts of gender identity and force the child to accept the radical notion of a gender-free society in which there are no differences in attitudes and occupations between men and women? Does it induce role reversals by showing women in hard physical-labor jobs and men as house-husbands?

21. Does it describe America as an unjust society (unfair to economic or racial groups or to women) rather than telling the truth that America has given more freedom and opportunity to more people than any nation in the history of the world?

22. Does it debunk the American private enterprise system and lead the child to believe that socialism is better? Does it make the child feel guilty about our high standard of living? Does it lead the child to believe that government spending programs are the formula for economic prosperity, rather than hard work and perseverance?

23. Does it propagandize for domestic spending programs, while attacking defense spending and economy in government? Does it lead the child to believe that disarmament rather than defense can prevent a future war?

24. Does it debunk or censor out our nation's heroes such as George Washington and Abraham Lincoln, but spend much time studying controversial contemporary figures?

25. Does it downgrade patriotism and lead the child to believe that other nations have better systems, or that some type of global one-world government or UN-control would be superior to ours and solve world problems? Does it use UNESCO-developed curricula to promote acceptance of a one-world government?

HOW TO EVALUATE SEX EDUCATION COURSES

1. Does it teach or imply that "responsible" sex is any sex that does not result in having a baby?

2. Does it omit all references to moral standards of right and wrong, teaching only animal-level sex? Does it try to eliminate all guilt for sin?

3. Does it urge boys and girls to seek help from or consult only or primarily public agencies rather than their parents or religious advisers?

4. Does it require instruction and discussion to take place in sex-integrated (coed) classes rather than separate classes for boys and girls?

5. Does it require boys and girls to discuss private parts and sexual behavior openly in the classroom, with explicit vocabulary, thereby destroying their natural modesty, privacy, and psychological defenses (especially of the girls) against immoral sex?

6. Does it omit mentioning chastity as a method (the only absolute method) of preventing teenage pregnancies and VD?

7. Does it assume that all boys and girls are engaging in immoral sex, thereby encouraging them to accept promiscuous sexual acts as normal?

8. Does it omit mention of the spiritual, psychological, emotional, and physical benefits of premarital chastity, marital fidelity, and traditional family life?

9. Does it omit mention of the spiritual, psychological, emotional, and physical penalties and risks of fornication, adultery and promiscuity?

10. Does it require boys and girls to engage in role-playing (pretending one is pregnant, pretending one has to admit having VD, pretending to use various types of contraceptives), thereby encouraging peer pressure to be exerted on the side of fornication rather than chastity?

11. Does it fail to stress marriage as the most moral, most fulfilling, and/or most socially acceptable method of enjoying sexual activity?

12. Does it encourage boys and girls *not* to tell their parents about the sex-ed curriculum, or about their sexual behavior or problems?

13. Does it present abortion as an acceptable method of birth control?

14. Does it use materials and references from the pro-abortion Planned Parenthood?

15. Does it present homosexual behavior as normal and acceptable?

16. Does it omit mention of the incurable types of VD which today affect millions of Americans? Does it falsely imply that all VD can be cured by treatment?

17. Does it give respectability to VD by listing famous people who had it?

18. Does it omit mention of the danger of cervical cancer in females from early promiscuity?

19. Does it give detailed descriptions of every type of normal and abnormal sexual activity?

20. Does it use a vocabulary which disguises immorality? For example, "sexually active" to mean fornication, "sexual partners" to mean sex in or out of marriage, "fetus" to mean baby, "termination of pregnancy" to mean killing a preborn baby.

21. Does it require boys and girls to draw or trace on paper intimate parts of the male and female bodies?

22. Does it ask unnecessary questions which cause boys and girls to doubt their parents' religious and social values ("is there a need for a wedding ceremony, religious or civil?")?

23. Does it force advanced concepts and vocabulary upon five to eight year old children too young to understand or be interested? (For example, selection of mate, Caesarian, pregnancy prevention, population control, ovulation, VD, sperm, ovum.)

24. Does it constantly propagandize for limiting the size of families by teaching that having more children means that each gets fewer economic benefits?

25. Can the sex-ed curriculum reasonably be described as a "how to do it" course in sexual acts (instruction which obviously encourages individual experimentation)?

Appendix B

SAMPLE LETTER FOR PARENTS

Here is a sample letter (prepared by the Maryland Coalition of Concerned Parents on Privacy Rights in Public Schools) which parents can copy and send to the president of their local School Board (with a copy to your child's school principal) in order to protect parental and student rights under the Hatch Amendment Regulations effective November 12, 1984. This letter does NOT ask for the removal of any course or material; it merely demands that the schools obey the law and secure written parental consent before subjecting children to any of the following. Parents are NOT required to explain their reasons for denying consent.

_____
_____

Date_____

To: School Board President_____
_____
_____

Dear_____:

I am the parent of _____ who attends _____ School. Under U.S. legislation and court decisions, parents have the primary responsibility for their children's education, and pupils have certain rights which the schools may not deny. Parents have the right to assure that their children's beliefs and moral values are not undermined by the schools. Pupils have the right to have and to hold their values and moral standards without direct or indirect manipulation by the schools through curricula, textbooks, audio-visual materials, or supplementary assignments.

Accordingly, I hereby request that my child be involved in NO school activities or materials listed below unless I have first reviewed all the relevant materials and have given my written consent for their use:
- Psychological and psychiatric examinations, tests, or surveys that are designed to elicit information about attitudes, habits, traits, opinions, beliefs, or feelings of an individual or group;
- Psychological and psychiatric treatment that is designed to affect behavioral, emotional, or attitudinal characteristics of an individual or group;
- Values clarification, use of moral dilemmas, discussion of religious or moral standards, role-playing or open-ended discussions of situations involving moral issues, and survival games including life/death decision exercises;
- Death education, including abortion, euthanasia, suicide, use of violence, and discussions of death and dying;

- Curricula pertaining to alcohol and drugs;
- Instruction in nuclear war, nuclear policy, and nuclear classroom games;
- Anti-nationalistic, one-world government or globalism curricula;
- Discussion and testing on inter-personal relationships; discussions of attitudes toward parents and parenting;
- Education in human sexuality, including premarital sex, extra-marital sex, contraception, abortion, homosexuality, group sex and marriages, prostitution, incest, masturbation, bestiality, divorce, population control, and roles of males and females; sex behavior and attitudes of student and family;
- Pornography and any materials containing profanity and/or sexual explicitness;
- Guided fantasy techniques; hypnotic techniques; imagery and suggestology;
- Organic evolution, including the idea that man has developed from previous or lower types of living things;
- Discussions of witchcraft, occultism, the supernatural, and Eastern mysticism;
- Political affiliations and beliefs of student and family; personal religious beliefs and practices;
- Mental and psychological problems and self-incriminating behavior potentially embarrassing to the student or family;
- Critical appraisals of other individuals with whom the child has family relationships;
- Legally recognized privileged and analogous relationships, such as those of lawyers, physicians, and ministers;
- Income, including the student's role in family activities and finances;
- Non-academic personality tests; questionnaires on personal and family life and attitudes;
- Autobiography assignments; log books, diaries, and personal journals;
- Contrived incidents for self-revelation; sensitivity training, group encounter sessions, talk-ins, magic circle techniques, self-evaluation and auto-criticism; strategies designed for self-disclosure (e.g., zig-zag);
- Sociograms; sociodrama, psychodrama; blindfold walks; isolation techniques.

The purpose of this letter is to preserve my child's rights under the Protection of Pupil Rights Amendment (the Hatch Amendment) to the General Education Provisions Act, and under its regulations as published in the *Federal Register* of Sept. 6, 1984, which became effective Nov. 12, 1984. These regulations provide a procedure for filing complaints first at the local level, and then with the U.S. Department of Education. If a voluntary remedy fails, federal funds can be withdrawn from those in violation of the law. I respectfully ask you to send me a substantive response to this letter attaching a copy of your policy statement on procedures for parental permission requirements, to notify all my child's teachers, and to keep a copy of this letter in my child's permanent file. Thank you for your cooperation.

copy to School Principal   Sincerely, _____

SUBJECT INDEX

Abortion, *37, 85, 113, 163, 260, 270*

Adoption, *176, 260*

Affective Test Development Project, *133*

Alcohol Education, *166, 212, 230, 262*

Alligator River, *80*

American Civil Liberties Union (ACLU), *45, 301*

Anti-Parent Pressure Program, *265*

Arizona, *128, 224, 228, 238, 244, 251, 277, 285*

Aspen Institute of Humanistic Studies, *348*

Astrology, *202, 365*

Athletics, *171*

Basic Educational Skills Through Technology (BEST) *396*

Biochemical treatment, *223*

Biofeedback, *35, 423*

Bionomics course, *258*

Birth of a baby film, *210, 404*

Boundary-breaking games, *199*

B-STEP Program, *149*

Butterick, *110*

California, *249*

Career Education Program, *204*

Cheating, *169, 324*

Choices: A Unit on Conflict and Nuclear War, *316, 412*

Christmas, *216*

Circle Times, *99*

Citizenship, *229, 231*

Colorado, *257*

Competency Based Education (CBE), *393*

Contraceptives, *146, 158, 189, 311*

Creative Problem Solving, *201*

Crime Resistance Program, *248*

Critical Thinking, *172, 263, 268*

Crossroads: Quality of Life in the Nuclear World, *316, 411*

Cumulative Files, *83*

Curriculum Innovations, Inc., *159*

Dear Mabel, *38*

Death Education, *34, 91, 284, 368, 403, 406*

Decision Categories, *56*

Decision Making in a Nuclear Age, *411*

Decision Making Skills Program, *238, 268*

Delphi Method, *69*

Department of Education, U.S., *131, 146, 181, 197, 314, 316, 328, 330, 396*

Diaries (see Journals)

Divorce, *34, 35, 91, 99, 124*

Dolls, *46, 245*

Drug Education, *70, 71, 132, 152, 196, 221, 259, 321, 326, 331, 346, 354, 401, 404, 424*

Dungeons and Dragons, *69, 210*

Easytrieve, *136*

Educational Community Opportunity for Stewardship (ECOS), *396*

Educators for Social Responsibility, *314*

Effecting Change, *51*

Elementary and Secondary Education Act (ESEA), *70, 126, 186, 232, 296, 311, 346, 354, 395*

Encounter groups, *76, 191*

Enrichment, *263*

Ethical Issues in Decision Making, *314*

Ethical Quest in a Democratic Society, 69, 421

Exemplary Center for Reading Instruction (ECRI), 184, 255, 285, 417

Facing History and Ourselves, 130, 193, 207, 292, 314, 411

Fallout Shelter Game, 267, 295

Family Living, 65, 115, 123, 144, 147

Family Planning, 311, 322

Fantasizing, 202, 423

Feely heads, 424

Flag, 113

Florida, 335, 341, 345, 351, 354, 357, 367, 370, 381

FOCUS, 248

Foresman, Scott, Spectra Series, 69, 70

Future Directions of Family Planning, 127, 311

Future Shock, 152

Future Studies, 53, 123, 189

Georgia, 393

Gifted programs (see also Talented & Gifted), 69, 201, 374

Global education, 69, 145, 189, 348, 422, 432

Gordon, Sol, films and comic books, 359, 368

Grab Bag, 407

Group Dynamics, 278

Guided Nurturance of Multi-Exceptional Students (GNOMES), 267

Hate, 183, 244

Health courses, 35, 36, 63, 85, 103, 117, 160, 169, 205, 234, 244, 264, 320, 371

Here's Looking at You Two Drug Program, 70, 71, 424

Home Economics, 69, 281

Homosexuality, 85, 301, 409

Humanist magazine, 119, 120

Hypnotism, 202, 423

Indiana, 417

Institute of World Order, 348

Journals and diaries, 103, 110, 112, 131, 151, 192, 208, 226, 245, 270, 279, 302, 344, 410, 429

Kansas, 202

Laidlaw Publishers, 110

Lifeboat situation, 63, 257, 262

Lottery, 152, 258

Louisiana, 362

Lying, 57, 62, 168, 183, 237, 261, 273, 332, 399

MACOS – Man: A Course of Study, 60, 130, 152

Magic Circle, 55, 61, 83, 144, 260, 269, 376, 398

Maine, 391

Mainstreaming, 330

Marriage and Parenthood, 110

Marriage Class, 115, 163

Maryland, 387, 420, 426

Massachusetts, 263, 307

Mastery Learning, 182, 185, 251, 255, 285

Me boxes, 144

ME Center, 202

Me-Me Drug Program, 132, 152, 196, 321, 326, 331

Mental Health, 71, 86, 170

Michigan, 107, 115, 138, 142, 146, 149, 150, 152, 156, 159

Middle States Evaluation Program, 388

Missouri, 184, 201

MS Magazine, 300

Music, 217

National Center for Educational Statistics, 390, 394

National Diffusion Network, 129, 177, 197, 207, 248, 292, 310, 314, 331, 336, 391, 394, 401, 404, 417, 421, 431

National Education Association (NEA), *155, 168, 190, 223, 292, 308, 316, 401, 412, 422*

National Institute of Education (NIE), *133, 155, 181, 189, 363, 390, 432*

National Institute of Mental Health, *241, 358*

National Organization for Women (NOW), *300*

Nebraska, *392*

New Basic Skills Program, *228*

New Frontiers, *248*

New Hampshire, *298, 310, 316, 320*

New Jersey, *126, 154*

New Model Me, *206, 431*

New Perspectives in Inter-Group Education, *432*

New School for Social Research, *180*

New York, *114, 130, 319, 407, 433*

North Carolina, *400, 404*

Northwest Regional Educational Laboratory, *48, 68, 71, 181*

Nuclear war courses, *319, 410*

Occult, *142, 210, 215, 282*

Oklahoma, *176, 177, 188, 416*

Ombudsman Drug Education Curriculum, *259, 401, 404*

Oregon, *27, 44, 50, 54, 60, 62, 65, 79, 85, 87, 93, 98, 102*

Pacesetters in Innovation, *369, 391, 420*

Parenting education, *357*

Parents, criticism of, *30, 50, 102, 159, 179, 183, 203, 205, 221, 244, 261, 323*

Parents, tricks on, *55, 57, 60, 61, 97, 235*

Parents—Who Needs Them?, *64*

Pennsylvania, *112, 418, 424*

Perspective on Loss Through Death and Divorce, *35, 87, 92, 98*

Physicians for the Prevention of Nuclear War, *314*

Planned Parenthood, *37, 43, 160, 234, 311, 339, 352, 416*

Planning, Programing, Budgeting Systems (PPBS), *196, 394*

Playboy, *162*

Pornography, *215, 234, 258, 413*

Positive Attitude Toward Learning, *293, 391*

Preparing for Tomorrow's World, *131*

Preventive Guidance Counseling Program, *27, 28, 46, 87, 92*

Project Challenge, *203*

Project Charlie, *221*

Project Instruct, *184*

Project Legal: Law Related Education, *131*

Psycho-drama, *161, 164, 182, 190, 194, 392, 431*

Quaker Schoolhouse, *418*

Quest, *206, 259*

Questionnaires/Surveys, *29, 34, 40, 43, 56, 57, 62, 83, 94, 101, 102, 116, 139, 154, 205, 222, 246, 275, 342, 355, 364, 371, 405*

REACH, *70*

Religion, *30, 120, 136, 161, 167, 183, 188, 214, 216, 245, 250, 269, 281, 400*

Right to Live, Who Decides?, *63*

Risk Taking, *50, 72, 74*

Role-playing, *99, 110, 120, 147, 204, 210, 212, 236, 294, 322, 392, 424*

Sarasota Drug Education Program, *346, 354*

Schools Without Failure, *303*

Seance, *204*

Self, *203*

Sensitivity training, *50, 190, 198, 301, 367, 402*

Sex education, *36, 37, 39, 85,*
127, 146, 155, 156, 160, 161, 311,
407, 413
Sex equity, *44*
Sex-role reversals, *45, 46, 47, 108*
Show Me, *258*
Simulation games, *149, 412*
Situation ethics, *160, 206, 236,*
261, 380
Sociodrama, *182, 430*
Sociograms, *428*
Something Else, *354*
Stealing, *55, 113, 122, 198, 237*
Suicide, *69, 71, 84, 92, 121, 122,*
140, 142, 170, 176, 201, 222,
262, 266, 271, 277, 308, 319,
338, 371, 405
Super Learning, *423*
Survival games, *63, 113, 176, 179,*
203, 234, 262, 267, 295, 403,
406, 431
Talented and Gifted Program
(TAG), *50, 64, 201*
Talents Unlimited, *131*
Taxonomy, *71, 182, 395*

Teaching Individuals Positive
Solutions (TIPS), *131, 236, 248,*
283
Texas, *190, 199*
Thinkabout, *396*
Time-testing, *417*
Touch therapy, *194*
Transactional Analysis, *55, 61,*
205, 264, 278, 283
Transcendental Meditation (TM),
142, 167, 370
Transition, *75*
Tribes, *206, 259*
United Nations, *422*
Values Appraisal Scale, *246*
Virginia, *236, 283*
Washington State, *36, 69, 71, 192,*
421
Whip, *411*
Wisconsin, *127, 194, 222, 311*
Witchcraft, *30, 204, 215, 282*
Women's Educational Equity Act
(WEEA), *44, 280*
WOW, *71*
Yoga, *142, 167, 202, 209, 214*

INDEX OF WITNESSES

Sylvia Allen, *269*

Frankie Anderson, *360*

Elaine Andreski, *149*

Sandra Bak, *171*

Theresa Bak, *109*

Gail Bjork, *370*

Mary Blaisdell, *320*

Evelyn Bonk, *115*

Eileen Bowie, *296*

Stephen Broady, *184*

Archie Brooks, *27*

Carrie Brooks, *44*

Janet Brossard, *36*

Delores Brown, *400*

Judith Brown, *285*

Patricia Broyles, *235*

Phyllis Chaplin, *398*

Mary Cole, *102*

Charlotte Cooney, *357*

Shirley Correll, *335*

George L. Crossley, Jr., *350*

Doris D'Antoni, *367*

Marion Darr, *114*

Snookie Dellinger, *404*

Marcella Donovan, *416*

Robert Duarte, *331*

Dr. Lawrence Dunegan, *169*

Carol Eremita, *303*

Ron Figuly, *310*

John Forrest, *120*

Kay Fradeneck, *159*

Robert Griggs, *209*

Patricia Hartnagle, *143*

Angela Hebert, *232*

Ruthellen Herzberg, *79*

Mary Park Hilles, *413*

Jim Hopkins, *316*

Nancy Hutchinson, *75*

Charlotte Iserbyt, *390*

Joyce Jensen, *249*

Larry Johnson, *62*

Sherri Katz, *255*

Myrtle Kelly, *175*

Naomi King, *424*

Glenda Knowles, *181*

Joan Lauterbach, *201*

Jacqueline Lawrence, *426*

Malcolm Lawrence, *387*

Wilma Leftwich, *177*

Alice Leidich, *118*

Gloria Lentz, *124*

Rabbi Yeduda Levin, *433*

Bettye Lewis, *107*

Kirk Lewis, *133*

Marilyn Lewis, *342*

Raymond O. Lewis, *338*

Joanne Lisac, *54*

Michael Lisac, *60*

Linda Mace, *277*

Shirley Mapes, *263*

Sandra Maynard, *93*

Anna Mayer, *187*

Ann McClellan, *244*

Sandra McDade, *362*

Marcy Meenan, *112*

Donna Muldrew, *190*

Anne Pfizenmaier, *306*

Mrs. Lee Phillips, *418*

Sherri Pitman, *238*

Barbara Powell, *146*

Frances Reilly, *168*

Nelda Reis, *378*

Flora Rettig, *138*

Shirley Riesz, *345*

Larry Rink, *206*

James Robert, *98*

Jayne Schindler, *257*

Phyllis Schlafly, *406*

Lynn Schmidt, *152*

William Dean Seaman, *87*

Cris Shardelman, *68*

Susan Simonson, *65*

Beth Skousen, *164*

Elizabeth Soper, *293*

Bryan Staff, *156*

Mary Jane Stanley, *179*

Mrs. George Staples, *166*

Shannon Stearns, *271*

Vandola Stevens, *123*

Dianna Storey, *71*

Sandra Tapasto, *129*

Helen Tapp, *251*

Jacquelyn Thaden, *375*

Alan C. Thomaier, *298*

Ada Thomas, *228*

Theresa Todd, *221*

John Tornicki, *154*

Beth Trotto, *420*

Valerie Walsh, *326*

Marcella Warila, *50*

Rev. Ronald Watson, *85*

Cindi Weatherly, *393*

Beth West, *354*

Shirley Whitlock, *224*

Diane Williams, *381*

Jil Wilson, *194*

Lois Wolthuis, *150*

Sandra Youngblood, *96*

Give

Child Abuse in the Classroom

. . . to Parents, Teachers, School Board Members, Elected Officials, Community Leaders, Media Personnel, Opinion Makers, and Concerned Citizens. Take it to every family in your neighborhood!

YOU can use this tool to . . .

* *make sure* YOUR child is never a victim of child abuse in the classroom. With this book, you know what to look for—and how to assert your parental rights.

* *stop* your local school from subjecting any child to "therapy" treatment in the classroom—unless their parents give informed consent in writing.

* *persuade* your State Legislature to pass a state "protection of pupil rights act" to protect children from classroom child abuse with state funds.

* *demand* that your local school board set up schools that teach traditional basics (including phonics) instead of classroom "therapy."

* *give* parents the confidence to make their own decisions as to whether they choose private schools, home teaching, or do battle to get the Pupil Rights Amendment fully enforced.

* *elect* national, state, and local candidates to office who will pledge full enforcement of the Pupil Rights Amendment, a return to parents' rights, and teaching of the traditional basics. (Any politician who promises to improve education by spending more money is a fraud; education problems are NOT financial.)

ELECT CANDIDATES WHO WILL REFORM EDUCATION NOW.

EDUCATION IS EVERYBODY'S BUSINESS!